Consistent Distributed Storage

Synthesis Lectures on Distributed Computing Theory

Editor
Michel Raynal, *University of Rennes, France and Hong Kong Polytechnic University*

Founding Editor
Nancy Lynch, *Massachusetts Institute of Technology*

Synthesis Lectures on Distributed Computing Theory was founded by Nancy Lynch of the Massachusetts Institute of Technology, and is now edited by Michel Raynal of the University of Rennes, France and Hong Kong Polytechnic University. The series publishes 50- to 150-page publications on topics pertaining to distributed computing theory. The scope largely follows the purview of premier information and computer science conferences, such as ACM PODC, DISC, SPAA, OPODIS, CONCUR, DialM-POMC, ICDCS, SODA, Sirocco, SSS, and related conferences. Potential topics include, but not are limited to: distributed algorithms and lower bounds, algorithm design methods, formal modeling and verification of distributed algorithms, and concurrent data structures.

Consistent Distributed Storage
Vincent Gramoli, Nicolas Nicolaou, and Alexander A. Schwarzmann
2021

Network Topology and Fault-Tolerant Consensus
Dimitris Sakavalas and Lewis Tseng
2019

Introduction to Distributed Self-Stabilizing Algorithms
Karine Altisen, Stéphane Devismes, Swan Dubois, and Franck Petit
2019

Distributed Computing Perls
Gadi Taubenfeld
2018

Decidability of Parameterized Verification
Roderick Bloem, Swen Jacobs, Ayrat Khalimov, Igor Konnov, Sasha Rubin, Helmut Veith, and Josef Widder
2015

Impossibility Results for Distributed Computing
Hagit Attiya and Faith Ellen
2014

Distributed Graph Coloring: Fundamentals and Recent Developments
Leonid Barenboim and Michael Elkin
2013

Distributed Computing by Oblivious Mobile Robots
Paola Flocchini, Giuseppe Prencipe, and Nicola Santoro
2012

Quorum Systems: With Applications to Storage and Consensus
Marko Vukolić
2012

Link Reversal Algorithms
Jennifer L. Welch and Jennifer E. Walter
2011

Cooperative Task-Oriented Computing: Algorithms and Complexity
Chryssis Georgiou and Alexander A. Shvartsman
2011

New Models for Population Protocols
Othon Michail, Ioannis Chatzigiannakis, and Paul G. Spirakis
2011

The Theory of Timed I/O Automata, Second Edition
Dilsun K. Kaynar, Nancy Lynch, Roberto Segala, and Frits Vaandrager
2010

Principles of Transactional Memory
Rachid Guerraoui and Michał Kapałka
2010

Fault-tolerant Agreement in Synchronous Message-passing Systems
Michel Raynal
2010

Communication and Agreement Abstractions for Fault-Tolerant Asynchronous
Distributed Systems
Michel Raynal
2010

The Mobile Agent Rendezvous Problem in the Ring
Evangelos Kranakis, Danny Krizanc, and Euripides Markou
2010

Consistent Distributed Storage

Vincent Gramoli, Nicolas Nicolaou, and Alexander A. Schwarzmann

ISBN: 978-3-031-00887-0   paperback
ISBN: 978-3-031-02015-5   eBook
ISBN: 978-3-031-00133-8   hardcover

DOI 10.1007/978-3-031-02015-5

A Publication in the Springer series
SYNTHESIS LECTURES ON DISTRIBUTED COMPUTING THEORY

Lecture #17
Series Editor: Michel Raynal, *University of Rennes, France and Hong Kong Polytechnic University*
Founding Editor: Nancy Lynch, *Massachusetts Institute of Technology*
Series ISSN
Print 2155-1626   Electronic 2155-1634

Consistent Distributed Storage

Vincent Gramoli
University of Sydney, Australia
EFPL, Switzerland

Nicolas Nicolaou
Algolysis Ltd., Cyprus

Alexander A. Schwarzmann
Augusta University, Georgia, USA

SYNTHESIS LECTURES ON DISTRIBUTED COMPUTING THEORY #17

ABSTRACT

Providing a shared memory abstraction in distributed systems is a powerful tool that can simplify the design and implementation of software systems for networked platforms. This enables the system designers to work with abstract readable and writable objects without the need to deal with the complexity and dynamism of the underlying platform. The key property of shared memory implementations is the consistency guarantee that it provides under concurrent access to the shared objects. The most intuitive memory consistency model is *atomicity* because of its equivalence with a memory system where accesses occur serially, one at a time. Emulations of shared atomic memory in distributed systems is an active area of research and development. The problem proves to be challenging, and especially so in distributed message passing settings with unreliable components, as is often the case in networked systems. We present several approaches to implementing shared memory services with the help of replication on top of message-passing distributed platforms subject to a variety of perturbations in the computing medium.

KEYWORDS

distributed shared memory, atomicity, read/write objects, quorum systems, reconfiguration, consensus, fault-tolerance, dynamism

Contents

Acknowledgments xi

Outline xiii

1   Introduction 1
  1.1   Shared Storage: A Landscape 1
  1.2   Distribution and Consistency 3

2   Model of Computation 7
  2.1   Distributed System 7
    2.1.1   Input/Output Automata and Executions 7
    2.1.2   Failures 9
    2.1.3   Communication 10
    2.1.4   Quorum Systems 11
  2.2   Consistency: Atomic Object Semantics 13
  2.3   Notation Summary 16
  2.4   Bibliographic Notes 17

3   The Static Environment 19
  3.1   Replication 19
  3.2   Communication and Rounds 19
  3.3   Efficiency Measures 20
  3.4   List of Symbols 21

4   The Single-Writer Setting 23
  4.1   SWMR Algorithm ABD: Basic Techniques 23
    4.1.1   Algorithm ABD Specification 24
    4.1.2   Algorithm ABD Correctness 25
    4.1.3   Efficiency of Algorithm ABD 29
  4.2   Algorithm FAST: Expediting Read Operations 30
    4.2.1   Algorithm FAST Specification 30
    4.2.2   Algorithm FAST Correctness 34

4.3   Lower Bound: Limitations of Fast Implementations 37

4.4   Algorithm Sliq: Introducing Quorum Views 38

    4.4.1   Algorithmic Technique: Quorum Views 39

    4.4.2   Algorithm Sliq Specification 40

    4.4.3   Algorithm Sliq Correctness 44

4.5   Bibliographic Notes 45

5   The Multiple-Writer Setting **47**

5.1   Algorithm mwABD: Multi-Writer ABD 47

    5.1.1   Algorithm mwABD Specification 47

    5.1.2   Algorithm mwABD Correctness 49

5.2   Algorithm CwFr: Quorum View Generalization 51

    5.2.1   Algorithmic Technique: MW Quorum Views 51

    5.2.2   Algorithm CwFr Specification 52

    5.2.3   Algorithm CwFr Correctness 57

5.3   Lower Bound: Inherent Limitations of mwmr on Fast Operations 60

5.4   Algorithm SfW: Expediting Write Operations 66

    5.4.1   Algorithmic Technique: Server Side Ordering (SSO) 67

    5.4.2   Algorithmic Technique: Enhanced Tagging 68

    5.4.3   Algorithm SfW Specification 69

    5.4.4   Algorithm SfW Correctness 73

5.5   Bibliographic Notes 77

6   The Dynamic Environment **79**

6.1   Consensus 80

6.2   Group Communication Services 81

6.3   Using Reconfiguration for Direct Implementations 82

7   RAMBO: Reconfigurable Dynamic Memory **83**

7.1   Models and Definitions 84

7.2   Rambo Service Specifications 86

    7.2.1   Rambo Service Specification 86

    7.2.2   Recon Service Specification 88

7.3   Implementation of Rambo 91

    7.3.1   Overall Architecture 92

    7.3.2   Implementation of Joiner 92

    7.3.3   Implementation of Reader-Writer 92

7.3.4   Implementation of the Recon Service 100

7.3.5   The Complete RAMBO Algorithm 102

7.4   Atomicity of RAMBO 102

7.5   Conditional Performance Analysis: Latency Bounds 105

7.6   Extensions of RAMBO 108

7.7   GeoQuorums—Adaptation of RAMBO for Mobile Settings 111

7.8   Bibliographic Notes 113

8   RDS: Integrated Reconfigurations 115

8.1   Preliminaries 115

8.2   The Paxos Consensus Algorithm 116

8.2.1   The Part-Time Parliament 116

8.2.2   Fast Paxos 117

8.2.3   Deciding Upon a New Configuration 118

8.3   Reconfigurable Distributed Storage 119

8.3.1   Signature and State 119

8.3.2   Read and Write Operations 121

8.3.3   Communication and Independent Transitions 122

8.3.4   Reconfiguration 125

8.4   Consensus of RDS 128

8.5   Conditional Performance Analysis 129

8.6   Bibliographic Notes 131

9   DynaStore: Incremental Reconfigurations 135

9.1   Preliminaries 136

9.1.1   Incremental Reconfiguration 137

9.1.2   Activity of Processes 137

9.1.3   Majority Assumption 138

9.2   The Weak Snapshot Automaton 138

9.3   The Reader-Writer-Recon Automaton 142

9.3.1   Partially Ordered Configurations 144

9.3.2   Adding New Configurations 145

9.3.3   Contacting Quorums 146

9.4   Correctness 147

9.5   Implementation and Performance Considerations 152

9.6   Bibliographic Notes 154

10 Concluding Remarks and Looking Ahead 155

Bibliography 159

Authors' Biographies 171

Index 173

Acknowledgments

The work includes results obtained in collaboration with several colleagues and by other researchers. The bibliographic notes throughout provide details on prior work.

The authors thank Nancy Lynch, the Series Founding Editor, for supporting this project and for her encouragement, and Michel Raynal, the Series Editor, for shepherding this project to completion. We thank the reviewers, Christian Cachin, Rachid Guerraoui, and Marko Vukolić, whose meaningful and insightful feedback helped improve the quality of this presentation. Special thanks are due to Diane Cerra, Editor at Morgan & Claypool Publishers, for her active role, encouragement, patience, and perseverance.

The work of the first author was partially supported by Australian Research Council Discovery Projects funding scheme (project number 180104030) and Future Fellowship funding scheme (project number 180100496). The work of the second author was in part supported by the European Commission Marie Skłodowska-Curie Action (project number 629088) and through the Cyprus Research and Innovation Foundation (POST-DOC/0916/0090) . This work of the third author was in part supported by the National Science Foundation (NSF) Grant 1017232 and Augusta University Research Foundation.

Finally, we would like to thank our families.

The first author wishes to thank his wife, Klara, his daughter, Zoé, and his two sons, Hugo and Roméo, for their patience during the writing of this monograph. The writing has taken longer than expected, but he notes in retrospect that the writing of this monograph is the perfect illustration of the French idiom "se bonnifier avec l'âge" because the result ended up exceeding his initial expectation.

The second author would like to express his gratitude to his wife, Andri, for her steady support, love, and patience during the journey of writing this book. It's been an unexpectedly long journey, and within this time she endured traveling by his side along with their three children to two continents for fulfilling personal goals. It would have been a major omission not to thank his three heroes, his children, Raphaela, Ioannis, and Chrysanthos, for they sat patiently waiting (most of the time) for some quality time with their daddy.

The third author is grateful to his wife, Sana, for her love, encouragement and support. This project did take longer than planned, but he notes with pride that his children had plenty of time to give him three grandsons. Finally he dedicates his work on this monograph to the Memory of his Father who would say, "It is about time you were done!"

Vincent Gramoli
Nicolas Nicolaou
Alexander A. Schwarzmann

Outline

This book contains ten chapters. Figure 1 shows some dependencies among chapters and suggests some reading orders.

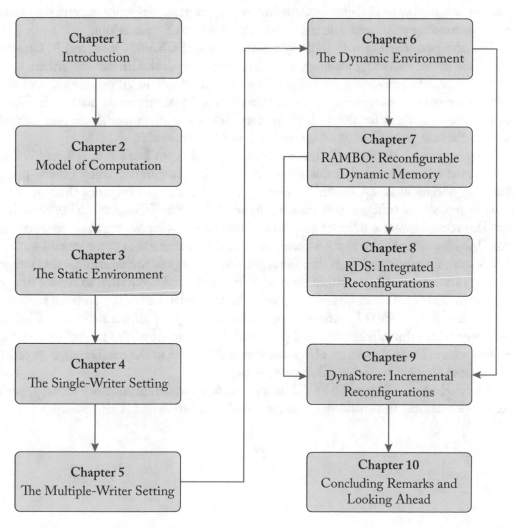

Figure 1: Suggested order of reading.

We begin the presentation in Chapter 1 where we discuss the general landscape of distributed shared storage systems, and introduce the challenges associated with combining replication and consistency in distributed settings.

In Chapter 2, we describe the model of computation, define consistency, and assumptions about communication and failure models. When a particular algorithm assumes a specialized model, we present model refinements and additional assumptions in the relevant section before presenting the algorithm.

The rest of the book is divided into two logical parts. In the first part we deal with static systems where the collection of failure-prone object replica servers is known a-priori. In the second part we deal with dynamic systems, where the set of participating servers may change over time as existing participants depart or fail, and as new participants join.

The first part, dealing with static systems, consists of Chapters 3, 4, and 5. Chapter 3 discusses additional modeling parameters. In Chapter 4, we deal with the algorithms for the single writer, multiple readers model that guarantee consistency in all executions, and where read and write operations terminate provided that a majority of servers do not fail. In Chapter 5, we present algorithms for the multiple writers, multiple readers model, and we exemplify techniques that can be used to speed up read and write operations.

The second part, dealing with dynamic systems, consists of Chapters 6, 7, 8, and 9. Chapter 6 discusses approaches to dynamic atomic memory implementation using general purpose distributed building blocks. Chapter 7 presents a framework to reconfigure a dynamic atomic memory by replacing a configuration of servers by another while offering availability of reads and writes. This reconfiguration relies on an external building block for servers to agree on configurations. The chapter concludes with a survey of several algorithms that optimize and specialize the framework for particular target environments. Chapter 8 presents algorithms that integrate the reconfiguration procedures within the atomic memory implementation to reduce time and message complexities. This integration improves the fault tolerance of the previous framework by minimizing the number of configurations needed at any point of the execution. Chapter 9 presents algorithms that obviate the need for including agreement within an explicit reconfiguration procedure. These algorithms accept incremental changes to the configuration in order to avoid the need for a consensus-based reconfiguration.

We conclude in Chapter 10 by discussing practical consistent memory services, performance considerations, and challenges associated with replication and reconfiguration.

Lastly, in addition to the reading orders proposed in Figure 1, the reader may benefit from the content of particular sections to fast-track to later chapters in the book. In particular, after reading Sections 4.1 and 5.1 (in this order) the reader may either choose to continue with the corresponding chapter sequels dealing with the static system, or may proceed to Chapter 6 and start reading about the dynamic systems.

Vincent Gramoli
Nicolas Nicolaou
Alexander A. Schwarzmann
June 2021

CHAPTER 1

Introduction

Reading, *'Riting*, and *'Rithmetic*, (i.e., *reading*, *writing*, and *arithmetic*) the three *R*'s underlying much of human intellectual activity, not surprisingly, also stand as a venerable foundation of modern computing technology. Indeed, both the Turing machine and von Neumann machine models operate by reading, writing, and computing, and all practical uniprocessor implementations are based on performing activities structured in terms of the three *R*'s. With the advance of networking technology, communication became an additional major systemic activity. However, at a high level of abstraction, it is apparently still more natural to think in terms of reading, writing, and computing. While it is hard to imagine distributed systems—such as those implementing the World-Wide Web—without communication, we often imagine browser-based applications that operate by retrieving or loading (i.e., reading) data, performing computation, and storing (i.e., writing) the results. In this monograph we deal with the storage of shared readable and writable data in distributed systems with the focus on implementations that provide resiliency and consistency in systems that are subject to perturbations in the underlying distributed platforms composed of computers and networks that interconnect them. The perturbations include failures of individual computers, dynamically changing collections of computers participating in the system, and failures and delays in the communication medium.

1.1 SHARED STORAGE: A LANDSCAPE

Shared storage services are at the core of most information-age systems. Shared memory systems we deal with provide objects supporting two access operations: *read* that obtains the current value of the object, and *write* that replaces the old value of the object with a new value. Such objects are often called *registers*. Although we do not include more complicated object semantics, such as transactions or integrated read-modify-write operations, there are common implementation challenges that any distributed storage system needs to resolve. Imagine a storage system that is implemented as a central server. The server accepts client requests to perform operations on its data objects and returns responses. While this is conceptually simple, this approach already presents two major problems. The first is that the central server is a performance bottleneck. The second is that the server is a single point of failure. The quality of service in such an implementation degrades rapidly as the number of clients grows, and the service becomes unavailable if the server crashes (imagine how inadequate a web news service would be were it implemented as a central server).

Thus, the system must, first of all, be *available*. This means that it must provide its services despite failures within the scope of its specification, for example, the system must be able to mask certain server and communication failures. The system must also support multiple concurrent accesses without imposing unreasonable degradation in performance. Fault-tolerance can only be provided through redundancy. In this context it means that object contents must be replicated at geographically distributed servers. Replication introduces the potential for designing systems that use redundancy to mask failures or disconnection of some servers.

It is also important to ensure data longevity and sustainability. A storage system may be able to tolerate failures of some servers, but over a long term it is conceivable that all initial servers may need to be replaced, because no servers are infallible, and furthermore planned upgrades may be needed. Additionally, in mobile settings, e.g., search-and-rescue or military operations, it may be necessary to provide migration of data from one collection of servers to another, so that the data can move as the needs dictate. Whether our concern is data longevity or mobility, the storage system must provide seamless runtime migration of data: one cannot stop the world and reconfigure the system in response to failures and changing environment.

A major challenge that comes with replication is *consistency*. How does the system find the latest value of a replicated object? This problem was not present with a central server implementation: the server always contains the latest value. In a replicated implementation, one may attempt to consult all replicas in search of the latest value, but this approach is expensive and not fault-tolerant as it assumes that all replicas are accessible. In any case, none of the implementation issues should be a concern for the clients of the distributed memory service. What the clients should expect to see is the illusion of a single-copy object that serializes all accesses so that each read operation returns the value of the preceding write operation, and that this value is at least as recent as that returned by any preceding read. More generally, the behavior of an object, as observed externally, must be consistent with the abstract sequential data type of the object, and in developing applications that use such objects the clients must be able to rely on the abstract data type of the object. This book focuses on this notion of consistency formalized as *atomicity* [71] or, equivalently, as *linearizability* [61]. Other notions can be found in a survey on consistency [111].

While there is no argument that atomicity is the most convenient notion of consistency, we note that weaker notions have also been proposed and implemented, motivated primarily by efficiency consideration. For example, several less-than-intuitive consistency definitions emerged from the domain of multi-processor memory systems, precipitating an anecdotal opinion that "no one can figure out these consistency models, but the memory access is fast." Atomicity provides strong guarantees, making it more expensive to provide than weaker consistency guarantees [7]. Weak consistency also needs to be considered in the partitionable network setting. Here Eric Brewer conjectured [18] that distributed storage systems cannot simultaneously provide *consistency*, *availability*, and *partition-tolerance*; known as the "CAP conjecture," this was later formalized as a theorem [47]. Thus, weaker consistency models need to be considered in some cases (cf. [19]). We take the view that it is nevertheless important to provide simple and intuitive atomic consistency. The situation reminiscent of the early days of programming languages when it was argued that assembly language is better because one can generate more efficient code, or the early days of graphical user interfaces when it was argued that command-line interfaces are better because they consume fewer resources. It is conceivable that such arguments will also pass in the case of atomicity. In the setting where network partitions are a concern, two approaches are considered. When partitions are intermittent and short-lived, one can deal with them as long(er) network delays, delegating the repair issues to lower level communication services. Otherwise, when partitions can be permanent, strong consistency can still be guaranteed using the approaches that constrain the service to *primary* partitions, with subsequent integration when partitions are merged. Notably, Barbara Liskov, a Turing Prize laureate, remarked that atomicity is not cheap but if we do not guarantee it, this creates headaches for developers.

Interestingly, some existing storage systems provide data access primitives implementing atomic *read-modify-write* operations. Such access primitives are much stronger than separate *read* and *write* primitives we consider here. Implementing this type of atomic operations is expensive, and at its core requires atomic updates that in practice are implemented by either reducing parts of the system to a *single-writer* model (e.g., Microsoft's Azure Storage), by depending on clock synchronization hardware (e.g., Google's Spanner), or by relying on mechanisms for resolving event ordering such as *vector clocks* (e.g., Amazon's Dynamo). Our exposition of atomic read/write storage illustrates challenges that are common to all distributed storage systems.

1.2   DISTRIBUTION AND CONSISTENCY

We now describe a general setting for implementing consistent shared memory services.

Modeling distributed platforms.   We model the system as a collection of interconnected computers, or nodes, that communicate by sending point-to-point messages. Each node has a unique identifier (cf. IP address), local storage, and it can perform local computation. A node may fail by *crashing* at any point of the computation. Any node that crashes stops operating: it does not perform any local computation, it does not send any messages, and any messages sent to it are not delivered.

The system is *asynchronous*, and the nodes have no access to a global clock or synchronization mechanisms. This means that relative processing speeds at the nodes can be arbitrary, and that the nodes do not know the upper bound on time that it takes to perform a local computation. The message delays can also be arbitrary, and the nodes do not know bounds on message latency (although such bounds may exist). Thus, the algorithms may not make assumptions about global time or delays, since the rate of processing at each node and message latencies are unknown.

We assume that messages can be reordered in transit, however, the messages cannot be corrupted, duplicated, or generated spontaneously. If a message is received then it must have been previously sent. The messages are not lost, but message loss can be modeled as long delays (we do not address techniques for constructing more dependable communication services, e.g., by using retransmission or gossip).

We categorize a distributed networked system as either *static* or *dynamic* as follows. In the *static* networked system the set of participating nodes is fixed, and each node may know the identity of every other participant; crashes (or voluntary departures) may remove nodes from the system. In the *dynamic* networked system the set of nodes may be unbounded, and the set of participating nodes may completely change over time as the result of crashes, departures, and new nodes joining; such changes may occur at any time. At this point we do not state assumptions on the magnitude of failures or "churn" in a dynamic setting, and we postpone this discussion until specific solutions are presented. Regardless of the dynamics, we require that consistency of the data is preserved. Perturbations in the computing medium may negatively affect the performance of the memory services we consider, however memory access operations are guaranteed to terminate under certain assumptions. For example, a static memory service guarantees that operations terminate when a majority of replicas is active and when the network delays are bounded. Dynamic memory services relax the static majority assumption and instead assume that dynamically changing subsets of replicas (e.g., dynamic quorums) are active during certain periods. If these assumptions are not satisfied, such services still guarantee atomicity, however some operations may be slow or may not terminate.

Overall, we consider the participating nodes to be "good citizens" in that they cooperate willingly when they are able to, and they do not act maliciously by intentionally or accidentally performing incorrect computation. Thus, we do not present techniques for dealing with malicious behaviors. Instead we direct the interested reader to related work that considers participants that may act nefariously, e.g., [57, 87, 102].

Distributed shared memory and consistency.   A *distributed shared memory* service emulates a shared memory space comprised of readable and writable objects (often called registers) over a networked platform consisting of distributed network nodes that communicate by message passing. Service implementations use replication to ensure survivability and availability of the objects, but the service makes this invisible to the clients. The contents of each object are replicated across several *servers* or *replica hosts*. Clients invoke read and write operations on the objects, where the clients that perform read operations are called *readers*, and those that perform write operations are called *writers* (a client may be both a reader and a writer).

In response to client requests the service invokes a *protocol* that involves communication with the replica hosts. This protocol determines the consistency guarantees of the memory system. Atomic consistency definition involves "shrinking" the duration of each operation in any execution to a chosen *serialization point* between the operation's invocation and response, and requiring that (i) the ordering of the operations, according to the serialization points, preserves their real-time ordering and (ii) the resulting behavior of the object is consistent with its sequential specification. In particular, if a read is invoked after a write completes, then the read is guaranteed to return either the value of that write, or a value written by a subsequent write that precedes the read. Additionally, if a read is invoked after another read completes, it returns the same or a "newer" value than the preceding read. (We present this more formally in the text.) It is due to these natural properties that atomicity is the most convenient and intuitive consistency guarantee.

Atomic registers were introduced by Lamport [71]. Herlihy and Wing [61] proposed an equivalent definition, called *linearizability*, that also extends the notion of atomicity to arbitrary data types. Lamport also defined weaker notions, viz. *safe* and *regular* registers. Safe registers guarantee that a read operation that follows a write operation returns the value written by the that write operation. No guarantees are provided on the value returned by reads that are concurrent with writes, other than they return a legal value. Regular registers provide a stronger guarantee. Here a read operation that is concurrent with a write operation must return either the value of a previous or the concurrent write. Atomicity is the strongest notion of consistency providing the most useful and intuitive memory access semantics, and we focus here on the *atomic shared memory systems*.

Here we present algorithms that implement the atomic shared memory abstraction, but differing in the availability and fault-tolerance guarantees they provide, and in their performance. We do not advocate a "one size fits all" solution, and we choose the algorithms to present that illustrate the main techniques used in implementing consistent shared objects in variety of setting, for example, single or multiple writers, and static or dynamic environments.

CHAPTER 2

Model of Computation

This chapter presents the formal model, definitions, and notations we use in the sequel of the book. The model presented here applies to all algorithms that follow, unless stated otherwise. Terminology, notations, and definitions that are specific to particular parts of the presentation are given separately. The reader is encouraged to use this chapter as a reference to what follows.

2.1 DISTRIBUTED SYSTEM

We consider a system that consists of a collection of *asynchronous* computing devices. Each device may contain multiple asynchronous, threads of computation. We refer to each thread as a *process*. Processes communicate by means of point-to-point channels. Processes are crash-prone, and each process may experience a failure at an arbitrary instant in time. Each process has a unique identifier (id) from a totally-ordered set $\mathcal{I}$. As we deal with implementations of *read/write shared objects*, the set of process ids includes two (not necessarily disjoint) sets of processes:

- set $\mathcal{W} \subseteq \mathcal{I}$ of writer identifiers,

- set $\mathcal{R} \subseteq \mathcal{I}$ of reader identifiers.

The sets $\mathcal{W}$ and $\mathcal{R}$ contain identifiers of processes that can, respectively, perform write and read operations on the shared object.

We consider two models of reader and writer participation. In the single writer, multiple readers model, henceforth denoted as SWMR, we have $|\mathcal{W}| = 1$ and $|\mathcal{R}| \geq 1$. For the multiple writers, multiple readers models, henceforth denoted as MWMR, we have $|\mathcal{W}| \geq 1$ and $|\mathcal{R}| \geq 1$.

The contents of a shared object may be replicated at a set of server processes with ids from the set $\mathcal{I}$:

- set $\mathcal{S} \subseteq \mathcal{I}$ of replica server (or host) identifiers.

In *static environments* the membership of $\mathcal{S}$ remains fixed (whether a server is active or failed), and each server maintains a replica of the object. In *dynamic environments* an object is replicated at a subset of servers in $\mathcal{S}$, and this subset may dynamically change over time.

2.1.1 INPUT/OUTPUT AUTOMATA AND EXECUTIONS

We use the *Input/Output Automata* formalism to formally describe algorithms. Each automaton is a state machine with states and transitions between states, where *actions* are associated with sets of state transitions. Actions are defined using the *precondition-effect* notation. There are input, output, and internal actions. A particular action is enabled if the preconditions of that action are satisfied in a given state. Input actions are always enabled. The statements given as effects are executed as a program started in the current state and indivisibly producing the next state as the result of the transition.

For example, let A be an automaton that contains set S in its state. The following transition defines an action that chooses an arbitrary element e from the set if it is not empty, delivers e to the A's environment, and deletes it from the set.

> **Output** extract(e)
>
> | | |
> |---|---|
> | **Precondition:** | $S \neq \emptyset \land e \in S$ |
> | **Effect:** | $S \leftarrow S \setminus \{e\}$ |

This specification defines transitions from all states in which the precondition is satisfied, where the action transforms the pre-state to the post-state by means of the effect. Input/Output Automata are composable, and a complete algorithm is constructed as the composition of the automata defining the behavior of each process in the algorithm. Next, we give the details of the formalism.

In the presentation of distributed data services an algorithm is modeled as automaton *Alg* that is constructed as a composition of component automata C_k. In our context, each C_k is either an automaton A_i for some $i \in \mathcal{I}$ that models the component assigned to process i, or an automaton $Ch_{i,j}$ for $(i, j) \in \mathcal{I} \times \mathcal{I}$ that models the channel from i to j. Thus, the overall system is modeled as a composition of automata for each process and the channels between the processes.

Each C_k is defined in terms of a set of states *states*(C_k) and a set of actions *actions*(C_k). Each state $\sigma \in states(C_k)$ is defined over a set of *state variables* each of some type T. The set *start*$(C_k) \subseteq states(C_k)$ denotes the set of initial states of C_k.

The set *actions*$(C_k) = in(C_k) \cup out(C_k) \cup int(C_k)$, where the sets $in(C_k)$, $out(C_k)$, and $int(C_k)$ denote the sets of *input*, *output*, and *internal* actions that can be performed by C_k, respectively. The *signature* of C_k, $sig(C_k)$, is the triple $\langle in(C_k), out(C_k), int(C_k) \rangle$. The signature $extsig(C_k) = \langle in(C_k), out(C_k), \emptyset \rangle$ represents the *external signature* or *external interface* of C_k.

Next, we define a set of *transitions* *trans*$(C_k) \subseteq states(C_k) \times actions(C_k) \times states(C_k)$. (Recall that transitions are given using the programmatic precondition-effect notation.) For each action $\alpha \in actions(C_k)$, this set contains a triple $\langle \sigma, \alpha, \sigma' \rangle$ defining the transition of C_k from state $\sigma \in states(C_k)$ to state $\sigma' \in states(C_k)$ as the result of action $\alpha \in actions(C_k)$. Such a triple is also called a *step* of C_k. For the step $\langle \sigma, \alpha, \sigma' \rangle$ we say that action α is *enabled* in state σ.

Two component automata C_k and C_ℓ can be *composed* if there exists an action $\alpha \in actions(C_k) \cap actions(C_\ell)$, and the automata are *compatible*, meaning that $out(C_k) \cap out(C_\ell) = \emptyset$ and $int(C_k) \cap int(C_\ell) = \emptyset$.

In the composition of automata, if C_k performs a step that involves α, so does C_ℓ that has α in its signature. Compatibility ensures that only one automaton in a composition controls the performance of a given output action and if an automaton performs an internal action this does not force the other automaton to take a step.

Every state of automaton Alg is a vector of the states of the component automata C_k. For a state σ of Alg, we let $\sigma[k]$ denote the state of automaton C_k in σ. Also, we let $\sigma[k].var$ denote the value of the state variable var of the process automaton C_k in state $\sigma[k]$. The transition set $trans(Alg)$ is the set of triples $\langle \sigma, \alpha, \sigma' \rangle$ such that if $\alpha \in actions(C_k)$ then $\langle \sigma[k], \alpha, \sigma'[k] \rangle \in trans(C_k)$; otherwise, $\sigma[k] = \sigma'[k]$. Such a triple is called a step of Alg.

An *execution fragment* ξ of automaton Alg is a finite or an infinite sequence $\sigma_0, \alpha_1, \sigma_1, \alpha_2, \ldots, \alpha_z, \sigma_z, \ldots$ of alternating states and actions, such that every $\sigma_s, \alpha_{s+1}, \sigma_{s+1}$ is a step of Alg. If an execution fragment begins with an initial state of C then it is called an *execution*. The set of all executions of Alg is denoted by $execs(Alg)$. We say that an execution fragment ξ' of Alg, *extends* a finite execution fragment ξ of Alg if the first state of ξ' is the last state of ξ. The *concatenation*, $\xi \circ \xi'$, of ξ and ξ' is the result of the extension of ξ by ξ' where the duplicate occurrence of the last state of ξ is eliminated, yielding an execution fragment of Alg.

We consider only the executions in which enabled actions get a fair chance of performing a step: execution ξ is *fair* if either it is finite and no action is enabled in the final state of ξ, or ξ is infinite, and if action α is enabled infinitely often then ξ contains infinitely many occurrences of α.

2.1.2   FAILURES

Failures are determined by an external entity, the *adversary*. The adversary determines which components of the system fail, what type of failure is inflicted, and at what step in the computation the failures occur. Here we assume that the adversary is *omniscient* and *on-line*, meaning that it has complete knowledge of the computation, and it makes instant and dynamic decisions during the course of the computation.

Let $\mathfrak{F}$ be a failure model that places certain constraint on the power of the adversary, e.g., a constraint on the maximum number of process failures. For an algorithm Alg we let $execs(Alg, \mathfrak{F})$ denote the set of all executions of Alg from $execs(Alg)$ in which the adversary obeys the constraint: $execs(Alg, \mathfrak{F}) \subseteq execs(Alg)$. We informally refer to such executions as *good*.

For some algorithm Alg we assume that the automaton A_i of each process i contains an action $\mathsf{fail}_i \in actions(A_i)$ that models crash failures. The adversary decides if and when a step $\langle \sigma_z, \mathsf{fail}_i, \sigma_{z+1} \rangle$ appears in an execution ξ. A fail_i event may change only the state of process i, and the state if i remains unchanged during the rest of the execution. That is, if a step $\langle \sigma_z, \mathsf{fail}_i, \sigma_{z+1} \rangle$ appears in ξ, then:

- $\langle \sigma_z[i], \mathsf{fail}_i, \sigma_{z+1}[i] \rangle \in trans(A_i)$,

- for any $z' > z + 1$, $\sigma_{z+1}[i] = \sigma_{z'}[i]$,

- for every process automaton A_j such that $i \neq j$ and $\sigma_z[j] = \sigma_{z+1}[j]$, and

- for every channel $Ch_{j,j'}$ for $j, j' \in \mathcal{I}$, $\sigma_z[(j, j')] = \sigma_{z+1}[(j, j')]$.

Furthermore, execution ξ after the $fail_i$ event contains no locally controlled (internal or output) actions of i. This means that once a process crashes (fails) then it does not take any further steps and its state remains the same in the execution following the fail action. We let $\mathfrak{C}$ be the failure model where the adversary is constrained to only cause crashes of processes. Process i *crashes* in an execution ξ, if ξ contains a fail step for i. We say that process i is *faulty* in an execution ξ if i crashes in ξ; otherwise process i is *correct*.

Definition 2.1   Crash Failure Model.   For algorithm Alg we define $\mathfrak{C}$ to be the failure model such that the set of executions $execs(Alg, \mathfrak{C})$ is the subset of $execs(Alg)$ that includes all executions ξ containing at most one (**crash**) step $\langle \sigma_y, fail_i, \sigma_{y+1} \rangle$ for each $i \in \mathcal{I}$, and if such step occurs in ξ, then it is the last locally controlled step involving i, and for any step $\langle \sigma_z, \alpha_{z+1}, \sigma_{z+1} \rangle$ in ξ, where $z \geq y + 1$, $\sigma_{y+1}[i] = \sigma_z[i] = \sigma_{z+1}[i]$.

The algorithms presented in the sequel are designed to tolerate crash failures, where, depending on the algorithm, additional constraints may be placed on the adversary. In the unconstrained adversary model, the adversary is allowed to crash any subset of writer and reader processes, and a proper subset of server processes in any execution. To constrain the adversary we place an upper limit on the number of server crashes the adversary is allowed to cause. We use f to denote the maximum allowed number of server failures. This yields the following model $\mathfrak{C}_f$.

Definition 2.2   Constrained Crash Failure Model.   For algorithm Alg we define $\mathfrak{C}_f$ to be the failure model such that the set of executions $execs(Alg, \mathfrak{C}_f)$ is the subset of $execs(Alg, \mathfrak{C})$ that includes all executions ξ in which $|\{\langle \sigma_k, fail_i, \sigma_{k+1} \rangle\}| \leq f$, i.e., in which there are at most f steps fail.

The value of f may depend on the ability of a particular algorithm to tolerate crashes. For certain settings there may be a need to constrain the adversary in other ways, for example, in dynamic systems giving a static constraint on the adversary is both unrealistic and impractical. We will explicitly deal with such cases when necessary.

2.1.3   COMMUNICATION

Recall that processes communicate by exchanging messages through point-to-point channels modeled by channel automata $Ch_{i,j}$, for each $i, j \in \mathcal{I}$. The external signature of automaton $Ch_{i,j}$ is defined by input action $send(m)_{i,j}$ and output action $recv(m)_{i,j}$, where m is a message from set $Msgs$ of all possible messages.

We say that process i *sends* a message m to process j in an execution ξ, if the event $send(m)_{i,j}$ appears in ξ. Similarly, we say that a process j *receives* m that is sent by process i if the event $recv(m)_{i,j}$ occurs in ξ; in this case we say that the message is *delivered*. A message m

is said to be *in-transit* in a state of ξ, if m is sent by i earlier in the execution but not received at j by that state.

The channels are *asynchronous* and do not guarantee ordered (FIFO) message delivery. The channels do not alter message contents and do not generate spontaneous messages. That is, if action $\mathsf{recv}(m)_{i,j}$ occurs in an execution then corresponding action $\mathsf{send}(m)_{i,j}$ occurs earlier in the execution.

The channels are assumed to be *reliable*. If action $\mathsf{send}(m)_{i,j}$ occurs in an execution and process j does not crash, then either action $\mathsf{recv}(m)_{i,j}$ occurs later in the (finite or infinite) execution, or if the execution is finite, then it can always be extended with an execution that contains action $\mathsf{recv}(m)_{i,j}$. The algorithms presented here assume such reliable channels.

A simple IOA representation of the channels we assume in this book appears in Automaton 1. The signature of the automaton includes the input send and output recv actions, while its state contains a local buffer variable to store the messages in transit. Notice that as we do not assume FIFO channels the buffer is an unordered set and there is not particular order in which the messages are taken out of this set.

Specification 1 $Ch_{i,j}$ Non-FIFO Channel Automaton: Signature, State, and Transitions

```
 1: Signature:                                   9: Input send(m)_{i,j}
 2:   Input:                                     10:   Effect:
 3:     send(m)_{i,j},  m ∈ Msgs,  i, j ∈ I      11:     Buffer ← Buffer ∪ {m}
 4:   Output:
 5:     recv(m)_{i,j},  m ∈ Msgs,  i, j ∈ I      12: Output recv(m)_{i,j}
                                                 13:   Precondition:
 6: State:                                       14:     m ∈ Buffer
 7:   Buffer ⊆ Msgs init ∅                       15:   Effect:
                                                 16:     Buffer ← Buffer \ {m}
 8: Transitions:
```

Remark 2.3 On message delays and loss: We note that in all algorithms presented here reliable delivery impacts only the liveness properties, while the safety properties do not depend on message delivery. Message loss can in principle be modeled as infinite delays between the send and receive events. It is not difficult to specify failure models that include message loss, and reason about the conditional liveness of algorithms under certain constraints on the adversary. Such exploration is outside of our scope.   **End remark**

2.1.4   QUORUM SYSTEMS

Quorum systems are basic mathematical tools that are used to achieve synchronization and coordination of concurrent actions on distributed data objects. Quorum systems and their variations, such as biquorum systems, majority sets, n-wise quorum systems, coteries, etc., are examples of *set systems*. A set system is defined as follows.

Definition 2.4   Set System.   A **set system** $\mathbb{S}$ over a universe U is a set of subsets of U.

A *Quorum System* is a set system, where every pair of its members, called *quorums*, have a non-empty intersection.

Definition 2.5   Quorum System.   A **quorum system** $\mathbb{Q}$ over a universe U is a set system over U such that for any $Q, Q' \in \mathbb{Q}$ it holds that $Q \cap Q' \neq \emptyset$.

We now generalize the definition of quorum systems based on the number of quorums that together have a non-empty intersection. Let $\mathbb{Q}^{[\ell]}$ denote any set of ℓ quorums from $\mathbb{Q}$.

Definition 2.6 n-Wise Quorum Systems.   A **quorum system** $\mathbb{Q}$ over a universe U is called n-**wise**, for $2 \leq n \leq |\mathbb{Q}|$, if $\forall \mathbb{Q}^{[n]} \subseteq \mathbb{Q}$, $\displaystyle\bigcap_{Q \in \mathbb{Q}^{[n]}} Q \neq \emptyset$.

It follows that any quorum system (Definition 2.5) is a 2-*wise* quorum system. Note that a $(k + 1)$-*wise* quorum system is also a k-*wise* quorum system, but not necessarily vice versa. Next, we define the intersection degree of a quorum system that gives the maximum intersection degree of a quorum system.

Definition 2.7   Intersection Degree.   A quorum system $\mathbb{Q}$ over a universe U has **intersection degree** δ, if $\mathbb{Q}$ is a δ-wise quorum system, but not a $(\delta + 1)$-wise quorum system.

From Definition 2.7 it follows that if a quorum system $\mathbb{Q}$ has intersection degree $\delta = |\mathbb{Q}|$, then there exists a common intersection among all quorums in $\mathbb{Q}$. A quorum system $\mathbb{Q}$ with intersection degree δ, for $2 \leq \delta \leq |\mathbb{Q}|$, is also a k-wise quorum system for $1 < k < \delta$.

Some of the algorithms implementing atomic memory rely on quorum systems over the set of server ids $\mathcal{S}$ to enforce consistency. Such algorithms assume the failure model where the adversary may fail *all but one* quorum Q of a quorum system $\mathbb{Q}$ in any execution ξ. We now define quorum system failures in executions of some algorithm *Alg*. For a quorum system $\mathbb{Q}$ over the set of identifiers $\mathcal{S}$, quorum Q becomes *faulty* in an execution if process i crashes for $i \in Q$.

Definition 2.8   Quorum Failure.   Let quorum system $\mathbb{Q}$ be defined over $\mathcal{S}$. Quorum $Q \in \mathbb{Q}$, is **faulty** in state σ_z of execution $\xi \in execs(Alg, \mathcal{C})$ if ξ contains a crash step $\langle \sigma_{y-1}, \mathsf{fail}_i, \sigma_y \rangle$, where $i \in Q$ and $y \leq z$.

If a quorum Q is not faulty in a state of an execution, then Q is *correct* in that state. We now define what it means for a quorum system to fail in an execution of an algorithm.

Definition 2.9   Quorum System Failure.   A quorum system $\mathbb{Q}$ over $\mathcal{S}$ is **faulty** in a state σ_z of execution $\xi \in execs(Alg, \mathcal{C})$, if $\forall Q \in \mathbb{Q}$, Q is faulty in σ_z of ξ.

Input:	Output:
$\text{read}_{x,i}$, $x \in X$, $i \in \mathcal{R}$	$\text{read-ack}(v)_{x,i}$, $i \in \mathcal{R}$, $x \in X$, $v \in V_x$
$\text{write}(v)_{x,i}$, $v \in V_x$, $x \in X$, $i \in \mathcal{W}$	$\text{write-ack}_{x,i}$, $i \in \mathcal{W}$, $x \in X$

Figure 2.1: External signature of a read/write atomic memory service.

If quorum system $\mathbb{Q}$ does not fail in an execution, then $\mathbb{Q}$ is *correct* in the execution. Given $\mathbb{Q}$ we define $\mathfrak{C}_{\mathbb{Q}}$ to be the adversary that is constrained to cause only the crashes that leave $\mathbb{Q}$ correct in all executions; such executions are deemed good with respect to $\mathbb{Q}$.

Definition 2.10 Quorum-Constrained Crash Failure Model.   For algorithm *Alg* we define $\mathfrak{C}_{\mathbb{Q}}$ to be the failure model such that the set of executions $execs(Alg, \mathfrak{C}_{\mathbb{Q}})$ is the subset of $execs(Alg, \mathfrak{C})$ that includes all executions ξ for which crashes do not cause $\mathbb{Q}$ to become faulty.

A *Biquorum System* is a pair of set systems such that any member of the first set system intersects with all members of the second.

Definition 2.11 Biquorum System.   A **biquorum system** $\mathbb{B}$ over a universe U is a pair of set systems $\langle \mathbb{B}_1, \mathbb{B}_2 \rangle$ over U such that for any $B_1 \in \mathbb{B}_1$ and any $B_2 \in \mathbb{B}_2$ it holds that $B_1 \cap B_2 \neq \emptyset$.

A biquorum system fails if all members of one of its two sets become faulty.

Definition 2.12 Biquorum System Failure.   Biquorum system $\mathbb{B} = \langle \mathbb{B}_1, \mathbb{B}_2 \rangle$ over $\mathcal{I}$ is **faulty** in state σ_z of execution $\xi \in execs(Alg, \mathfrak{C})$, if for some $k \in \{1, 2\}$ it holds that $\forall B \in \mathbb{B}_k$, B is faulty in σ_z.

2.2   CONSISTENCY: ATOMIC OBJECT SEMANTICS

Here we formalize the consistency property of distributed shared object implementations in terms of atomicity. We model the clients of a distributed shared memory service as sequential processes that (concurrently) access shared objects by means of read and write operations. Each memory access operation begins with an operation *invocation* and concludes with a *response*. Let x be the name of a shared object, i be the id of the client process, and v be a value the object can store. A read operation includes the invocation $\text{read}_{x,i}$ and the response $\text{read-ack}(v)_{x,i}$, similarly a write operation includes the invocation $\text{write}(v)_{x,i}$ and the response $\text{write-ack}_{x,i}$.

The signature (interface) of the service implementing shared objects is given in Figure 2.1 using the I/O Automata notation. Here X is a (countable) set of object identifiers and V_x, for $x \in X$, is the set of values object x can assume, where $(v_0)_x \in V_x$ is the initial value of the object. A *read/write* object $x \in X$ is modeled by automaton A_x with input actions $in(A_x) =$

$\{$read$_{x,i}$, write$(v)_{x,i}\}$, and output actions $out(A_x) = \{$read-ack$(v')_{i,x}$, write-ack$_{i,x}\}$, where $v, v' \in V_x$ and $i \in \mathcal{I}$.

Atomic objects are composable. This allows one to construct a complete shared memory as the composition of automata A_x, for $x \in X$. Thus, in the sequel we deal with just one atomic object implementation, and we omit mention of x to reduce clutter in notation.

We generally use ρ to denote a read operation invoked by some reader, ω to denote a write operation invoked by some writer, and π to denote an operation that is either a read or a write. We say that process r, for $r \in \mathcal{R}$, invokes a read operation on an object in an execution ξ if the invocation step $\langle \sigma_k, $read$_r, \sigma_{k+1} \rangle$, appears in ξ. Process r completes the read operation if the corresponding response step $\langle \sigma_{k'}, $read-ack$(v)_r, \sigma_{k'+1} \rangle$ appears later in ξ. Similarly, we say that process w, for $w \in \mathcal{W}$, invokes a write operation on x in an execution ξ if the invocation step $\langle \sigma_z, $write$(v)_w, \sigma_{z+1} \rangle$ appears in ξ. Process w completes the write operation if the corresponding response step $\langle \sigma_{z'}, $write-ack$_w, \sigma_{z'+1} \rangle$ appears later in ξ.

For a read or a write operation π we let $inv(\pi)$ stand for its invocation step, and we let $res(\pi)$ stand for its response step. We now define operation completeness.

Definition 2.13 Operation Completeness.   Operation π is **incomplete** in an execution $\xi \in execs(\mathcal{M})$, if ξ contains $inv(\pi)$ but does not contain $res(\pi)$; otherwise we say that π is **complete**.

We assume that the read and write clients are well-formed. Namely, a process does not invoke a new operation until it receives the response for a previously invoked operation. This notion is captured by the following definition.

Definition 2.14 Well-Formedness.   An execution is **well-formed** if for any process i that invokes a read or a write operation π in step $inv(\pi)$, the execution does not contain invocation step $inv(\pi')$ of another operation π' at process i before the response step $res(\pi)$ of π.

In an execution, we say that operation π_1 *precedes* another operation π_2, or that π_2 *succeeds* π_1, if the response step of π_1 precedes the invocation step of π_2 in the execution; this is denoted by $\pi_1 \rightarrow \pi_2$. Two operations are *concurrent* if neither precedes the other. This is captured in the following definition.

Definition 2.15 Precedence Relations.   Let two operations π_1 and π_2 take place in execution ξ. We say that

- π_1 **precedes** π_2, denoted by $\pi_1 \rightarrow \pi_2$, if $res(\pi_1)$ appears before $inv(\pi_2)$ in ξ,

- π_1 **succeeds** π_2, denoted by $\pi_2 \rightarrow \pi_1$, if $inv(\pi_1)$ appears after $res(\pi_2)$ in ξ, and

- π_1 is **concurrent** with π_2, denoted by $\pi_1 \leftrightarrow \pi_2$, if neither $\pi_1 \rightarrow \pi_2$, nor $\pi_2 \rightarrow \pi_1$ in ξ.

Correctness of an implementation of an atomic read/write object is defined in terms of *atomicity* (safety) and *termination* (liveness) properties.

Atomicity of shared memory (also called linearizability) is often defined in terms of equivalence with a serial memory. We assume that clients are well-formed. Let us consider a system of several clients that perform sequences of actions that may include operations on objects. Consider some execution ξ of the system, that is, an alternating sequence of global states and actions of the clients.

$$s_0, a_1, s_1, a_2, \ldots s_{k-1}, a_k, s_k, \ldots$$

Here $\{s_k\}$ are the externally observed global states, where s_0 is the initial state, and $\{a_k\}$ are the actions. Each action a_k occurs at some global time $time(a_k)$; this time is unknown to the clients. Let us pick some object x and assume that all invocations of operations on x have corresponding responses. For each client and each matching pair (I_j, R_j) of invocations I_j and responses R_j we are going to assume that these pairs of actions occur indivisibly at some unique global time between $time(\text{I}_j)$ and $time(\text{R}_j)$. We call this time the *serialization point*; in essence, we shrink the duration of each operation to some instant between the invocation and the response for that operation. Now let us construct from execution ξ and the serialization points the following sequence:

$$v_0, \text{I}_1, \text{R}_1, v_1, \text{I}_2, \text{R}_2, v_2, \ldots v_{j-1}, \text{I}_j, \text{R}_j, v_j, \ldots$$

Here each pair (I_j, R_j) appears in the order of the corresponding chosen serialization point, v_0 is the value of x in the initial state, and v_j is the value of x in the state that immediately follows R_j in ξ.

A memory system implementation of object x is *atomic* if for any ξ it is possible to choose such serialization points so that

(i) each v_{j-1} is the value of x in the state immediately preceding I_j in ξ and

(ii) any quadruple $(v_{j-1}, \text{I}_j, \text{R}_j, v_j)$ is consistent with the abstract sequential data type of x, i.e., if the corresponding operation is invoked in a state with $x = v_{j-1}$, then upon completion of the operation we have $x = v_j$.

Although the above definition provides good intuition, identifying serialization points is not the easiest way to reason about the properties of an implementation. Thus, we provide another, equivalent, definition. This definition is given in terms of a partial order on operations in any well-formed execution.

Definition 2.16 Atomicity. An implementation of a read/write object is *atomic* if the following holds. Let the set Π contain all complete operations in any well-formed execution of the implementation. Then for operations in Π there exists an irreflexive partial ordering $\prec$ satisfying the following.

A1. If for operations π_1 and π_2 in Π, $\pi_1 \to \pi_2$, then it cannot be the case that $\pi_2 \prec \pi_1$.

A2. If $\pi \in \Pi$ is a write operation and $\pi' \in \Pi$ is any operation, then either $\pi \prec \pi'$ or $\pi' \prec \pi$.

A3. The value returned by a read operation is the value written by the last preceding write operation according to $\prec$ (or the initial value if there is no such write).

A major reason that makes atomicity attractive is *compositionality*: a system composed of multiple atomic object implementations preserves atomicity. This makes it possible to provide an implementation for a single atomic object, and then provide a complete memory system by composing the implementations for individual objects.

Last, we define the termination property of an implementation.

Definition 2.17 Termination.   We say that an implementation of shared memory $\mathcal{M}$ in a given model of computation and failures satisfies the termination property if for any execution $\xi \in execs(\mathcal{M})$, either ξ is finite, or if ξ contains an invocation step for an operation at a correct process i, then ξ contains the corresponding response step.

In other words, termination ensures that an operation invoked from a process i is going to terminate as long as i is correct.

In the sequel, taking advantage of compositionality of atomic object implementations, we focus on the implementation of a single atomic read/write object abstraction. We henceforth omit the names of the objects to reduce notational clutter.

2.3   NOTATION SUMMARY

This section presents a list of the notation presented in this chapter together with a short description for easy reference.

$\mathcal{I}.$	a totally-ordered set of process identifiers	7
$\mathcal{W} \subseteq \mathcal{I}$	set of writer identifiers in $\mathcal{I}$	7
$\mathcal{R} \subseteq \mathcal{I}$	set of reader identifiers in $\mathcal{I}$	7
$\mathcal{S} \subseteq \mathcal{I}$	set of replica host (server) identifiers in $\mathcal{I}$	7
A_i	automaton assigned to process i	8
$Ch_{i,j}$	channel from i to j	8
σ	a state of automaton A	9
$\sigma[k]$	the state of automaton C_k in the state σ of Alg	9
$\sigma[k].var$	value of variable var in the state $\sigma[k]$ of automaton C_k	9
$\langle \sigma, \alpha, \sigma' \rangle$	a transition (or step) from the state σ of automaton Alg to the state σ' of Alg as a result of action α in $actions(Alg)$	9

ξ	an execution fragment which is a finite or infinite sequence of steps of A	9
$execs(Alg)$	set of all executions of automaton Alg	9
f	number of maximum server (replica host) failures	10
$execs(Alg, \mathfrak{C}_f)$	the set of all executions of Alg with at most f crashes	10
$\mathbb{Q}$	a quorum system	12
$\mathbb{Q}^{[\ell]}$	set of ℓ quorums from $\mathbb{Q}$	12
$execs(Alg, \mathfrak{C}_{\mathbb{Q}})$	the set of all executions of Alg in which quorum system $\mathbb{Q}$ remains correct	13
$\mathbb{B}$	a biquorum system	13
X	a set of object identifiers.................................	13
V_x	the set of values object x can store	13
$(v_0)_x \in V_x$	the initial value of an object x	13
ρ	a read operation	14
ω	a write operation.......................................	14
π	a read or write operation	14
$inv(\pi)$	the step in an execution that invokes operation π	14
$res(\pi)$	the step in an execution that completes operation π	14

2.4   BIBLIOGRAPHIC NOTES

In this chapter we described our computation and communication model, and we provided the necessary notation and definitions for the presentation of the context of this book. The Input/Output Automata specification framework, as presented by Lynch and Tuttle in [84], is adopted here for algorithm specification.

Quorum systems have been exploited in the context of distributed systems with the seminal work of Gifford [45] and Thomas [108]. Quorum systems are used extensively for process coordination and synchronization in different applications in distributed computing [58, 70, 72, 73, 108, 113]. Biquorum systems were first introduced in [51] whereas the *n-wise* and *intersection degree* definitions were first used in [36].

Atomicity was one of the consistency semantics introduced by Lamport in [71] to specify the behavior of concurrent read and write operations on a register object. Later, Herlihy and Wing [61] introduced *linearizability*, an equivalent notion, but that can be applied to any concurrent object type in addition to read/write objects. Linearizability is a *local* property in the sense that if each object is linearizable then the systems of composed of such object is linearizable. In particular, atomicity is *compositional* in the same way [80]. Finally, Definition 2.16 of atomicity follows from Lemma 13.16 from the book by Lynch [80].

CHAPTER 3

The Static Environment

We now begin the exposition of emulations of atomic readable and writable shared objects in a *static* distributed setting. Here each shared object is replicated among a predefined set of networked hosts, also called *servers*. The set of servers remains fixed during the computation, and only *crashes (or voluntary departures)* may remove servers from the system. However, the remaining servers always constitute a subset of the initial set of servers.

Algorithms designed for static setting must accommodate certain dynamic behavior, such as asynchrony (delays) and permanent crashes within certain limits. Generally speaking, if the limits on the crashes of the servers are exceeded, then the liveness and performance cannot be guaranteed. However, the safety (correctness) of the system, that is atomicity, must be maintained in all executions regardless of the length of the delays and the number of crashes. Studying static systems is interesting and important for several reasons. First, dealing with static environments helps us understand the inherent limitations in designing atomic shared memory emulations. Second, developing solutions for static settings prepares the stage for developing more dynamic services in the following part of the book. Indeed, some algorithmic techniques for static settings can be revised and used in algorithms for dynamic environments.

In this chapter we describe the model, a protocol structuring technique, measures of efficiency, and relevant definitions and notation.

3.1 REPLICATION

In the static environment we consider a fixed set of server processes, each of which maintains a copy of the distributed shared object. Let $\mathcal{S} \subseteq \mathcal{I}$ be the set of identifiers of all processes that host a copy of the shared object. The algorithms for static settings assume that every process $i \in \mathcal{W} \cup \mathcal{R}$ knows $\mathcal{S}$.

3.2 COMMUNICATION AND ROUNDS

Communication between processes is over reliable point-to-point communication channels. When process i performing operation π sends a message to process j, it associates a local counter with the message; process i increments the counter for each new message to j. Each message is uniquely identified by the process identifiers of the sender and receiver, by the operation π during which the message is sent, and by the value of the message counter at the sender process when the message is sent. When replying to a message number c from process i, process j includes c as the message number, thus enabling process i to identify this message as the reply. We let the context of the protocol serve to identify certain messages as replies. We denote by $m(\pi, c)_{i,j}$ the message sent by process i with number c to process j during operation π. For some variable *var*, we use $m(\pi, c)_{i,j}.var$ to denote the value of variable *var* contained in the message $m(\pi, c)_{i,j}$.

We say that process i *contacts* a subset of processes $G \subseteq \mathcal{I}$, within operation π in execution ξ, if process i sends messages $m(\pi, c)_{i,j}$ to processes $j \in H$, where $G \subseteq H \subseteq \mathcal{I}$, and for every process $j \in G$:

(a) process j receives message $m(\pi, c)_{i,j}$ sent by i,

(b) process j sends a reply message $m(\pi, c)_{j,i}$ to i, and

(c) process i receives the reply $m(\pi, c)_{j,i}$ from j.

We denote by $cont(\pi, G)_i$ the occurrence of such events.

Let set H be equal to $\mathcal{S}$ and let M be the set of reply messages received by process i when it contacts set G. Next we define a predicate $\mathcal{PR} : \mathcal{S} \times M \rightarrow \{true, false\}$ that is evaluated on inputs that are sets of processes that send replies and sets of messages received as replies. For example, a majority predicate $\mathcal{PR}_{maj}(G, M)$, returns true if $|G| > \frac{|\mathcal{S}|}{2}$ (in this case regardless of M).

This leads us to the definition of a *communication round*, or simply *round*. When process i performing operation π sends a message to all processes in $\mathcal{S}$ with the result of process i contacting the set of processes G such that $\mathcal{PR}(G, M)$ evaluates to *true*, we say that process i performs a communication round within operation π.

In other words, a round is performed when a process sends messages to the set of servers and then awaits replies from the servers. The round terminates when the process receives enough replies that together contain the information needed to terminate the round. Once the process terminates a round, the process may initiate another round. In algorithms that employ the round structure no process sends messages outside the round structure.

3.3   EFFICIENCY MEASURES

Performance of algorithms implementing atomic shared memory is assessed primarily in terms of the latency of read and write operations. There are two factors that affect the latency of each operation: (a) *computation time* and (b) *operation latency* that is typically due to communication dclays.

Computation is measured in the usual way counting the steps that an algorithm takes in performing an operation.

Latency of operations is measured in terms of the number of communication rounds performed during an operation. If the worst case communication delay for point-to-point messaging is d, then a single round takes time at most $2d$ because it involves a communication round trip. It is important to note that d may be used to assess operation latency, but this quantity is unknown to the algorithm (and thus cannot be used anywhere in the code).

It is usually the case that computation time is insignificant compared to communication delays. However, we need to keep in mind that this is not always true, and so it is important to confirm that computation time can indeed be ignored in assessing latency.

We now define the notions of fast operations and fast implementations of atomic data services. An operation π is called *fast* if it completes after it performs a single communication round. Let algorithm *Alg* be an implementation of an atomic data service designed for a particular failure model $\mathfrak{F}$.

Definition 3.1   Fast Operations.   For implementation *Alg* and failure model $\mathfrak{F}$, let π be the operation that is invoked by process i in an execution $\xi \in execs(Alg, \mathfrak{F})$. If process i performs a single round after which the operation completes, then we say that π is a **fast** operation; otherwise π is **slow**.

An implementation is called *fast* if in each execution all operations are fast.

Definition 3.2   Fast Implementation.   Implementation *Alg* of an atomic shared memory is called **fast** if every execution $\xi \in execs(Alg, \mathfrak{F})$ contains only fast operations.

3.4   LIST OF SYMBOLS

This list consists of a quick reference to the notation that was introduced in this section together with a short description. This notation is going to be used in Chapters 4 and 5 along with notation presented in Chapter 2.

$\mathcal{S} \subseteq \mathcal{I}$ set of server (replica host) identifiers in $\mathcal{I}$ 19

$m(\pi, c)_{i,j}$ message sent from i with number c to j during operation π 20

$m(\pi, c)_{i,j}.var$ value of variable *var* contained in the message $m(\pi, c)_{i,j}$ 20

$cont(\pi, G)_i$ i contacts set $G \subseteq \mathcal{I}$, for operation π, if it sends messages to and receives messages from every process in G 20

CHAPTER 4

The Single-Writer Setting

This chapter presents algorithms that implement atomic shared memory for the single-writer, multiple-reader (SWMR) setting. Here the sole writer performs one write operation at a time to modify the value of any object in the shared memory, and this yields a natural total order to the write operations and, in turn, to the values written. This helps reasoning about the correctness of SWMR implementations. However it is still challenging to develop efficient implementations and to study trade-offs between fault-tolerance and efficiency.

We begin by presenting in Section 4.1 the seminal implementation by Attiya, Bar-Noy, and Dolev, commonly referred to as algorithm ABD. This work won the Dijkstra Prize in Distributed Computing in 2011. The algorithm implements SWMR atomic memory using replication to achieve fault-tolerance and availability. The algorithm tolerates crashes of any minority of replica nodes. Write operations are fast, that is, they take one round, and read operations take two rounds.

In Section 4.2 we present an algorithm that trades fault-tolerance for speed. Here all operations are fast, terminating optimally in a single round. To achieve this performance, the algorithm places a constraint on the number of readers with respect to the number of tolerated crashes. Specifically, the number of readers is inversely proportional to the number of crashes that can be tolerated.

In Section 4.3 we consider the limitations on the number of readers and on fault-tolerance of fast implementations. These results motivate the development of algorithms that allow together fast (single-round) and slow (two-round) operations, while removing the constraint on the number of readers. We present such an algorithm in Section 4.4.

4.1 SWMR ALGORITHM ABD: BASIC TECHNIQUES

Algorithm ABD implements SWMR atomic memory, where read and write operations are structured in terms of communication rounds, with reads performing two rounds and writes performing a single round. The algorithm replicates a shared object among the servers in $\mathcal{S}$ and tolerates crashes of any minority of servers. That is, the adversary is constrained by the failure model $\mathfrak{C}_{\lfloor |\mathcal{S}|/2 \rfloor}$.

Each replica server maintains the local value of the object and a tag (in this case an integer value), associated with the object that is assigned by the sole writer. Tag values are used as logical timestamps to order write operations, and therefore determine the values that subsequent read operations return.

Write operations have one phase that includes a single communication round. In each write operation the writer increments the tag and sends the new value along with the tag to all servers. The writer then awaits responses from a majority of servers and terminates the operation.

Read operations are implemented in two phases, called *query* and *propagation*, where each phase consists of a single communication round. In the first phase the reader queries replica servers for their values and associated tags, and awaits responses from a majority of severs. The reader extracts the value corresponding to the maximum tag in the responses and performs the second phase, in which it propagates this value and the maximum tag to the servers. Read operation terminates after responses are received from a majority of servers.

Note that each phase is guaranteed to terminate because there is always a majority of correct servers according to the assumed failure model $\mathfrak{C}_{\lfloor |\mathcal{S}|/2 \rfloor}$.

The correctness of this implementation, i.e., atomicity, is based on the observation that for any pair of operations, when one follows another, at least one correct server witnesses both operations because any two majority sets of servers have at least one server in common. This ensures that the second operation will always "see" the value that is at least as recent as that of the most recent preceding operation.

Next, we present the specification and additional details.

4.1.1   ALGORITHM ABD SPECIFICATION

Algorithm ABD is the composition of the following component automata: ABD_w that defines the protocol of the sole writer, ABD_r that defines the protocol of each reader $r \in \mathcal{R}$, ABD_s that defines the protocol of each server $s \in \mathcal{S}$, and $Ch_{i,j}$ for each channel for $i, j \in \mathcal{I}$. We now describe the specification of each automaton.

Writer ABD_w (Specification 2). The sole writer in the system receives write(v) requests from the clients to write the value v to the object. The writer increments a local counter (the tag) and associates it with v (line 27). It then sends the tag and the value to all servers (lines 29–35) and waits for responses. Once the writer receives replies from a majority (lines 40–45) it returns an acknowledgment to the client (lines 46–50) and terminates the write operation.

Reader ABD_r (Specification 3). A read operation has two phases, *query* and *propagation*, each consisting of one round. When a reader r receives a read request through the action read$_r$ from a client (lines 23–29), it sends read messages to the servers (lines 30–36), querying servers for their information, and waits for and collects their replies (lines 37–40). Once a majority of servers replies, the reader discovers the maximum tag (and its associated value) in the collected replies (lines 52–64). Next the reader propagates this tag and value by sending these to the servers (lines 41–47) and waits for and collects replies from servers (lines 48–51). Once a majority of servers replies (lines 65–70), the reader returns the discovered value to the client and terminates the operation (lines 71–76).

Specification 2 ABD_w Writer Automaton: Signature, State, and Transitions

---

```
 1:  Data Types:
 2:      Msgs, same as in Automaton 4

 3:  Signature:
 4:    Input:
 5:        write(v)_w, v ∈ V
 6:        recv(msg)_{s,w}, msg ∈ Msgs, s ∈ S
 7:        fail_w
 8:    Output:
 9:        send(msg)_{w,s}, msg ∈ Msgs, s ∈ S
10:        write-ack_w
11:    Internal:
12:        write-fix_w

13:  State:
14:        ts ∈ ℕ init 0
15:        v ∈ V init ⊥
16:        wCounter ∈ ℕ init 0
17:        srvAck ⊆ S init ∅
18:        status ∈ {idle, active, done, failed} init idle
19:        destSet ⊆ S init S

20:  Transitions:
21:    Input write(val)_w
22:      Effect:
23:          if status = idle then
24:              status ← active
25:              srvAck ← ∅
26:              destSet ← S
27:              (v, ts) ← (val, ts + 1)
28:              wCounter ← wCounter + 1
```

```
29:    Output send((WRITE, t, val, wC))_{w,s}
30:      Precondition:
31:          status = active
32:          s ∈ destSet
33:          (t, val, wC) = (ts, v, wCounter)
34:      Effect:
35:          destSet ← destSet \ {s}

36:    Input recv((W-ACK, wC))_{s,w}
37:      Effect:
38:          if status = active ∧ wCounter = wC then
39:              srvAck ← srvAck ∪ {s}

40:    Internal write-fix_w
41:      Precondition:
42:          status = active
43:          |srvAck| ≥ (|S| + 1)/2
44:      Effect:
45:          status ← done

46:    Output write-ack_w
47:      Precondition:
48:          status = done
49:      Effect:
50:          status ← idle

51:    Input fail_w
52:      Effect:
53:          status ← failed
```

Server ABD_s (Specification 4). Each server maintains a replica of the shared object and the associated tag. The initial value of each replica is v_0 and the corresponding tag is 0. When a server receives a message from phase 1 of a reader (lines 25–29), it prepares a response message containing the local tag and the value. When a server receives a message from the writer or from phase 2 of a reader, it examines the received tag, and if it is greater than the local tag, then the server updates its replica value and the tag to those received (lines 22–24), and prepares a response message. The outgoing messages are sent in the send action (lines 30–35).

4.1.2   ALGORITHM ABD CORRECTNESS

First we note that, although the value returned by a read operation is determined at the end of phase 1, skipping phase 2 can easily lead to violations of atomicity when read operations are concurrent with a write operation as illustrated in Figure 4.1. The figure shows two executions of the algorithm with five servers $\{s_1, \ldots, s_5\}$. Let us allow read operations to terminate in a single round at the conclusion of phase 1. The execution in Figure 4.1a contains a complete write operation that receives replies from servers s_1, s_2, and s_3, followed by read operation ρ_1 that receives replies from s_3, s_4, s_5. Here the execution is atomic since the read returns the

Specification 3 ABD_r Reader Automaton: Signature, State, and Transitions

1:   **Data Types:**
2:     $Msgs$, same as in Automaton 4

3:   **Signature:**
4:     **Input:**
5:       read_r, $r \in \mathcal{R}$
6:       $\text{recv}(m)_{s,r}$, $m \in Msgs$, $r \in \mathcal{R}$, $s \in \mathcal{S}$
7:       fail_r, $r \in \mathcal{R}$
8:     **Output:**
9:       $\text{send}(m)_{r,s}$, $m \in Msgs$, $r \in \mathcal{R}$, $s \in \mathcal{S}$
10:       $\text{read-ack}(val)_r$, $val \in V$, $r \in \mathcal{R}$
11:     **Internal:**
12:       $\text{read-phase1-fix}(maxt, val)_r$, $maxt \in \mathbb{N}$, $val \in V$
13:       read-phase2-fix_r

14:   **State:**
15:     $ts \in \mathbb{N}$ **init** 0
16:     $v \in V$ **init** $\perp$
17:     $rCounter \in \mathbb{N}$ **init** 0
18:     $status \in$
19:       $\{idle, phase1, phase2, done, failed\}$ **init** $idle$
20:     $srvAck \subseteq Msgs \times \mathcal{S}$ **init** $\emptyset$
21:     $destSet \subseteq \mathcal{S}$ **init** $\mathcal{S}$

22:   **Transitions:**
23:     **Input read_r**
24:       **Effect:**
25:         **if** $status = idle$ **then**
26:           $status \leftarrow phase1$
27:           $srvAck \leftarrow \emptyset$
28:           $destSet \leftarrow \mathcal{S}$
29:           $rCounter \leftarrow rCounter + 1$

30:     **Output $\text{send}(\langle \text{READ}, rC \rangle)_{r,s}$**
31:       **Precondition:**
32:         $status = phase1$
33:         $s \in destSet$
34:         $rC = rCounter$
35:       **Effect:**
36:         $destSet \leftarrow destSet \setminus \{s\}$

37:     **Input $\text{recv}(\langle \text{R-ACK}, t, val, rC \rangle)_{s,r}$**
38:       **Effect:**
39:         **if** $status = phase1 \wedge rCounter = rC$ **then**
40:           $srvAck \leftarrow srvAck \cup \{(\langle \text{R-ACK}, t, val, rC \rangle, s)\}$

41:     **Output $\text{send}(\langle \text{WRITE}, t, val, rC \rangle)_{r,s}$**
42:       **Precondition:**
43:         $status = phase2$
44:         $s \in destSet$
45:         $(t, val, rC) = (ts, v, rCounter)$
46:       **Effect:**
47:         $destSet \leftarrow destSet \setminus \{s\}$

48:     **Input $\text{recv}(\langle \text{W-ACK}, rC \rangle)_{s,r}$**
49:       **Effect:**
50:         **if** $status = phase2 \wedge rCounter = rC$ **then**
51:           $srvAck \leftarrow srvAck \cup \{(\langle \text{W-ACK}, rC \rangle, s)\}$

52:     **Internal read-phase1-fix_r**
53:       **Precondition:**
54:         $status = phase1$
55:         $|srvAck| \geq (|\mathcal{S}| + 1)/2$
56:       **Effect:**
57:         $maxT \leftarrow max(\{m.t : (m, *) \in srvAck\})$
58:         $(maxt, val) \leftarrow (m.t, m.val)$ such that
59:           $(m, *) \in srvAck \wedge m.t = maxT$
60:         $(ts, v) \leftarrow (maxt, val)$
61:         $status \leftarrow phase2$
62:         $srvAck \leftarrow \emptyset$
63:         $destSet \leftarrow \mathcal{S}$
64:         $rCounter \leftarrow rCounter + 1$

65:     **Internal read-phase2-fix_r**
66:       **Precondition:**
67:         $status = phase2$
68:         $|srvAck| \geq (|\mathcal{S}| + 1)/2$
69:       **Effect:**
70:         $status \leftarrow done$

71:     **Output $\text{read-ack}(val)_r$**
72:       **Precondition:**
73:         $status = done$
74:         $val = v$
75:       **Effect:**
76:         $status \leftarrow idle$

77:     **Input fail_r**
78:       **Effect:**
79:         $status \leftarrow failed$

value previously written, in this case value 1. Consider now the execution in Figure 4.1b. The write operation here is *incomplete*, as only server s_3 receives the new value. Read operation ρ_1 obtains values from s_3, s_4, s_5 as in Figure 4.1a. Since the state of servers s_3-s_5 is the same in both executions, then ρ_1 cannot distinguish between them and returns 1 as before. Read operation ρ_2 follows ρ_1, and obtains values from s_2, s_4, s_5, but these servers still have the old value 0. Thus, ρ_2 returns 0. This violates atomicity since ρ_2 succeeds ρ_1, and yet returns an older value than ρ_1.

Specification 4 ABD_s Server Automaton: Signature, State, and Transitions

1: **Data Types:**
2:   $Msgs_1 \subseteq \{\text{WRITE,R-ACK}\} \times \langle \mathbb{N} \times V \rangle \times \mathbb{N}$
3:   $Msgs_2 \subseteq \{\text{READ, W-ACK}\} \times \mathbb{N}$
4:   $Msgs = Msgs_1 \cup Msgs_2$

5: **Signature:**
6:   **Input:**
7:     $\text{recv}(m)_{i,s}, \ m \in Msgs, \ s \in \mathcal{S}, \ i \in \mathcal{R} \cup \{w\}$
8:     fail_s
9:   **Output:**
10:    $\text{send}(m)_{s,i}, \ m \in Msgs, \ s \in \mathcal{S}, \ i \in \mathcal{R} \cup \{w\}$

11: **State:**
12:   $ts \in \mathbb{N} \ \textbf{init} \ 0$
13:   $v \in V \ \textbf{init} \ v_0$
14:   $Counter(i) \in \mathbb{N}, \ i \in \mathcal{R} \cup \{w\} \ \textbf{init} \ 0$
15:   $status \in \{active, failed\} \ \textbf{init} \ active$
16:   $replySet \subset Msgs \times \mathcal{I} \ \textbf{init} \ \emptyset$

17: **Transitions:**
18:   **Input** $\text{recv}(\langle \text{WRITE}, t, val, C \rangle)_{i,s}$
19:     **Effect:**

20:     **if** $status = active \wedge C > Counter(i)$ **then**
21:       $Counter(i) \leftarrow C$
22:       **if** $t > ts$ **then**
23:         $(ts, v) \leftarrow (t, val)$
24:       $replySet \leftarrow replySet \cup \langle \langle \text{W-ACK}, C \rangle, i \rangle$

25: **Input** $\text{recv}(\langle \text{READ}, C \rangle)_{i,s}$
26:   **Effect:**
27:     **if** $status = active \wedge C > Counter(i)$ **then**
28:       $Counter(i) \leftarrow C$
29:       $replySet \leftarrow replySet \cup \langle \langle \text{R-ACK}, ts, v, C \rangle, i \rangle$

30: **Output** $\text{send}(m)_{s,i}$
31:   **Precondition:**
32:     $status = active$
33:     $\langle m, i \rangle \in replySet$
34:   **Effect:**
35:     $replySet \leftarrow replySet \setminus \{\langle m, i \rangle\}$

36: **Input** fail_s
37:   **Effect:**
38:     $status \leftarrow failed$

To prove correctness of ABD we need to show that any execution $\xi \in execs(\text{ABD}, \mathfrak{C}_f)$, for $|\mathcal{S}| > 2f$, satisfies liveness (i.e., termination) and safety (i.e., atomicity) properties. Termination is easy to show because of the constraint on the adversary and the fact that in read and write operations each communication round depends only on the correct majority of servers. Indeed, since $|\mathcal{S}| > 2f$, there is always a majority of servers that participate in any operation. Next, we reason about atomicity.

Theorem 4.1   *Algorithm* ABD *implements a SWMR atomic object.*

Proof. According to Definition 2.16, for each execution ξ there must exist a partial order $\prec$ on the set of operations Π that satisfy conditions **A1**, **A2**, and **A3**. Let $tag(\pi)$ be the value of the tag that is established by the writer when π is a write, and the tag computed as the maximum tag at the conclusion of phase 1 when π is a read. With this we define the partial order on operations as follows. For two operations π_1 and π_2 when π_1 is any operation and π_2 is a write we let $\pi_1 \prec \pi_2$ if $tag(\pi_1) < tag(\pi_2)$. For two operations π_1 and π_2, when π_1 is a write and π_2 is a read we let $\pi_1 \prec \pi_2$ if $tag(\pi_1) \leq tag(\pi_2)$. The rest of the order is established by transitivity. Note that reads with the same tags are not ordered. Now we use this definition of the order and the fact any two majorities intersect to reason about each of the three conditions of Definition 2.16.

A1 If for operations π_1 and π_2 in Π, $\pi_1 \rightarrow \pi_2$, then it cannot be the case that $\pi_2 \prec \pi_1$.

Let us assume that the opposite holds: $\pi_2 \prec \pi_1$. If π_2 is a write, then this is impossible because the write operation increments the tag, thus any other tag in the system is

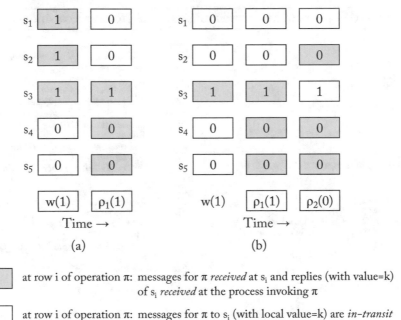

s_1	1	0	
s_2	1	0	
s_3	1	1	
s_4	0	0	
s_5	0	0	
	w(1)	$\rho_1(1)$	

Time →

(a)

s_1	0	0	0
s_2	0	0	0
s_3	1	1	1
s_4	0	0	0
s_5	0	0	0
	w(1)	$\rho_1(1)$	$\rho_2(0)$

Time →

(b)

k	at row i of operation π: messages for π *received* at s_i and replies (with value=k) of s_i *received* at the process invoking π

k	at row i of operation π: messages for π to s_i (with local value=k) are *in-transit*

Figure 4.1: (a) Execution with a complete *write* followed by a complete *read*. The read returns the value previously written, preserving atomicity. (b) Execution with an incomplete *write* followed in sequence by two complete *reads*. The first read cannot distinguish this execution from the one in 4.1(a) and returns 1. The second read does not observe 1 and returns 0, thus violating atomicity.

strictly smaller. If π_2 is a read, then in phase 1 it obtains the maximum tag from a majority of servers. Because any two majorities intersect, this tag is at least as large as any tag recorded in the servers by any complete operation. Therefore, $tag(\pi_1) \leq tag(\pi_2)$. If $tag(\pi_1) < tag(\pi_2)$ then it cannot be the case that $\pi_2 \prec \pi_1$. If $tag(\pi_1) = tag(\pi_2)$ and π_1 is a write, then π_2 is ordered after π_1 by definition. Finally, if π_1 is a read, then the two reads with the same tags are not ordered, and again it cannot be the case that $\pi_2 \prec \pi_1$.

A2 If ω is a write operation and π is any operation, then either $\omega \prec \pi$ or $\pi \prec \omega$.

If $tag(\omega) > tag(\pi)$ then $\pi \prec \omega$ follows directly. If $tag(\omega) = tag(\pi)$ then it must be that π is a read that obtains its tag from a server written to by ω using the intersection property, and $\omega \prec \pi$ follows again from the definition of the order. If $tag(\omega) < tag(\pi)$ then $\omega \prec \pi$ follows directly.

A3 The value returned by a read operation is the value written by the last preceding write operation according to $\prec$ (or the initial value if there is no such write).

Let ω be the last write operation preceding the read operation ρ. This means that $tag(\omega) \leq tag(\rho)$. If $tag(\omega) = tag(\rho)$, then either (a) ρ returns the value written by ω because the majority of servers responding to ρ in phase 1 includes at least one server written to by ω for which ρ obtains its maximum tag, or (b) if this is not the case, then it must be the case that ρ returns the value propagated in phase 2 of another read with the same tag. If $tag(\omega) < tag(\rho)$, then ρ obtains a larger tag that can only be originating by a write that follows ω, thus ω is not the preceding write, but this cannot be the case. Finally, if $tag(\rho) = 0$, then there are no preceding writes, and ρ returns the initial value.

This completes the proof. □

4.1.3 EFFICIENCY OF ALGORITHM ABD

It follows from the specification of the algorithm that write operations consist of a single phase that includes exactly one communication round. Thus, the latency of writes is at most $2d$, where d is the maximum message delay (and of course d is unknown to the algorithm).

Read operations consist of two phases, where as before each phase includes exactly one round. Thus, the latency of reads is at most $4d$.

For both operations we assume that the local processing time is insignificant compared to the worst case messaging delay. Note that most of the computation by the writer and the readers in a given round is due to the number of messages that must be processed, specifically $|\mathcal{S}|/2$. Once the reader or the writer deals with a majority of messages, it can ignore and/or discard any other message pertaining to the round.

This leads us to the final observation. Recall that in using majorities the only property that algorithm ABD relies on is that any two majorities intersect. That is, we use majorities as a particular quorum construction. The algorithm remains correct if instead of majorities we use an arbitrary quorum system $\mathbb{Q}$ over server ids $\mathcal{S}$. We call the result algorithm $\text{ABD}_{\mathbb{Q}}$. It is easy to construct quorum systems such that each quorum has cardinality $\Theta(\sqrt{|\mathcal{S}|})$. For example, we can arrange the server ids into a square (using padding as necessary if $|\mathcal{S}|$ is not a perfect square) and define each quorum as a union of server ids in one row and one column. The cardinality of the resulting quorums is $2\sqrt{|\mathcal{S}|} - 1 = o(|\mathcal{S}|)$, thus it becomes substantially smaller than $|\mathcal{S}|/2$ when the number of servers grows. With this parameterization only $\Theta(\sqrt{|\mathcal{S}|})$ of messages must be processed by readers and the writer in each round of algorithm $\text{ABD}_{\mathbb{Q}}$. The latency is unchanged.

What does change with algorithm $\text{ABD}_{\mathbb{Q}}$ is the failure model. Instead of failure model $\mathfrak{C}_{|\mathcal{S}|/2-1}$, algorithm $\text{ABD}_{\mathbb{Q}}$ is designed for the failure model $\mathfrak{C}_{\mathbb{Q}}$. Note that either algorithm ensures atomicity for any pattern of failures in model $\mathfrak{C}$, and only the termination of operations depends on the more restricted model: $\mathfrak{C}_{|\mathcal{S}|/2-1}$ for algorithm ABD and $\mathfrak{C}_{\mathbb{Q}}$ for algorithm $\text{ABD}_{\mathbb{Q}}$.

4.2 ALGORITHM FAST: EXPEDITING READ OPERATIONS

Algorithm ABD is conceptually simple and it efficiently implements SWMR memory. The write operations take a single round and this operation latency cannot be improved: the writer must contact at least one object server and receive a response. However, the read operation takes two rounds, which led to the commonly accepted intuition that "atomic reads must write." As it turns out, the question of whether it is possible to have single-round read implementations, or recalling Definition 3.2, whether *fast* implementation are possible is answered in the affirmative.

We present algorithm FAST of Dutta et al. that implements *fast* read and write operations. To achieve this the algorithm constrains the number of readers in $\mathcal{R}$ with respect to the number of replica hosts in $\mathcal{S}$ and the number of crashes f. Specifically, the algorithm assumes that $|\mathcal{R}| < \frac{|\mathcal{S}|}{f} - 2$. Thus, in order to support at least two readers the algorithm assumes that $f < \frac{|\mathcal{S}|}{4}$.

To impose an order to the written values, FAST uses tags associated with values as in ABD. Also, similarly to algorithm ABD, each operation waits for $|\mathcal{S}| - f$ server replies. When a write operation is invoked, the writer increments its local tag, it sends the tag and the associated value to the servers, and waits for $|\mathcal{S}| - f$ replies before completing.

The main departure of algorithm FAST lies in the server and reader implementations. In addition to maintaining the object replica, the servers record the ids of processes to which they reply. The record is used by the read operations to determine their return value.

When a read operation is invoked, the reader sends query messages to the servers and awaits $|\mathcal{S}| - f$ replies. Upon receiving the replies the reader evaluates a predicate over the number of servers that replied with the maximum tag, in relation to the number of participants that witnessed this tag based on the records received from the servers. If the tag was received from "enough" servers and was seen by a "sufficient" number of participants, then the reader returns the value associated with the maximum tag, otherwise the reader returns the value associated with the previous tag. We next present the algorithmic details and the reasoning about the predicate.

4.2.1 ALGORITHM FAST SPECIFICATION

Algorithm FAST is composed of the following automata: FAST_w that defines the protocol for the sole writer, FAST_r that defines the protocol for each reader $\rho \in \mathcal{R}$, FAST_s that defines the protocol for each server $s \in \mathcal{S}$, and $Ch_{i,j}$ for each channel for $i, j \in \mathcal{I}$. The failure model $\mathfrak{C}$ is further restricted to f crashes such that $|\mathcal{R}| < \frac{|\mathcal{S}|}{f} - 2$, that is, the algorithm assumes failure model $\mathfrak{C}_{\frac{|\mathcal{S}|}{|\mathcal{R}|+2} - 1}$.

Algorithm FAST (unlike algorithm ABD) maintains *two* values for each tag: the current values, and the previous value. Readers return either the current value or the previous value depending on the information they gather from the servers; we discuss this in detail later.

Writer FAST_w (Specification 5). The writer protocol follows algorithm ABD. A write operation is invoked with the action write(val)$_w$ (lines 22–29). The writer increments its local tag,

Specification 5 FAST_w Writer Automaton: Signature, State, and Transitions

1: **Data Types:**
2:      *Msgs*, same as in Automaton 8

3: **Signature:**
4:      **Input:**
5:          $\text{write}(v)_w,\ v \in V$
6:          $\text{recv}(m)_{s,w},\ m \in \textit{Msgs}, s \in \mathcal{S}$
7:          fail_w
8:      **Output:**
9:          $\text{send}(m)_{w,s},\ m \in \textit{Msgs}, s \in \mathcal{S}$
10:         write-ack_w
11:     **Internal:**
12:         write-fix_w

13: **State:**
14:     $ts \in \mathbb{N}$ **init** 0 // object tag
15:     $v \in V$ **init** v_0 // object value
16:     $vp \in V$ **init** v_0 // previous value
17:     $wCounter \in \mathbb{N}$ **init** 0
18:     $srvAck \subseteq \mathcal{S}$ **init** $\emptyset$
19:     $destSet \subseteq \mathcal{S}$ **init** $\mathcal{S}$
20:     $status \in \{idle, active, done, failed\}$ **init** $idle$

21: **Transitions:**
22:     **Input** $\text{write}(val)_w$
23:         **Effect:**
24:             **if** $status = idle$ **then**
25:                 $status \leftarrow active$
26:                 $srvAck \leftarrow \emptyset$
27:                 $destSet \leftarrow \mathcal{S}$
28:                 $(vp, v, ts) \leftarrow (v, val, ts + 1)$

29:                 $wCounter \leftarrow wCounter + 1$

30: **Output** $\text{send}(\langle \text{WRITE}, t, val, valp, wC\rangle)_{w,s}$
31:     **Precondition:**
32:         $status = active$
33:         $s \in destSet$
34:         $(t, val, valp, wC) = (ts, v, vp, wCounter)$
35:     **Effect:**
36:         $destSet \leftarrow destSet \setminus \{s\}$

37: **Input** $\text{recv}(\langle \text{W-ACK}, wC\rangle)_{s,w}$
38:     **Effect:**
39:         **if** $status = active \wedge wCounter = wC$ **then**
40:             $srvAck \leftarrow srvAck \cup \{s\}$

41: **Internal** write-fix_w
42:     **Precondition:**
43:         $status = active$
44:         $|srvAck| \geq |\mathcal{S}| - f$
45:     **Effect:**
46:         $status \leftarrow done$

47: **Output** write-ack_w
48:     **Precondition:**
49:         $status = done$
50:     **Effect:**
51:         $status \leftarrow idle$

52: **Input** fail_w
53:     **Effect:**
54:         $status \leftarrow failed$

stores the current value as the previous value, and initializes the current value to *val* (line 28). Then the writer sends messages containing these values and the tag to the servers (lines 30–36), and waits for $|\mathcal{S}| - f$ servers to reply before terminating the operation (lines 37–46).

Specification 6 FAST_r Reader Automaton: Signature and State

1: **Data Types:**
2:      *Msgs*, same as in Specification 8

3: **Signature:**
4:      **Input:**
5:          $\text{read}_r,\ r \in \mathcal{R}$
6:          $\text{recv}(m)_{s,r},\ m \in \textit{Msgs}, r \in \mathcal{R}, s \in \mathcal{S}$
7:          $\text{fail}_r,\ r \in \mathcal{R}$
8:      **Output:**
9:          $\text{send}(m)_{r,s},\ m \in \textit{Msgs}, r \in \mathcal{R}, s \in \mathcal{S}$
10:         $\text{read-ack}(val)_r,\ val \in V, r \in \mathcal{R}$
11:     **Internal:**
12:         read-phase1-fix_r

13: **State:**
14:     $ts \in \mathbb{N}$ **init** 0
15:     $v \in V$ **init** $\perp$
16:     $vp \in V$ **init** $\perp$
17:     $retvalue \in V$ **init** $\perp$
18:     $rCounter \in \mathbb{N}$ **init** 0
19:     $status \in \{idle, active, done, failed\}$ **init** $idle$
20:     $srvAck \subseteq \textit{Msgs} \times \mathcal{S}$ **init** $\emptyset$
21:     $maxTack \subseteq \textit{Msgs}$ **init** $\emptyset$
22:     $maxTsSrv \subseteq \mathcal{S}$ **init** $\emptyset$
23:     $destSet \subseteq \mathcal{S}$ **init** $\mathcal{S}$

Specification 7 FAST$_r$ Reader Automaton: Transitions

```
 1: Transitions:                                            21: Internal read-fix_r
 2:   Input read_r                                          22:   Precondition:
 3:     Effect:                                             23:     status = active
 4:       if status = idle then                             24:     |srvAck| ≥ |S| − f
 5:         status ← active                                 25:   Effect:
 6:         srvAck ← ∅                                      26:     ts ← max{m.t : (m, ∗) ∈ srvAck}
 7:         destSet ← S                                     27:     maxTack ← {m : (m, ∗) ∈ srvAck ∧ m.t = ts}
 8:         rCounter ← rCounter + 1                         28:     (v, vp) ← (m.val, m.valp) s.t. m ∈ maxTack
                                                            29:     if ∃α ∈ [1, |R| + 1]  ∧  ∃MS ⊆ maxTack :
 9:   Output send(⟨READ, t, val, valp, rC⟩)_r,s            30:       |MS| ≥ |S| − αf
10:     Precondition:                                       31:       ∧ | ∩_{m∈MS} m.seen| ≥ α then
11:       status = active                                   32:       retvalue ← v
12:       s ∈ destSet                                       33:     else
13:       (t, val, valp, rC) = (ts, v, vp, rCounter)        34:       retvalue ← vp
14:     Effect:                                             35:     status ← done
15:       destSet ← destSet \ {s}
                                                            36: Output read-ack(val)_r
                                                            37:   Precondition:
16:   Input recv(⟨R-ACK, t, val, valp, seen, C⟩)_s,r        38:     status = done
17:     Effect:                                             39:     val = retvalue
18:       if status = active ∧ rCounter = C then            40:   Effect:
19:         srvAck ←                                        41:     status ← idle
20:           srvAck ∪ {((R-ACK, t, val, valp, seen, C), s)} 42: Input fail_r
                                                            43:   Effect:
                                                            44:     status ← failed
```

Reader FAST$_r$ (Specifications 6 and 7). The reader automaton is much different from the reader in ABD$_r$ as the reader needs to terminate at the single communication round. The read operation is invoked with action read (lines 2–8 of Automaton 7). The reader sends read messages to the servers (lines 9–13), and waits for $|S| - f$ servers to reply (line 24). Once the necessary replies are received, the reader determines the maximum tag among the replies (line 26), records the replies from the servers containing this tag in set $maxTack$ (line 27), and checks whether that tag was seen by a "sufficient" number of processes. This check is the heart of the algorithm and this is accomplished by the predicate that appears in lines 29–31.

The predicate is designed to guarantee atomicity through the following two key properties.

(1) The predicate holds when the write that originated the computed maximum tag completes before the current read.

(2) If the predicate is true for the current read, then it is also true for all subsequent reads, provided there is no write with a higher tag.

Let us examine the idea behind the predicate. Read operations terminate after a single round. Since f servers may fail, operations cannot wait for more than $|S| - f$ servers to reply. Consider execution ξ_1 of algorithm FAST that contains a complete write operation ω succeeded by a complete read operation ρ. The write operation sends a value associated with a tag tag_ω to all servers. A certain set S_ω of $|S| - f$ servers receives these messages and each of these servers reply, allowing the write operation to complete. All other messages of ω remain in transit in ξ_1

and are not received by any server $s \in \mathcal{S} \setminus \mathcal{S}_\omega$. Read operation ρ similarly sends messages to all servers and receives replies from a set $\mathcal{S}_\rho$, also containing $|\mathcal{S}| - f$ servers, however $\mathcal{S}_\rho$ does not include f servers that replied to ω. It follows that $|\mathcal{S}_\omega \cap \mathcal{S}_\rho| = |\mathcal{S}| - 2f$. To preserve atomicty, read ρ must return the value associated with tag_ω.

Consider now a second execution ξ_2 of algorithm FAST, where the write operation is incomplete, and propagates the value associated with the tag tag_ω only to servers in $\mathcal{S}_\omega \cap \mathcal{S}_\rho$. We extend ξ_2 by read operation ρ_1 performed by reader r_1 that receives replies from servers in $\mathcal{S}_\rho$. Read ρ_1 cannot distinguish executions ξ_1 from ξ_2 as the only servers that reply to the read operation with tag_ω in both executions are the ones in $\mathcal{S}_\omega \cap \mathcal{S}_\rho$. Thus, ρ_1 also returns the value associated with tag_ω. Extend now ξ_2 by a second read ρ_2 performed by reader r_2 that receives replies from servers in set $\mathcal{S}_{\rho_2}$, but that does include f servers from $\mathcal{S}_\omega \cap \mathcal{S}_\rho$. It is easy to see that ρ_2 receives the tag tag_ω from the servers in $|\mathcal{S}_\omega \cap \mathcal{S}_\rho \cap \mathcal{S}_{\rho_2}| = |\mathcal{S}| - 3f$. Since ρ_1 returns tag_ω and $\rho_1 \rightarrow \rho_2$, then ρ_2 has to return the value associated with tag_ω to preserve atomicity.

Note that in ξ_2, r_1 receives tag_ω from $|\mathcal{S}| - 2f$ servers and tag_ω is seen by at least 2 processes—the writer w and r_1. Also, ρ_2 receives tag_ω from $|\mathcal{S}| - 3f$ servers and tag_ω is seen by at least 3 processes—the writer w, r_1 and r_2. So it is easy to see that a predicate that enables fast reads must depend on the number of servers, as well as the number of readers, that have seen the most recent tag. Since there no limitations on the crashes of readers, no reader can expect to be able to exchange information with other readers. The only way for any reader to learn about other readers is collect information about other readers indirectly via the servers. Thus, along with the object copy, every server needs to maintain the set of processes (a subset of the readers plus the writer) to which the server has replied after updating its tag to tag_ω (including the reader or the writer that updated the tag of the server to tag_ω). This information is kept in the set *seen*, a state variable of server FAST$_s$ (Specification 8).

Generalizing the above argument gives us the desired predicate: if there is $\alpha \geq 1$ such that the reader receives the maximum tag from at least $|\mathcal{S}| - \alpha f$ servers, and there are at least α processes that are in the list *seen* of each of those $|\mathcal{S}| - \alpha f$ messages, then the predicate is true. Formally, the predicate is the following.

Reader predicate in FAST$_r$:

$$\exists\, \alpha \in \|\mathcal{R}| + 1], \ \exists\, MS \subseteq maxTack :$$

$$|MS| \geq |\mathcal{S}| - \alpha f \ \textbf{and} \ |\bigcap_{m \in MS} m.seen| \geq \alpha.$$

If the predicate holds then the reader returns value v associated with the maximum tag (line 32); otherwise, it returns value vp associated with the previous tag (line 34).

Note that correctness, in the case of a reader returning the previous value vp, depends on the existence of a single well-formed writer. Thus, the invocation of the write operation with for the maximum tag that a reader discovers (in line 26) implies the completion of the previous write operation with the tag associated with vp. When the read operation decides to return the value associated with the discovered maximum tag, then the safety of the algorithm relies on the correctness of the predicate.

Specification 8 FAST_s Server Automaton: Signature, State, and Transitions

---

1: **Data Types:**
2: $\quad Msgs_1 \subseteq \{\text{READ},\text{WRITE}\} \times \langle \mathbb{N} \times V \times V \rangle \times \mathbb{N}$
3: $\quad Msgs_2 \subseteq \{\text{R-ACK}\} \times \langle \mathbb{N} \times V \times V \rangle \times 2^{\mathcal{I}} \times \mathbb{N}$
4: $\quad Msgs_3 \subseteq \{\text{W-ACK}\} \times \mathbb{N}$
5: $\quad Msgs = Msgs_1 \cup Msgs_2 \cup Msgs_3$

6: **Signature:**
7: $\quad$ **Input:**
8: $\qquad \text{recv}(m)_{i,s}, \ m \in Msgs, s \in \mathcal{S}, i \in \mathcal{R} \cup \{w\}$
9: $\qquad \text{fail}_s$
10: $\quad$ **Output:**
11: $\qquad \text{send}(m)_{s,i}, \ m \in Msgs, s \in \mathcal{S}, i \in \mathcal{R} \cup \{w\}$

12: **State:**
13: $\quad ts \in \mathbb{N} \textbf{ init } 0$
14: $\quad v \in V \textbf{ init } v_0$
15: $\quad vp \in V \textbf{ init } v_0$
16: $\quad seen \subseteq \mathcal{R} \cup \mathcal{W} \textbf{ init } \emptyset$
17: $\quad Counter(i) \in \mathbb{N}, \ \forall i \in \mathcal{R} \cup \{w\} \textbf{ init } 0$
18: $\quad status \in \{active, failed\} \textbf{ init } idle$
19: $\quad replySet \subseteq Msgs \times \mathcal{I} \textbf{ init } \emptyset$

20: **Transitions:**
21: **Input** $\text{recv}(\langle msgT, t, val, valp, C \rangle)_{i,s}$

22: **Effect:**
23: $\quad$ **if** $status = active \wedge C > Counter(i)$ **then**
24: $\qquad Counter(i) \leftarrow C$
25: $\qquad$ **if** $t > ts$ **then**
26: $\qquad\quad (ts, v, vp) \leftarrow (t, val, valp)$
27: $\qquad\quad seen \leftarrow \{i\}$
28: $\qquad$ **else**
29: $\qquad\quad seen \leftarrow seen \cup \{i\}$
30: $\qquad$ **if** $msgT = \text{READ}$ **then**
31: $\qquad\quad replySet \leftarrow replySet$
32: $\qquad\qquad \cup \{(\langle \text{R-ACK}, ts, v, vp, seen, C \rangle, i)\}$
33: $\qquad$ **else**
34: $\qquad\quad replySet \leftarrow replySet \cup \{(\langle \text{W-ACK}, C \rangle, i)\}$

35: **Output** $\text{send}(m)_{s,i}$
36: **Precondition:**
37: $\quad status = active$
38: $\quad (m, i) \in replySet$
39: **Effect:**
40: $\quad replySet \leftarrow replySet \setminus \{(m, i)\}$

41: **Input** fail_s
42: **Effect:**
43: $\quad status \leftarrow failed$

Server FAST_s (Specification 8). Servers in algorithm FAST perform two functions: (i) they maintain a copy of the atomic object; and (ii) they implement a bookkeeping mechanism that allows read operations to complete in a single round. The state of each server s includes the current tag tag, associated value v, and the previous value vp, with the respective initial values $0, v_0$, and v_0. The state of server s also includes set $seen$ that records the ids of the processes to which the server replied with its largest tag and the associated values.

The server acts as follows. When action recv from process i occurs (line 21), server s compares the tag t enclosed in the message to its local tag tag (line 25). If the received tag is larger, then the server updates its replica information and sets the $seen$ set to $\{i\}$ (lines 26–27). Else the server just adds the sender id to set $seen$ (line 29). The server then prepares a response message (lines 30–34). If process i is a reader, the server encloses in the message its replica information and set $seen$. If process i is the writer, the message is just an acknowledgment. The response messages are sent in action send.

4.2.2 ALGORITHM FAST CORRECTNESS

We need to show that any execution $\xi \in execs(\text{FAST}, f)$, for $|\mathcal{S}| > 2f$, satisfies liveness (i.e., termination) and safety (i.e., atomicity) properties. Termination is guaranteed as each operation expects $|\mathcal{S}| - f$ replies and no more than f servers are allowed to fail. So the key property we need to proof is that of atomicity.

Theorem 4.2   *Algorithm Fast implements a read/write atomic object.*

Proof. According to Definition 2.16, for each execution ξ there must exist a partial order $\prec$ on the set of operations Π that satisfy conditions **A1**, **A2**, and **A3**. Similar to Theorem 4.1, we denote by tag_π the value of the new tag generated by the writer when π is a write, and the tag associated with the returned value when π is a read. Note that a read in FAST may return either the value associated with the maximum tag, i.e., $maxTS$ or the value associated with the previous tag, i.e., $maxTS - 1$. With this we define the partial order on operations as follows. For two operations, π_1 and π_2, when π_1 is any operation and π_2 is a write, we let $\pi_1 \prec \pi_2$ if $tag_{\pi_1} < tag_{\pi_2}$. For two operations π_1 and π_2 when π_1 is a write and π_2 is a read we let $\pi_1 \prec \pi_2$ if $tag_{\pi_1} \leq tag_{\pi_2}$. The rest of the order is established by transitivity. Note that reads with the same tags are not ordered. Now we use this definition of the order to reason about each of the three conditions of Definition 2.16.

A1 If for operations π_1 and π_2 in Π, $\pi_1 \rightarrow \pi_2$, then it cannot be the case that $\pi_2 \prec \pi_1$.

Let us assume that $\pi_2 \prec \pi_1$. If π_2 is a write, then the sole writer will generate a new tag by incrementing the largest tag in the system. Thus, any other tag will be strictly smaller than tag_{π_2} and hence, $tag_{\pi_1} < tag_{\pi_2}$. By our ordering definition it follows that $\pi_1 \prec \pi_2$ contradicting our assumption. It remains to examine the case where π_2 is a read and π_1 is either a write or a read.

Let us begin with the case where π_1 is a write, and π_2 is a read. Operation π_1 propagates its tag to $|\mathcal{S}| - f$ servers before completing, and π_2 discovers the maximum tag among $|\mathcal{S}| - f$ server replies. Since $f < \frac{|\mathcal{S}|}{2}$, then π_2 receives a tag greater or equal than tag_{π_1} from the intersection of the two majority sets, i.e., from at least $|\mathcal{S}| - 2f$ servers. Let $maxTS$ be the maximum of those tags. There are two cases for π_2. Either it discovers (i) that $maxTS > tag_{\pi_1}$, or (ii) that $maxTS = tag_{\pi_1}$. The reader returns a tag (and thus its associated value) such that either $tag_{\pi_2} = maxTS$ or $tag_{\pi_2} = maxTS - 1$. If $maxTS > tag_{\pi_1}$ then $tag_{\pi_2} \geq tag_{\pi_1}$, and thus $\pi_1 \prec \pi_2$, in either case. If $maxTS = tag_{\pi_1}$ then the predicate at π_2 holds for $\alpha = 2$, $|MS| = |\mathcal{S}_{\pi_1} \cap \mathcal{S}_{\pi_2}| \geq |\mathcal{S}| - 2f$, and $|\bigcap_{(s,m)\in MS} m.seen| \geq 2$ since every server in the intersection added the writer and the reader process in its *seen* set before replying. Thus, the *read* returns the tag $tag_{\pi_2} = tag_{\pi_1}$. Hence, in any case $tag_{\pi_2} \geq tag_{\pi_1}$, and thus $\pi_1 \prec \pi_2$ by our definition, contradicting again our initial assumption that $\pi_2 \prec \pi_1$.

It remains to examine the case where both π_1 and π_2 are read operations. This is the most challenging case to proof as *reads* do not propagate the tag they return before completing. Assume that r_1 and r_2 invoke π_1 and π_2, respectively. As before, π_1 may return either $tag_{\pi_1} = maxTS - 1$ or $tag_{\pi_1} = maxTS$. If π_1 returns $tag_{\pi_1} = maxTS - 1$, then the writer completed the write operation that propagated the tag $maxTS - 1$ and invoked the operation that propagated the tag $maxTS$ before the completion of π_1. Since $\pi_1 \rightarrow \pi_2$ then π_2 succeeds the write that propagated the tag $maxTS - 1$. Thus, as we showed above, π_2 returns a tag $tag_{\pi_2} \geq maxTS - 1$. If $tag_{\pi_2} > tag_{\pi_1}$, then $\pi_1 \prec \pi_2$, otherwise the two operations cannot be ordered. Thus, it cannot be the case that $\pi_2 \prec \pi_1$.

So it remains to investigate the case where π_1 returns $maxTS$. This happens when the predicate holds for π_1. If the reader r_2 is already in the set that satisfies the predicate for π_1, then it follows that r_2 discovered $maxTS$ in an older read operation. As r_2 will send a tag greater or equal to $maxTS$ during π_2, then π_2 will return a tag $tag_{\pi_2} \geq maxTS$ and hence either $\pi_1 \prec \pi_2$ or the two operations cannot be ordered.

If r_2 is not in the set observed during π_1, then let MS_1 be the set of servers that replied with $maxTS$ and satisfy the predicate for π_1. Also, let MS_2 be the messages received at r_2 and contain $maxTS$. Then,

$$|MS_1 \cap MS_2| \geq |\mathcal{S}| - (\alpha + 1) f.$$

Since $\alpha \leq |\mathcal{R}|$ and $|\mathcal{R}| < \frac{|\mathcal{S}|}{f} - 2$, then $|\mathcal{S}| - (\alpha + 1) f > f$. So any reader operation will observe the value returned by π_1. Since $\pi_1 \rightarrow \pi_2$, then every server $s \in MS_2 \cap MS_1$ replies to r_1 before replying to r_2. Hence for every message m send by any server $s \in MS_2 \cap MS_1$ it holds that $r_1 \in m.seen$ set, and s adds r_2 in its $seen$ set before replying for π_2. If we denote by $seen_1 = | \bigcap_{(m,s) \in MS_1} m.seen |$ then it follows that $seen_1 \cup \{r_2\} \subseteq \bigcap_{(m,s) \in MS_2 \cap MS_1} m.seen$. Since $|seen_1| \geq \alpha$ and $r_2 \notin seen_1$ then $| \bigcap_{(m,s) \in MS_2 \cap MS_1} m.seen | \geq \alpha + 1$. So the predicate holds for π_2 in this case for $\alpha + 1$. Thus, in any case π_2 returns $tag_{\pi_2} = tag_{\pi_1} = maxTS$, and hence the two operations cannot be ordered. So it cannot be the case that $\pi_2 \prec \pi_1$ in this case either.

A2 If ω is a write operation and π is any operation, then either $\omega \prec \pi$ or $\pi \prec \omega$.

If $tag_\omega > tag_\pi$ then $\pi \prec \omega$ follows directly. If $tag_\omega = tag_\pi$ then it must be that π is a read that obtains its tag from a server written to by ω using the intersection property, and $\omega \prec \pi$ follows again from the definition of the order. If $tag_\omega < tag_\pi$ then $\omega \prec \pi$ follows directly.

A3 The value returned by a read operation is the value written by the last preceding write operation according to $\prec$ (or the initial value if there is no such write).

Let ω be the last write operation preceding the read operation ρ. This means that $tag_\omega \leq tag_\rho$. If $tag_\omega = tag_\rho$, then ρ discovered the value written by ω in a set of servers MS that satisfy its predicate, i.e., $MS \leq |\mathcal{S}| - \alpha f$ and $| \bigcap_{m \in MS} m.seen | \geq \alpha$. For this to happen either: (a) at least $|\mathcal{S}| - f$ servers in MS received messages from ω, or (b) the servers in MS replied to $\alpha - 1$ reads before replying to ρ. If $tag_\omega < tag_\rho$, then ρ obtains a larger tag that can only be originating by a write that follows ω, thus ω is not the preceding write, but this cannot be the case. Finally, if $tag_\rho = 0$, then there are no preceding writes, and ρ returns the initial value.

This completes the proof. $\qquad\qquad\qquad\qquad\qquad\qquad\qquad\qquad\qquad\qquad\qquad\qquad\qquad$ $\square$

4.3 LOWER BOUND: LIMITATIONS OF FAST IMPLEMENTATIONS

Algorithm FAST assumes that the number of crashes f in the failure model $\mathfrak{C}_f$ is constrained to be inversely proportional to the number of readers: $f \leq |\mathcal{S}|/(|\mathcal{R}| + 2)$. This begs the question of whether it is possible to increase the number of readers in fast implementations without negatively affecting the ability to tolerate crashes. Here, we answer this question in the negative.

Theorem 4.3   *A fast atomic read/write object implementation is possible iff* $|\mathcal{R}| < \frac{|\mathcal{S}|}{f} - 2$.

Proof Sketch. We consider a series of execution fragments that contain only fast operations. Let us assume that there exist an atomic object implementation when $|\mathcal{R}| = \frac{|\mathcal{S}|}{f} - 1$.

For our construction we split the servers $\mathcal{S}$ into $k = \frac{|\mathcal{S}|}{f}$ disjoint subsets $(\mathcal{S}_1, \dots, \mathcal{S}_k)$ such that the size of every subset is $|\mathcal{S}_i| \leq f$. Since we assume that f servers may fail, then to guarantee termination each operation cannot wait for more than $|\mathcal{S}| - f$ servers to reply. Thus, each operation may receive replies from *at least all but one* subsets in $\{\mathcal{S}_1, \dots, \mathcal{S}_k\}$. We say that an operation π *communicates* with a subset $\mathcal{S}_i$ if every server $s \in \mathcal{S}_i$ receives the message sent from the invoking process i for π during its first round and i receives the reply from s; otherwise the messages from i to any $s \in \mathcal{S}_i$ for π remain in transit.

Let us begin the construction of our execution series with an execution ξ_1 that contains the following operations: (i) a complete *write* $\omega(v)$ that communicates with the subsets $\mathcal{S}_1, \dots, \mathcal{S}_{k-1}$, succeeding by (ii) a complete *read* ρ_1 that communicates with the subsets $\mathcal{S}_2, \dots, \mathcal{S}_k$. Since $\omega \to \rho_1$ then ρ_1 returns v to preserve atomicity.

Consider now an execution ξ_1' which contains the following operations: (i) an incomplete *write* $\omega(v)$ that communicates with the subsets $\mathcal{S}_2, \dots, \mathcal{S}_{k-1}$, and (ii) a complete *read* ρ_1 that communicates with the subsets $\mathcal{S}_2, \dots, \mathcal{S}_k$. Notice that only the servers in $\mathcal{S}_1$ can distinguish ξ_1 from ξ_1'. Since ρ_1 does not receive any replies from the servers in $\mathcal{S}_1$, then it cannot distinguish ξ_1 from ξ_1'. Thus, ρ_1 returns v in ξ_1' as well. We extend ξ_1' with a complete read operation ρ_2 that communicates with the subsets $\mathcal{S}_1, \mathcal{S}_3, \dots, \mathcal{S}_k$ (it skips $\mathcal{S}_2$) to obtain ξ_2. Since $\rho_1 \to \rho_2$ and ρ_1 returns v in ξ_2 then ρ_2 returns v in ξ_2 to preserve atomicity.

Consider now ξ_2' which is similar with ξ_2 but with both the write ω and the read ρ_1 to be incomplete. In particular ξ_2' contains: (i) an incomplete *write* $\omega(v)$ that communicates with the subsets $\mathcal{S}_3, \dots, \mathcal{S}_{k-1}$, (ii) an incomplete *read* ρ_1 that communicates with the subsets $\mathcal{S}_3, \dots, \mathcal{S}_k$, and (iii) a complete *read* ρ_2 that communicates with the subsets $\mathcal{S}_1, \mathcal{S}_3, \dots, \mathcal{S}_k$. Notice that only the servers in S_2 may distinguish ξ_2 from ξ'_2. Since ρ_2 does not receive replies from the servers in S_2 it cannot distinguish ξ_2 from ξ'_2 and thus it returns v in ξ'_2 as well.

Continuing in the same pattern we construct execution ξ_ℓ, for $\ell \leq k - 2$, by extending execution $\xi'_{\ell-1}$ and is composed of the following operations: (i) an incomplete *write* $\omega(v)$ that communicates with the subsets $S_\ell, \ldots, S_{k-1}$, (ii) a series of incomplete *reads* ρ_z, for $1 \leq z < \ell$, from reader r_z each communicating with the subsets $S_1, \ldots, S_{z-1}, S_\ell, \ldots, S_k$, and (iii) a complete *read* ρ_ℓ from r_ℓ that communicates with the subsets $S_1, \ldots, S_{\ell-1}, S_{\ell+1}, \ldots, S_k$. We also construct ξ'_ℓ where the write and each of the incomplete reads do not communicate with the servers in S_ℓ. Since the servers in S_ℓ do not reply to ρ_ℓ then ρ_ℓ cannot distinguish ξ'_ℓ from ξ_ℓ. With a simple induction on ℓ we can show that ρ_ℓ returns v in both ξ_ℓ and ξ'_ℓ.

Consider now the case where $\ell = k - 1$. The execution ξ_{k-1} extends execution ξ'_{k-2} with a complete read ρ_{k-1} from r_{k-1} that communicates with the subsets $S_1, \ldots, S_{k-2}, S_k$. Since $\rho_{k-2} \to \rho_{k-1}$ and ρ_{k-2} returns v in ξ'_{k-2} (and thus ξ_{k-1}) then ρ_{k-1} returns v in ξ_{k-1} as well to preserve atomicity. Finally, we construct execution ξ'_{k-1} that does not contain any write operation and the read ρ_{k-2} is incomplete by not receiving replies from any server in the subset S_{k-1}. Notice that only the servers in subset S_{k-1} can distinguish executions ξ_{k-1} from ξ'_{k-1} as they are the only servers that the messages received change between the two executions. Since ρ_{k-1} does not communicate with any server in S_{k-1} then it cannot distinguish between the two executions. Thus, ρ_{k-1} returns v in ξ'_{k-1} as well. This, however, violates atomicity as ρ_{k-1} returns a value that was never written. As ρ_{k-1} was invoked by the $k - 1$th reader then this contradicts our assumption that atomicity is preserved when $|\mathcal{R}| = k - 1 = \frac{S}{f} - 1$. □

4.4 ALGORITHM SLIQ: INTRODUCING QUORUM VIEWS

We now present algorithm SLIQ that relaxes the strict environmental conditions by adopting a different approach than algorithm FAST (see Section 4.2). In contrast to FAST, that requires *all* operations to complete in a single round, SLIQ allows *some reads* to perform *two* rounds, and relaxes the restrictions on the participation of the service (allowing unbounded number of readers). The algorithm uses a quorum system over replica servers. To ensure operation termination, the adversary is constrained so that at *least a single quorum* is correct in any execution.

Briefly, the algorithm adopts the technique of using tags associated with values (as in FAST) to order the values written on the atomic object. Each *write* associates a tag with a tuple $\langle v, vp \rangle$ containing both the new value to be written v and the previous value written vp. A *read* collects replies from a quorum of servers during its first round. To specify the "speed" of a *read*, SLIQ utilizes a client-side decision tool, called *Quorum Views*, to examine the distribution of an *object value* among the server replies. This aims to help the reader determine the status of the *write* that propagated that object value. If the status of a write is determinable then the read terminates in one round otherwise it performs a second round before completing. The reader may return either v or vp depending on the quorum view observed.

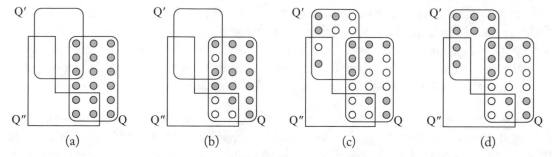

Figure 4.2: (a) **QV1**, (b) **QV2**, (c) **QV3** with incomplete write, and (d) **QV3** with complete write.

4.4.1   ALGORITHMIC TECHNIQUE: QUORUM VIEWS

We first present *quorum views* which are the heart of SLIQ. A quorum view refers to the distribution of an object value as it is witnessed by a read operation during a communication round. As each value is associated with a unique tag, we define quorum views in terms of the tag distribution instead of the actual written value. Let $maxT$ denote the maximum tag that a read discovers during some round. Also, let $m(\rho, c)_{s,r}.ts$ denote the tag that server s sends during the cth round of the read operation ρ to the invoking reader r. Given this notation, quorum views are defined as follows.

Definition 4.4   Quorum Views.   Any read ρ that receives replies from all the members of a quorum $Q \in \mathbb{Q}$ in some round c, witnesses one of the following **quorum views**.

    QV1. $\forall s \in Q : m(\rho, c)_{s,r}.ts = maxT$,

    QV2. $\forall Q' \in \mathbb{Q}, Q \neq Q', \exists A \subseteq Q \cap Q'$, s.t. $A \neq \emptyset$ and $\forall s \in A : m(\rho, c)_{s,r}.ts < maxT$, and

    QV3. $\exists s' \in Q : m(\rho, c)_{s',r}.ts < maxT$ and $\exists Q' \in \mathbb{Q}, Q \neq Q'$ and $\forall s \in Q \cap Q' :$ $m(\rho, c)_{s,r}.ts = maxT$.

    Under the assumption that servers always maintain the largest tag they receive and given that a single quorum is guaranteed to be non-faulty (thus an operation may wait from a single quorum to reply), these three types of quorum views may reveal the status of a *write* operation (complete or incomplete). Next, we describe the idea behind each quorum view. An example of the three quorum views can be depicted in Figure 4.2 assuming that the read operation ρ receives replies from the servers in Q. The dark nodes maintain the maximum tag ($maxT$) and white nodes or "blank" quorums maintain an older tag.

QV1: Here read ρ obtains $maxT$ from every server $s \in Q$ (as seen in Figure 4.2a). This implies that s received a message from the writer, updated its tag to $maxT$, and replied to the writer before receiving and replying to the *read* message from ρ. Since the write operation cannot wait for more than a single quorum to reply, then ω has to complete as soon as the replies are delivered to the writer. Note that no process except from the writer w can distinguish whether the replies are delivered and the *write* completed or the replies are in-transit and the *write* is incomplete. Thus, for any process $i \neq w$, **QV1** implies a potentially operation.

QV2: This is the negation of the other two views, **QV1** and **QV3** (given below), establishing a quorum where the new value is neither distributed to the full quorum nor distributed fully in any of its intersections. Observe that, by Definition 2.5, every two quorums intersect, i.e., $\forall Q, Q' \in \mathbb{Q}, Q \cap Q' \neq \emptyset$. Therefore, if there exists a quorum Q' such that $\forall s \in Q', m(\rho, c)_{s,r}.ts = maxT$, then it follows that $\forall Q \in \mathbb{Q}, s' \in Q' \cap Q$ replies with $m(\rho, c)_{s',r}.ts = maxT$ to ρ. That is, all servers in any intersection of Q' must reply with $maxT$ to a read operation ρ. From this observation, **QV2** reveals an *incomplete write* operation. Recall that, by **QV2**, ρ witnesses a subset of servers that maintain a tag older than $maxT$ in *each intersection* of Q (see Figure 4.2b). This implies that the write operation (which propagates $maxT$) has not yet received replies from any full quorum and thus, has not yet completed.

QV3: Here there is insufficient information regarding the status of the write operation. If an operation receives replies from a quorum Q (that contains some servers with a tag less than $maxT$) and witnesses some intersection $Q \cap Q'$ that contains $maxTS$ in all of its servers, then a write operation might: (i) have been completed and contacted Q' (see Figure 4.2d) or (ii) be incomplete and contacted a subset of servers B such that $Q \cap Q' \subseteq B$ and $\forall Q'' \in \mathbb{Q}, Q'' \nsubseteq B$ (see Figure 4.2c).

4.4.2 ALGORITHM SLIQ SPECIFICATION

Algorithm SLIQ is composed of four types of automata: $SLIQ_w$ that specifies the write operation protocol for the writer process w; $SLIQ_r$ specifies the read protocol for each $r \in \mathcal{R}$; $SLIQ_s$ that specifies the server protocol for each $s \in \mathcal{S}$; and $Ch_{i,j}$ that specifies the communication channels (see Section 2.1.3). As in the previous algorithms we assume that the initial value of each replica is v_0 and the tag variable, ts, in each process is initially set to 0. Also, for each writer and reader process the variable $\mathbb{Q}$ stores initially the quorum system membership.

Writer Protocol (Specification 9, $SLIQ_w$). The writer protocol in SLIQ is very similar to the writer protocol in FAST (see Specification 5, $FAST_w$). In particular, when a write(v) action occurs (lines 23–29) the writer increments its local tag and assigns it to both the new value to be written v and the previous written value vp. The writer sends *write* messages to each server when action send occurs (lines 32–36) and receives their replies when action recv occurs (lines 37–40). The writer terminates when it receives replies from a *quorum* of servers. This can be seen in line 44 of the write-fix action and is the main departure from the write protocol of FAST that instead was expecting a majority ($\mathcal{S} - f$) of servers to reply.

Specification 9 SLIQ_w Writer Automaton: Signature, State, and Transitions

1: **Data Types:**
2:   *Msgs*, same as in Specification 11

3: **Signature:**
4:   **Input:**
5:     $\text{write}(val)_w, \; v \in V$
6:     $\text{recv}(m)_{s,w}, \; m \in Msgs, \; s \in \mathcal{S}$
7:     fail_w
8:   **Output:**
9:     $\text{send}(m)_{w,s}, \; m \in Msgs, \; s \in \mathcal{S}$
10:     write-ack_w
11:   **Internal:**
12:     write-fix_w

13: **State:**
14:   $ts \in \mathbb{N} \text{ init } 0$
15:   $v \in V \text{ init } \bot$
16:   $vp \in V \text{ init } \bot$
17:   $wCounter \in \mathbb{N}^+ \text{ init } 0$
18:   $srvAck \subseteq \mathcal{S} \text{ init } \emptyset$
19:   $status \in \{idle, active, done, failed\} \text{ init } idle$
20:   $destSet \subseteq \mathcal{S} \text{ init } \mathcal{S}$

21: **Transitions:**
22:   **Input** $\text{write}(val)_w$
23:     **Effect:**
24:       **if** $status = idle$ **then**
25:         $status \leftarrow active$
26:         $srvAck \leftarrow \emptyset$
27:         $destSet \leftarrow \mathcal{S}$
28:         $(vp, v, ts) \leftarrow (v, val, ts + 1)$
29:         $wCounter \leftarrow wCounter + 1$

30:   **Output** $\text{send}(\langle \text{WRITE}, t, val, valp, C \rangle)_{w,s}$
31:     **Precondition:**
32:       $status = active$
33:       $s \in destSet$
34:       $(t, val, valp, C) = (ts, v, vp, wCounter)$
35:     **Effect:**
36:       $destSet \leftarrow destSet \setminus \{s\}$

37:   **Input** $\text{recv}(\langle \text{W-ACK}, wC \rangle)_{s,w}$
38:     **Effect:**
39:       **if** $status = active \wedge wCounter = wC$ **then**
40:         $srvAck \leftarrow srvAck \cup \{s\}$

41:   **Internal** write-fix_w
42:     **Precondition:**
43:       $status = active$
44:       $\exists Q \in \mathbb{Q} : Q \subseteq srvAck$
45:     **Effect:**
46:       $status \leftarrow done$

47:   **Output** write-ack_w
48:     **Precondition:**
49:       $status = done$
50:     **Effect:**
51:       $status \leftarrow idle$

52:   **Input** fail_w
53:     **Effect:**
54:       $status \leftarrow failed$

Reader Protocol (Specification 10, SLIQ_r). The read protocol is the heart of SLIQ and distinguishes the algorithm from both FAST and ABD. Any read operation may take one or two rounds to complete (fast or slow) independently whether the *read* is concurrent with any other operation (*read* or *write*). The decision on the number of communication rounds is based on the quorum views that the reader obtains during its first communication round .

A read operation is invoked when the SLIQ_r automaton receives a read_r request from its environment (lines 28–32). The *status* variable becomes $active$. and the reader sends messages to each server $s \in \mathcal{S}$ through action $\text{send}(m)_{r,s}$ (lines 35–39) to obtain the value of the object replicas. The $\text{recv}(m)_{s,r}$ action (lines 49–51) is triggered when a reply from a server s is received. The reader collects the identifiers of the servers that replied to the current operation and their messages in the *srvAck* set. When the set *srvAck* contains the members of at least a single quorum Q of the quorum system $\mathbb{Q}$ (line 59), the reader examines the distribution of the maximum tag and its associated values ($\langle maxT, v, vp \rangle$) within that quorum by collecting the servers that replied with $maxT$ in the $maxTsSrv$ set (line 65). This distribution characterizes a quorum view.

Specification 10 SLIQ_r Reader Automaton: Signature and State

---

1: **Data Types:**
2:   $Msgs$, same as in Specification 11

3: **Signature:**
4:   **Input:**
5:     $read_r$, $r \in \mathcal{R}$
6:     $recv(m)_{s,r}$, $m \in Msgs$, $r \in \mathcal{R}$, $s \in \mathcal{S}$
7:     $fail_r$, $r \in \mathcal{R}$
8:   **Output:**
9:     $send(m)_{r,s}$, $m \in Msgs$, $r \in \mathcal{R}$, $s \in \mathcal{S}$
10:     $read\text{-}ack(val)_r$, $val \in V$, $r \in \mathcal{R}$
11:   **Internal:**
12:     read-phase1-fix$_r$
13:     read-phase2-fix$_r$

14: **State:**
15:   $ts \in \mathbb{N}$ **init** 0
16:   $v \in V$ **init** $\perp$
17:   $vp \in V$ **init** $\perp$
18:   $retvalue \in V$ **init** $\perp$
19:   $rCounter \in \mathbb{N}^+$ **init** 0
20:   $status \in$
21:     $\{idle, done, failed, phase1, phase2\}$ **init** $idle$
22:   $srvAck \subseteq Msgs \times \mathcal{S}$ **init** $\emptyset$
23:   $maxTsSrv \subseteq \mathcal{S}$ **init** $\emptyset$
24:   $destSet \subseteq \mathcal{S}$ **init** $\mathcal{S}$

25: **Transitions:**
26:   **Input** read$_r$
27:     **Effect:**
28:       if $status = idle$ then
29:         $status \leftarrow phase1$
30:         $srvAck \leftarrow \emptyset$
31:         $destSet \leftarrow \mathcal{S}$
32:         $rCounter \leftarrow rCounter + 1$

33:   **Output** send$(\langle \text{READ}, t, val, valp, rC \rangle)_{r,s}$
34:     **Precondition:**
35:       $status = phase1$
36:       $s \in destSet$
37:       $(t, val, valp, rC) = (ts, v, vp, rCounter)$
38:     **Effect:**
39:       $destSet \leftarrow destSet \setminus \{s\}$

40:   **Output** send$(\langle \text{INFORM}, t, val, valp, rC \rangle)_{r,s}$
41:     **Precondition:**
42:       $status = phase2$
43:       $s \in destSet$
44:       $(t, val, valp, rC) = (ts, v, vp, rCounter)$
45:     **Effect:**
46:       $destSet \leftarrow destSet \setminus \{s\}$

47: **Input** recv$(\langle \text{R-ACK}, t, val, valp, rC \rangle)_{s,r}$
48:   **Effect:**
49:     if $status = phase1 \wedge rCounter = rC$ then
50:       $srvAck \leftarrow srvAck \cup$
51:         $\{(\langle \text{R-ACK}, t, val, valp, rC \rangle, s)\}$

52: **Input** recv$(\langle \text{I-ACK}, rC \rangle)_{s,r}$
53:   **Effect:**
54:     if $status = phase2 \wedge rCounter = rC$ then
55:       $srvAck \leftarrow srvAck \cup \{(\langle \text{I-ACK}, rC \rangle, s)\}$

56: **Internal** read-phase1-fix$_r$
57:   **Precondition:**
58:     $status = phase1$
59:     $\exists Q \in \mathbb{Q} : Q \subseteq srvAck$
60:   **Effect:**
61:     $ts \leftarrow max(\{m.ts : (m, s) \in srvAck \wedge s \in Q\})$
62:     $maxAck \leftarrow$
63:       $\{(m, s) : (m, s) \in srvAck \wedge m.ts = ts\}$
64:     $(v, vp) \leftarrow (m.val, m.valp)$ s.t. $(m, *) \in maxAck$
65:     $maxTsSrv \leftarrow \{s : s \in Q, (s, m) \in maxAck\}$
66:     if $Q \subseteq maxTsSrv$ then   // QV1
67:       $retvalue \leftarrow v$
68:       $status \leftarrow done$
69:     else
70:       if $\exists Q' \in \mathbb{Q}, Q' \neq Q$
71:         s.t. $Q \cap Q' \subseteq maxTsSrv$ then
           // QV3
72:           $retvalue \leftarrow v$
73:           $status \leftarrow phase2$
74:           $srvAck \leftarrow \emptyset$
75:           $destSet \leftarrow \mathcal{S}$
76:           $rCounter \leftarrow rCounter + 1$
77:       else   // QV2
78:         $retvalue \leftarrow vp$
79:         $status \leftarrow done$

80: **Internal** read-phase2-fix$_r$
81:   **Precondition:**
82:     $status = phase2$
83:     $\exists Q \in \mathbb{Q} : Q \subseteq srvAck$
84:   **Effect:**
85:     $status \leftarrow done$

86: **Output** read-ack$(val)_r$
87:   **Precondition:**
88:     $status = done$
89:     $val = retvalue$
90:   **Effect:**
91:     $status \leftarrow idle$

92: **Input** fail$_r$
93:   **Effect:**
94:     $status \leftarrow failed$

If the quorum view observed is either **QV1** or **QV2** then the reader terminates in the first round; otherwise if the quorum view is **QV3** the reader proceeds to a second round. If

QV1 is observed (i.e., $maxTsSrv = Q$), then the write operation that propagates $\langle maxT, v, vp \rangle$ is potentially completed and thus, the read returns v (lines 66–68).

If **QV3** is observed (i.e., $\exists Q' \in \mathbb{Q}$ s.t. $maxTsSrv \cap Q' = Q \cap Q'$), then the reader cannot determine the status of the write operation and, thus, proceeds to a second round (lines 71–76). During this round, the reader sends $\langle maxT, v, vp \rangle$ to all the servers. Once the reader gets replies from a full quorum, the read completes and returns v (lines 82–85).

If neither **QV1** nor **QV3** is observed then **QV2** is observed, and the write operation that propagates $\langle maxT, v, vp \rangle$ has not yet completed. Since we have a single well-formed writer, the detection of $maxT$ implies the completion of the *write* that propagated the previous value vp (associated with $maxT - 1$). Thus, in case the reader observes **QV2** it returns the value vp in a single round (lines 78–79).

Specification 11 SLIQ$_s$ Server Automaton: Signature, State, and Transitions

---

```
 1:  Data Types:
 2:      Msgs₁ ⊆ {WRITE,INFORM} × ⟨ℕ × V × V⟩ × ℕ
 3:      Msgs₂ ⊆ {READ,R-ACK} × ⟨ℕ × V × V⟩ × ℕ
 4:      Msgs₃ ⊆ {W-ACK,I-ACK} × ℕ
 5:      Msgs = Msgs₁ ∪ Msgs₂ ∪ Msgs₃

 6:  Signature:
 7:      Input:
 8:          recv(m)ᵢ,ₛ, m ∈ Msgs, s ∈ S, i ∈ R ∪ W
 9:          failₛ
10:      Output:
11:          send(m)ₛ,ᵢ, m ∈ Msgs, s ∈ S, i ∈ R ∪ W

12:  State:
13:      ts ∈ ℕ init 0
14:      v ∈ V init ⊥
15:      vp ∈ V init ⊥
16:      Counter(i) ∈ ℕ⁺, i ∈ R ∪ {w} init 0
17:      status ∈ {active, failed} init active
18:      replySet ⊆ Msgs × I init ∅

19:  Transitions:
20:      Input failₛ
21:      Effect:
```

```
22:          status ← failed

23:      Input recv(⟨msgT,t,val,valp,C⟩)ᵢ,ₛ
24:      Effect:
25:          if status = active ∧ C > Counter(i) then
26:              Counter(i) ← C
27:          if t > ts then
28:              (ts,v,vp) ← (t,val,valp)
29:          if msgT = WRITE then
30:              m ← ⟨W-ACK, Counter(i)⟩
31:          if msgT = READ then
32:              m ← ⟨R-ACK, ts, v, vp, Counter(i)⟩
33:          if msgT = INFORM then
34:              m ← ⟨I-ACK, Counter(i)⟩
35:          replySet ← replySet ∪ {(m,i)}

36:  Output send(m)ₛ,ᵢ
37:      Precondition:
38:          status = active
39:          ⟨m,i⟩ ∈ replySet
40:      Effect:
41:          replySet ← replySet \ {(m,i)}
```

Server Protocol (Specification 11, SLIQ$_s$). The server protocol in SLIQ is very similar to the server protocol in ABD (see Specification 4, ABD$_s$). Each server maintains a passive role; it waits to receive *read* and *write* requests (lines 25–35), updates its local object replica if the tag attached in the message received is greater than the server's local tag (lines 27–28), and replies to those requests (lines 38–41).

4.4.3   ALGORITHM SLIQ CORRECTNESS

We need to show that any execution $\xi \in execs(\text{SLIQ}, \mathbb{Q})$, for any quorum system $\mathbb{Q}$, satisfies liveness (i.e., termination) and safety (i.e., atomicity) properties. Liveness follows from the observation that any operation initiated at a correct process is guaranteed to terminate since that process never waits for more than any single quorum to reply, and there is always at least one correct quorum in $\mathbb{Q}$. So it remains to show that ξ preserves atomicity.

Theorem 4.5   *Algorithm* SLIQ *implements a read/write atomic object.*

Proof. We order operations with respect to the timestamps written and return similar to Theorem 4.2. In particular, by Definition 2.16, for each execution ξ there must exist a partial order $\prec$ on the set of operations Π that satisfy conditions **A1**, **A2**, and **A3**. Similar to Theorem 4.1, we denote by tag_π the value of the new tag generated by the writer when π is a write, and the tag associated with the returned value when π is a read. Note that a read in SLIQ may return either the value associated with the maximum tag, i.e., $maxTS$ or the value associated with the previous tag, i.e., $maxTS - 1$ (similar to FAST algorithm in Section 4.2). With this we define the partial order on operations as follows. For two operations, π_1 and π_2, when π_1 is any operation and π_2 is a write we let $\pi_1 \prec \pi_2$ if $tag_{\pi_1} < tag_{\pi_2}$. For two operations π_1 and π_2 when π_1 is a write and π_2 is a read we let $\pi_1 \prec \pi_2$ if $tag_{\pi_1} \leq tag_{\pi_2}$. The rest of the order is established by transitivity. Note that reads with the same tags are not ordered. Now we use this definition of the order to reason about each of the three conditions of Definition 2.16.

A1 If for operations π_1 and π_2 in Π, $\pi_1 \rightarrow \pi_2$, then it cannot be the case that $\pi_2 \prec \pi_1$.

Let us assume that $\pi_2 \prec \pi_1$. If π_2 is a write, then the sole writer will generate a new tag by incrementing the largest tag in the system. Thus, any other tag will be strictly smaller than tag_{π_2} and hence, $tag_{\pi_1} < tag_{\pi_2}$. By our ordering definition it follows that $\pi_1 \prec \pi_2$ contradicting our assumption. It remains to examine the case where π_2 is a read and π_1 is either a write or a read.

Let us begin with the case where π_1 is a write, and π_2 is a read. Operation π_1 propagates its tag to the servers of at least a single quorum, say $Q \in \mathbb{Q}$, before completing. During phase 1, π_2 sends *read* messages to all the servers and waits for the servers of a quorum, say $Q' \in \mathbb{Q}$ to reply. Since $Q \cap Q' \neq \emptyset$ then every server $s \in Q \cap Q'$ replies with a tag $\geq tag_{\pi_1}$. So π_2 observes a maximum tag $maxT \geq tag_{\pi_1}$. If $maxT = ts_{\pi_1}$, then π_2 will observe either **QV1** or **QV2** since every server in the intersection $Q \cap Q'$ replies with $maxT$. In either case π_2 returns $tag_{\pi_2} = maxT = tag_{\pi_1}$. If $maxT > tag_{\pi_1}$, then π_2 returns a tag at least as small as $maxT - 1$ so $tag_{\pi_2} \geq tag_{\pi_1}$ in this case as well. Hence, in any case $tag_{\pi_2} \geq tag_{\pi_1}$, and thus $\pi_1 \prec \pi_2$ by our definition, contradicting again our initial assumption that $\pi_2 \prec \pi_1$.

It remains to examine the case where both π_1 and π_2 are read operations. Assume that r_1 and r_2 invoke π_1 and π_2, respectively. We will examine the possible quorum views that π_1

may witness during its phase 1: **QV1**, **QV2**, and **QV3**. If π_1 discovers **QV3**, then it proceeds to a propagation phase before completing, propagating the tag is about to return to a quorum of servers, say Q_1. During phase 1, π_2 receives replies from a quorum of servers, say Q_2. Since by Definition 2.5, $Q_1 \cap Q_2 \neq \emptyset$, then every server $s \in Q_1 \cap Q_2$ replies with a tag $\geq tag_{\pi_2}$. With similar arguments as before we can show that $tag_{\pi_2} \geq tag_{\pi_1}$ in this case. Let us examine now what happens in the cases where π_1 discovers **QV1** or **QV2** and completes in one round. If π_1 discovers **QV1** then all the servers of a complete quorum, say Q, replied to π_1 with a tag tag_{π_1}. Thus, again all the servers in $Q \cap Q_2$ will reply to π_2 with a tag at least as large as tag_{π_1}. Hence, as before π_2 returns $tag_{\pi_2} \geq tag_{\pi_1}$ in this case as well. If π_1 discovers **QV2**, then it returns $tag_{\pi_1} = maxT - 1$. Since π_1 witnessed a tag $maxT$ then, by well-formedness, the writer completed the write operation that propagated the tag $maxTS - 1$ and invoked the operation that propagated the tag $maxTS$ before the completion of π_1. Since $\pi_1 \to \pi_2$ then π_2 succeeds the write that propagated the tag $maxTS - 1$. Thus, as we showed above, π_2 returns a tag $tag_{\pi_2} \geq maxTS - 1$. So, $tag_{\pi_2} \geq tag_{\pi_1}$ in this case as well. If $tag_{op_2} > tag_{op_1}$, then $\pi_1 \prec \pi_2$, otherwise the two operations cannot be ordered. Thus, it cannot be the case that $\pi_2 \prec \pi_1$ contradicting our assumption.

A2 If ω is a write operation and π is any operation, then either $\omega \prec \pi$ or $\pi \prec \omega$.

If $tag_\omega > tag_\pi$ then $\pi \prec \omega$ follows directly. If $tag_\omega = tag_\pi$ then it must be that π is a read that obtains its tag from a server written to by ω using the intersection property, and $\omega \prec \pi$ follows again from the definition of the order. If $tag_\omega < tag_\pi$ then $\omega \prec \pi$ follows directly.

A3 The value returned by a read operation is the value written by the last preceding write operation according to $\prec$ (or the initial value if there is no such write).

Let ω be the last write operation preceding the read operation ρ. This means that $tag_\omega \leq tag_\rho$. If $tag_\omega = tag_\rho$, then ρ discovered the value written by ω in a quorum of servers Q and the distribution of the tag in Q satisfies either **QV1** or **QV3**. If $tag_\omega < tag_\rho$, then ρ obtains a larger tag that can only be originating by a write that follows ω, thus ω is not the preceding write, but this cannot be the case. Finally, if $tag_\rho = 0$, then there are no preceding writes, and ρ returns the initial value.

This completes the proof. □

4.5   BIBLIOGRAPHIC NOTES

Implementations of SWMR atomic read and write object in the asynchronous message passing environment attracted the attention of researchers in the last two decades. Attiya, Bar Noy, and Dolev adopted ideas presented for the shared memory model by [109] and introduced ABD (Section 4.1) in [5]. It wasn't until 2004 that Dutta et al. [34, 35] improved the operation latency of ABD by introducing Fast (Section 4.2), an algorithm that allows all operations to complete in a single communication round. That paper proved that fast behavior comes with the cost of bounding the readers with respect to the servers and failures in the system. A work by Anta et al. [4] showed that the algorithm presented in [34] is computationally heavy. They proposed a modified algorithm, without compromising determinism, operation latency, and consistency, but adhering the same bounds on the reader and writer participation. A series of papers followed [34] in an attempt to relax the bound on the readers by sacrificing the speed of some read operations. Among those is algorithm SF developed by Georgiou et al. in [43] that uses *virtual groups* to enable unbounded readers in the system with the cost of "some" slow read operations. Subsequently, Georgiou et al. developed algorithm SLIQ (Section 4.4) to enable fast operations over the use of quorum systems and unbounded reader participants. Guerraoui and Vukolic [58] defined the *refined quorum systems* that were used to implement SWMR atomic objects with fast operations under some timing assumptions over the underlying asynchronous environment. In that work the authors followed Guerraoui [56], where "luck" on contention conditions sometimes allows fast operations. More recently Hadjistasi et al. [59] examined the possibility of allowing operations to complete in 3 *message exchanges* or equivalently in one-and-a-half rounds. They achieve such performance by allowing server-to-server communication. In particular, each client was performing a read operation by communicating with all the servers, each server receiving this request was sending a message to the rest of the servers, and if a server receives reply from a majority replies to the reader. Once a majority of replies are received at the reader then the read completes.

CHAPTER 5

The Multiple-Writer Setting

In this chapter we consider algorithms for the setting with *multiple* writers, thus removing the assumption that there is single writer. The new challenge in this multiple-writer, multiple-reader (MWMR) environment is the ordering of the concurrent write operations necessary to guarantee atomicity.

We present several results for atomic MWMR memory. Section 5.1 presents the algorithm that extends the SWMR algorithm ABD (Section 4.1) for multiple writers. Section 5.2 explores the application of techniques used in SWMR implementations to improve the communication complexity in the MWMR setting. Section 5.3 examines the inherent bounds on the latency of operations in the multi-writer setting. Finally, in Section 5.4 we present the algorithm that improves the communication performance of both *write* and *read* operations in the MWMR setting.

5.1   ALGORITHM MWABD: MULTI-WRITER ABD

The original algorithm ABD algorithm (Section 4.1) can violate atomicity even if there are only two writers. Consider what happens if two writers concurrently perform write operations starting with the same initial local tag value 0. The tags are incremented and then each written value is propagated to some majorities of servers along with the tag value 1. At the completion of the write operations there may be servers that still have the initial replica value, some that have value written by the first writer and some that have the value written by the second writer. Even if one could somehow reason about the order of the two writes, there is no guarantee that a subsequent read will return the most recent value because both written values have the same tag at the servers.

There are two causes that lead to such scenarios. The first is due to the fact that the tags used by the writers are not unique. The second is that in executions with multiple writers the different writers do not "see" one another. This leads to the idea of revising the write protocol so that the writers are required to "learn" about the latest write operation, and so that the tags are created to be unique before writing a new value to the object. In some sense a writer should *read before writing*. We now present algorithm MWABD that employs this idea in implementing a MWMR atomic object.

5.1.1   ALGORITHM MWABD SPECIFICATION

Now we make precise the two aspects in which the multi-writer algorithm differs from algorithm ABD.

1. Integer sequence numbers are used in algorithm ABD as tags to impose an order on write operations. With multiple writers we need to disambiguate timestamps originating at different writers. For this purpose, algorithm mwABD associates with each written value a tag that is now a pair consisting of a sequence number *seq* and the writer id *wid*, thus we have $\langle seq, wid \rangle \in \mathbb{N} \times \mathcal{W}$. Tags are ordered lexicographically. Given two tags tag_i and tag_j, $tag_i > tag_j$ if either:

   - $tag_i.seq > tag_j.seq$, or

   - $tag_i.seq = tag_j.seq$ and $tag_i.wid > tag_j.wid$

   We will use this order on the tags to define a partial order on the read and write operations when reasoning about correctness.

2. Each write operation now performs *two* phases:

   - the first queries the servers for the tags and it is called the *query* phase, and

   - the second propagates the new value with new tag that is larger than any tag seen in the first phase to the servers, and it is called the *propagation* phase.

The first change precipitates a slight revision of the reader and server automata to handle the new tag type. The communication protocol itself does not change. We refer the reader to the description of algorithm ABD in Section 4.1 for the implementation of the reader and server automata (ABD_r and ABD_s) with the only difference being the new tag that is now a pair from $\mathbb{N} \times \mathcal{W}$. The second change results in a substantial revision of the writer automaton and we present it next.

Writer Protocol (Specification 12, mwABD$_w$). The new writer protocol is perhaps surprisingly similar to the reader protocol and it consists of two phases. The goal of the first (query) phase is to identify the highest tag (instead of finding the most recent value), and the goal of the second (propagation) phase is to propagate the new value (instead of the most recent prior value).

In more detail, when a writer operation is invoked with action write(val)$_w$, writer w prepares the first phase (lines 25–31). Then the writer sends READ messages to all replica servers and waits for their replies. When a majority of servers replies, the writer discovers the *largest* tag, $maxT$, among the replies (line 59). It then generates a new tag by incrementing the sequence number found in $maxT$ and including its own identifier (line 60). Then the writer commences its second phase in which it sends WRITE messages containing the generated new tag together with the value to be written to the servers. Once the writer receives replies from a majority of servers it terminates and returns an acknowledgment (lines 67–70).

Specification 12 MWABD_w Writer Automaton: Signature, State, and Transitions

1: **Data Types:**
2:   $Msgs_1 \subseteq \{\text{READ,WRITE,R-ACK}\} \times \langle\langle \mathbb{N} \times \mathcal{W}\rangle \times V\rangle \times \mathbb{N}$
3:   $Msgs_2 \subseteq \{\text{W-ACK}\} \times \mathbb{N}$
4:   $Msgs = Msgs_1 \cup Msgs_2$

5: **Signature:**
6:   **Input:**
7:     $\text{write}(v)_w, \ v \in V, w \in \mathcal{W}$
8:     $\text{recv}(m)_{s,w}, \ m \in Msgs, w \in \mathcal{W}, s \in \mathcal{S}$
9:     $\text{fail}_w, \ w \in \mathcal{W}$
10:   **Output:**
11:     $\text{send}(m)_{w,s}, \ m \in Msgs, w \in \mathcal{W} \ s \in \mathcal{S}$
12:     $\text{write-ack}_w, \ w \in \mathcal{W}$
13:   **Internal:**
14:     $\text{write-fix}_w, \ w \in \mathcal{W}$

15: **State:**
16:   $tag = \langle ts, w\rangle \in \mathbb{N} \times \mathcal{W} \text{ init } \langle 0, w\rangle$
17:   $v \in V \text{ init } \bot$
18:   $wCounter \in \mathbb{N}^+ \text{ init } 0$
19:   $srvAck \subseteq Msgs \times \mathcal{S} \text{ init } \emptyset$
20:   $status \in$
21:     $\{idle, phase1, phase2, done, failed\}, \text{ init } idle$
22:   $destSet \subseteq \mathcal{S}, \text{ init } \mathcal{S}$

23: **Transitions:**
24:   **Input write**$(val)_w$
25:   **Effect:**
26:     **if** $status = idle$ **then**
27:       $status \leftarrow phase1 \text{ f}$
28:       $srvAck \leftarrow \emptyset$
29:       $destSet \leftarrow \mathcal{S}$
30:       $v \leftarrow val$
31:       $wCounter \leftarrow wCounter + 1$

32:   **Output send**$(\langle\text{READ}, wC\rangle)_{w,s}$
33:   **Precondition:**
34:     $status = phase1$
35:     $s \in destSet$
36:     $wC = wCounter$
37:   **Effect:**
38:     $destSet \leftarrow destSet \setminus \{s\}$

39: **Input recv**$(\langle\text{R-ACK}, t, val, wC\rangle)_{s,r}$
40:   **Effect:**
41:     **if** $status = phase1 \wedge wCounter = wC$ **then**
42:       $srvAck \leftarrow srvAck \cup \{(\langle\text{R-ACK}, t, val, wC\rangle, s)\}$

43: **Output send**$(\langle\text{WRITE}, t, val, wC\rangle)_{w,s}$
44:   **Precondition:**
45:     $status = phase2$
46:     $s \in destSet$
47:     $(t, val, wC) = (tag, v, wCounter)$
48:   **Effect:**
49:     $destSet \leftarrow destSet \setminus \{s\}$

50: **Input recv**$(\langle\text{W-ACK}, wC\rangle)_{s,r}$
51:   **Effect:**
52:     **if** $status = phase2 \wedge wCounter = wC$ **then**
53:       $srvAck \leftarrow srvAck \cup \{(\langle\text{W-ACK}, wC\rangle, s)\}$

54: **Internal write-phase1-fix**$_r$
55:   **Precondition:**
56:     $status = phase1$
57:     $|srvAck| \geq (|\mathcal{S}| + 1)/2$
58:   **Effect:**
59:     $maxT \leftarrow max(\{m.t : (m, *) \in srvAck\})$
60:     $tag \leftarrow \langle maxT.ts + 1, w\rangle$
61:     $status \leftarrow phase2$
62:     $srvAck \leftarrow \emptyset$
63:     $destSet \leftarrow \mathcal{S}$
64:     $wCounter \leftarrow wCounter + 1$

65: **Internal write-phase2-fix**$_r$
66:   **Precondition:**
67:     $status = phase2$
68:     $|srvAck| \geq (|\mathcal{S}| + 1)/2$
69:   **Effect:**
70:     $status \leftarrow done$

71: **Output write-ack**$_w$
72:   **Precondition:**
73:     $status = done$
74:   **Effect:**
75:     $status \leftarrow idle$

76: **Input fail**$_w$
77:   **Effect:**
78:     $status \leftarrow failed$

5.1.2 ALGORITHM MWABD CORRECTNESS

It is easy to see that any execution $\xi \in execs(\text{MWABD}, f)$, for $|\mathcal{S}| > 2f$, satisfies liveness (i.e., termination) property. Due to the similarity of this algorithm to the ABD, termination is satisfied with the same arguments used in the proof of Theorem 4.1. So it remains to show that ξ guarantees atomicity.

Theorem 5.1 *Specification* MWABD *implements a* MWMR *read/write atomic object.*

Proof. We use similar reasoning an in Theorem 4.1 to order the operations based on the tags they write and return. More precisely, for each execution ξ of mwABD there must exist a partial order $\prec$ on the set of completed operations Π that satisfy conditions **A1**, **A2**, and **A3** of Definition 2.16. Let tag_π be the value of the tag at the completion of π (i.e., at the conclusion of write-phase2-fix) when π is a write, and the tag computed as the maximum tag at the conclusion of read-phase1-fix when π is a read. With this we define the partial order on operations as follows. For two operations π_1 and π_2 when π_1 is any operation and π_2 is a write, we let $\pi_1 \prec \pi_2$ if $tag_{\pi_1} < tag_{\pi_2}$. For two operations π_1 and π_2 when π_1 is a write and π_2 is a read we let $\pi_1 \prec \pi_2$ if $tag_{\pi_1} \leq tag_{\pi_2}$. The rest of the order is established by transitivity and reads with the same tags are not ordered.

A1 If for operations π_1 and π_2 in Π, $\pi_1 \to \pi_2$, then it cannot be the case that $\pi_2 \prec \pi_1$.

By contradiction we assume that it holds $\pi_2 \prec \pi_1$. We need to examine all the cases for π_1 and π_2 for being writes or reads.

Let us first assume that π_2 is a write operation. Then, according to our model, $\pi_2 \prec \pi_1$ holds if $tag_{\pi_2} < tag_{\pi_1}$. Since $\pi_1 \to \pi_2$, then, by MWABD, the operation π_1 (either read or write) propagates tag_{π_1} to a majority of servers before completing (during phase 2). When π_2 is invoked, it queries a majority of servers during phase 1. Since any two majorities intersect, then there should be at least a single server that reply to both the phase 2 of π_1 and phase 1 of π_2. This server, say s, receives the write message from π_1 before receiving the read message from π_2. Since the tag in each server monotonically increments, then s replies to π_2 with a tag $tag_s \geq tag_{\pi_1}$. So π_2 discovers a maximum tag $maxT \geq tag_s \geq tag_{\pi_1}$. Since π_2 generates a new tag $tag_{\pi_2} = \langle maxT.seq + 1, w \rangle$ then $tag_{\pi_2} > maxT$ and hence $tag_{\pi_2} > tag_{\pi_1}$, contradicting our initial assumption.

Let us assume now that π_2 is a read, then in phase 1 it obtains the maximum tag from a majority of servers. Since (a) π_1 propagates tag_{π_1} to a majority before completing phase 2, (b) the servers increment monotonically their tag, and (c) any two majorities intersect, then π_2 will observe a maxtag $maxT \geq tag_{\pi_1}$ when receiving messages from a majority of servers during phase 1. Therefore, $tag_{\pi_1} \leq tag_{\pi_2}$. If $tag_{\pi_1} < tag_{\pi_2}$ then it cannot be the case that $\pi_2 \prec \pi_1$. If $tag_{\pi_1} = tag_{\pi_2}$ and π_1 is a write, then π_2 is ordered after π_1 (thus $\pi_1 \prec \pi_2$) by definition. Finally, if π_1 is a read, then the two reads with the same tags are not ordered, and again it cannot be the case that $\pi_2 \prec \pi_1$.

A2 If ω is a write operation and π is any operation, then either $\omega \prec \pi$ or $\pi \prec \omega$.

If $tag(\omega) > tag(\pi)$ then $\pi \prec \omega$ follows directly. If $tag(\omega) = tag(\pi)$ then it must be that π is a read that obtains its tag from a server written to by ω using the intersection property, and $\omega \prec \pi$ follows again from the definition of the order. If $tag(\omega) < tag(\pi)$ then $\omega \prec \pi$ follows directly.

A3 The value returned by a read operation is the value written by the last preceding write operation according to $\prec$ (or the initial value if there is no such write).

Let ω be the last write operation preceding the read operation ρ. This means that $tag_\omega \leq tag_\rho$. Notice that tag_ρ is equal to the maximum tag ($maxT$) that ρ received from a server during its phase 1. So if $tag_\omega = tag_\rho$, then $tag_\omega = maxT$ and either (a) ρ returns the value written by ω because the majority of servers responding to ρ in phase 1 includes at least one server written to by ω, or (b) another read ρ' propagated tag_ω during its phase 2 to a server that replied to ρ in phase 1. If $tag_\omega < tag_\rho$, then ρ obtains a larger tag that can only be originating by a write that follows ω, thus ω is not the preceding write, but this cannot be the case. Finally, if $tag_\rho = 0$, then there are no preceding writes, and ρ returns the initial value.

This completes the proof. □

5.2   ALGORITHM CWFR: QUORUM VIEW GENERALIZATION

Algorithm MWABD presented in the previous section implements a MWMR atomic read/write object with a two round protocol for both *reads* and *writes*. So a natural question arises: *Is it possible to allow fast operations in a* MWMR *setting?* We next exploit techniques used in the SWMR setting and we present algorithm CwFR that generalizes the idea of Quorum Views (Section 4.4) to enable fast read operations. The algorithm implements operation as follows:

(i) writes use the two-round query and propagate technique (as in MWABD), and

(ii) reads use the analysis of Quorum Views for allowing fast (single round) operations.

As we will see, read operations can be fast in CwFR even when they are invoked concurrently with one or multiple write operations. In the MWMR setting, a *read* may witness multiple values written concurrently. So it is not clear which value a *read* may choose to return if it is to terminate in a single round. To impose a total ordering on the written values, algorithm CwFR uses tags associated with the written values as before. Again, a *tag* is a tuple of the form $\langle ts, w \rangle \in \mathbb{N} \times \mathcal{W}$, where ts is the timestamp and w is a writer identifier. Tags are compared lexicographically.

5.2.1   ALGORITHMIC TECHNIQUE: MW QUORUM VIEWS

CwFR uses the three quorums views of Definition 4.4 in Section 4.4.

Recall that by Definition 4.4, **QV1** requires that all servers in some quorum reply with the same tag. **QV3** requires that some servers in the quorum contain an older value, but there exists an intersection where all of its servers contain the new value. Finally, **QV2** is the negation of the other two views, establishing a quorum where the new value is neither distributed to the full quorum nor distributed fully in any of its intersections. An example of the three quorum

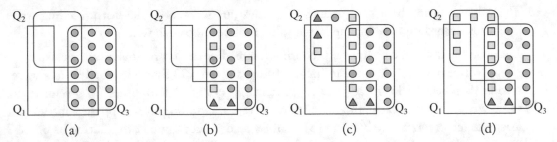

Figure 5.1: (a) **QV1**, (b) **QV2**, (c) **QV3**: incomplete Write, and (d) **QV3**: complete write. Quorum views with multiple concurrent values.

views in the MWMR setting is depicted in Figure 5.1. The shapes in the figure represent three different values of the register that are potentially written concurrently. Notice that in the case of **QV3** we cannot determine with certainty the status of the write operation. In **QV1** the write potentially completed by receiving replies from Q_3 and in **QV2** we determine that the write that propagates the latest write has not yet competed.

5.2.2   ALGORITHM CWFR SPECIFICATION

The original quorum views algorithm as presented in Section 4.4 relies on the existence of a single writer. If a quorum view is able to predict the non-completeness of the latest *write*, it is immediately understood that—by the well-formedness of the single writer—any previous write operation is already completed. Multiple writers invalidate such a conclusion: different values (and tags) may be written concurrently. Hence, the discovery of a write operation that propagates some tag does not imply the completion of the write operations that propagate a smaller tag. Consequently, algorithm CWFR incorporates an iterative technique around quorum views that not only predicts the completion status of a write operation, but also detects the last potentially complete write operation. Below we provide a description of CWFR and present the main idea behind it. The algorithm is composed of four automata: CWFR$_w$, that handles the *write* requests, CWFR$_r$, that handles the *read* requests, CWFR$_s$, that handles the read and write messages at the replica hosts, and $Ch_{i,j}$ to establish the asynchronous reliable communication channels. The algorithm uses a quorum system to group servers into intersecting quorums. The quorum system is known to every participant and it is initially stored in variable $\mathbb{Q}$.

Writer Protocol (Specification 13, CWFR$_w$). The automaton for writer process w completes a write operation in two phases and is very similar to the write protocol of MWABD. During the first round the writer sends read messages to all servers (line 38) and waits for replies from all the members of some quorum. Once the writer receives replies from a full quorum (line 59), he discovers the maximum tag $maxTag$ among the replies (line 61). He then generates a new tag $tag_w = \langle maxTag.seq + 1, w \rangle$ in which it encloses the incremented sequence

Specification 13 CwFR_w Writer Automaton: Signature, State, and Transitions

---

1: **Data Types:**
2:   *Msgs*, same as in Specification 16

3: **Signature:**
4:   **Input:**
5:     $\text{write}(val)_w$, $val \in V$, $w \in \mathcal{W}$
6:     $\text{recv}(m)_{s,w}$, $m \in Msgs$, $s \in \mathcal{S}$, $w \in \mathcal{W}$
7:     fail_w, $w \in \mathcal{W}$
8:   **Output:**
9:     $\text{send}(m)_{w,s}$, $m \in Msgs$, $s \in \mathcal{S}$, $w \in \mathcal{W}$
10:     write-ack_w, $w \in \mathcal{W}$
11:   **Internal:**
12:     $\text{write-phase1-fix}_w$, $w \in \mathcal{W}$
13:     $\text{write-phase2-fix}_w$, $w \in \mathcal{W}$
14: **State:**
15:   $tag = \langle ts, w \rangle \in \mathbb{N} \times \mathcal{W}$ init $\{0, w\}$
16:   $v \in V$ init $\perp$
17:   $vp \in V$ init $\perp$
18:   $maxT \in \mathbb{N}$ init 0
19:   $wCounter \in \mathbb{N}^+$ init 0
20:   $status \in$
21:     $\{idle, done, phase1, phase2, failed\}$ init $idle$
22:   $srvAck \subseteq \mathcal{S} \times Msgs$ init $\emptyset$
23:   $destSet \subseteq \mathcal{S}$ init $\mathcal{S}$
24: **Transitions:**
25:   **Input** $\text{write}(val)_w$
26:     **Effect:**
27:       if $status = idle$ then
28:         $status \leftarrow phase1$
29:         $srvAck \leftarrow \emptyset$
30:         $destSet \leftarrow \mathcal{S}$
31:         $vp \leftarrow v$
32:         $v \leftarrow val$
33:         $wCounter \leftarrow wCounter + 1$

34:   **Output** $\text{send}(\langle \text{READ}, t, valp, wC \rangle)_{w,s}$
35:     **Precondition:**
36:       $status = phase1$
37:       $s \in destSet$
38:       $(t, valp, wC) = (tag, vp, wCounter)$
39:     **Effect:**
40:       $destSet \leftarrow destSet \setminus \{s\}$

41:   **Input** $\text{recv}(\langle \text{R-ACK}, t, wC \rangle)_{s,w}$
42:     **Effect:**

43:       if $status = phase1 \wedge rCounter = wC$ then
44:         $srvAck \leftarrow srvAck \cup \{((\text{R-ACK}, t, wC), s)\}$

45:   **Output** $\text{send}(\langle \text{WRITE}, t, val, wC \rangle)_{w,s}$
46:     **Precondition:**
47:       $status = phase2$
48:       $s \in destSet$
49:       $(t, val, wC) = (tag, v, wCounter)$
50:     **Effect:**
51:       $destSet \leftarrow destSet \setminus \{s\}$

52:   **Input** $\text{recv}(\langle \text{W-ACK}, wC \rangle)_{s,w}$
53:     **Effect:**
54:       if $status = phase2 \wedge rCounter = wC$ then
55:         $srvAck \leftarrow srvAck \cup \{((\text{W-ACK}, wC), s)\}$

56:   **Internal** $\text{write-phase1-fix}_w$
57:     **Precondition:**
58:       $status = phase1$
59:       $\exists Q \in \mathbb{Q} : Q \subseteq \{s : (s,m) \in srvAck\}$
60:     **Effect:**
61:       $maxTag \leftarrow \max_{s \in Q \wedge (s,m) \in srvAck}(m.t)$
62:       $tag = \langle maxTag.ts + 1, w \rangle$
63:       $status \leftarrow phase2$
64:       $srvAck \leftarrow \emptyset$
65:       $destSet \leftarrow \mathcal{S}$
66:       $wCounter \leftarrow wCounter + 1$

67:   **Internal** $\text{write-phase2-fix}_w$
68:     **Precondition:**
69:       $status = phase2$
70:       $\exists Q \in \mathbb{Q} : Q \subseteq \{s : (s,m) \in srvAck\}$
71:     **Effect:**
72:       $status \leftarrow done$

73:   **Output** write-ack_w
74:     **Precondition:**
75:       $status = done$
76:     **Effect:**
77:       $status \leftarrow idle$

78:   **Input** fail_w
79:     **Effect:**
80:       $status \leftarrow failed$

---

number of the maximum tag, and the writer's identifier (line 62). Once the new tag is generated, the writer proceeds to phase 2, during which the writer associates the value to be written with the new tag and it sends the pair to all servers. Once the servers of some quorum reply, the writer marks the *status* variable as *done* and completes the write (lines 69–72).

Reader Protocol (Specification 15, CwFR_r). Any read operation requires *one or two phases* (rounds) to complete (fast or slow). The decision on the number of communication rounds is based on the quorum views that the reader establishes during its first round. The reader r invokes

---

Specification 14 CwFR_r Reader Automaton: Signature and State

---

1: **Data Types:**
2:   *Msgs*, same as in Specification 16

3: **Signature:**
4:   **Input:**
5:     $read_r$, $r \in \mathcal{R}$
6:     $recv(m)_{s,r}$, $m \in Msgs$, $r \in \mathcal{R}$, $s \in \mathcal{S}$
7:     $fail_r$, $r \in \mathcal{R}$
8:   **Output:**
9:     $send(m)_{r,s}$, $m \in Msgs$, $r \in \mathcal{R}$, $s \in \mathcal{S}$
10:     $read\text{-}ack(val)_r$, $val \in V$, $r \in \mathcal{R}$
11:   **Internal:**
12:     read-phase1-fix$_r$
13:     read-phase2-fix$_r$
14:     read-qview-eval$_r$

15: **State:**
16:   $tag = \langle ts, wid \rangle \in \mathbb{N} \times \mathcal{W}$ **init** $\langle 0, \min(\mathcal{W}) \rangle$
17:   $maxTag = \langle ts, wid \rangle \in \mathbb{N} \times \mathcal{W}$ **init** $\langle 0, \min(\mathcal{W}) \rangle$
18:   $v \in V$ **init** $\perp$
19:   $retvalue \in V$ **init** $\perp$
20:   $rCounter \in \mathbb{N}^+$ **init** 0
21:   $status \in$
22:     $\{idle, phase1, phase2, eval, done, failed\}$ **init** *idle*
23:   $srvAck \subseteq Msgs \times \mathcal{S}$ **init** $\emptyset$
24:   $maxAck \subseteq Msgs \times \mathcal{S}$ **init** $\emptyset$
25:   $maxTagSrv \subseteq \mathcal{S}$ **init** $\emptyset$
26:   $replyQ \subseteq \mathcal{S}$ **init** $\emptyset$
27:   $destSet \subseteq \mathcal{S}$ **init** $\mathcal{S}$

---

a read operation when the CwFR_r automaton receives a $read_r$ request from its environment (lines 4–8).

At first, the reader sends a read message to all servers (line 11) and waits for some quorum to reply (line 34). Once all servers in quorum Q reply, the reader discovers the maximum tag $maxTag$ among the replies (line 38). Then the reader *iteratively* analyzes the distribution of the $maxTag$ among the members of the responding quorum Q, in an attempt to determine the latest, potentially complete, write operation. This is done by the read-qview-eval$_r$ action (lines 47–69).

Initially, the reader checks if the distribution of the $maxTag$ in Q matches either quorum view **QV1** or **QV3**. Namely, it checks if all the servers in Q replied with $maxTag$ (**QV1**), or if there exists an intersection of Q with some other quorum $Q' \in \mathbb{Q}$ s.t. every server in that intersection replied with $maxTag$ (**QV3**). If **QV1** is detected, the read completes and the value associated with the discovered $maxTag$ is returned (line 57). If **QV3** is detected (line 61) the reader continues to the second round, sending the latest tag ($maxTag$) and its associated value to all the servers. When a full quorum replies in the second round, the read returns the value associated with $maxTag$ (lines 72–75).

If none of the previous quorum views hold (and thus **QV2** holds), then it must be the case that the write that yielded the maximum tag is not yet completed. At this point we try to discover the latest potentially completed *write*. Note that this is not necessarily the *write* that propagates the previous tag as multiple write operations may be invoked concurrently, each propagating a different tag. The key idea behind this iteration lies on the fact that servers *overwrite older with newer values*. So we can assume that the servers that replied with the maximum tag, potentially stored and overwritten an older tag. Thus, we can replace the values of the servers that replied with the maximum tag with the second higher tag. We can achieve the same effect, as seen in Figure 5.2, by removing all servers with the highest tag from Q. Once we do that we repeat the

Specification 15 CwFr$_r$ Reader Automaton: Transitions

1: **Transitions:**
2:   **Input read$_r$**
3:     **Effect:**
4:       if $status = idle$ then
5:         $status \leftarrow phase1$
6:         $srvAck \leftarrow \emptyset$
7:         $destSet \leftarrow S$
8:         $rCounter \leftarrow rCounter + 1$

9:   **Output send**$(\langle \text{READ}, t, val, rC \rangle)_{r,s}$
10:     **Precondition:**
11:       $status = phase1$
12:       $s \in destSet$
13:       $(t, val, rC) = (maxTag, v, rCounter)$
14:     **Effect:**
15:       $destSet \leftarrow destSet \setminus \{s\}$

16:   **Input recv**$(\langle \text{R-ACK}, t, rC \rangle)_{s,r}$
17:     **Effect:**
18:       if $status = phase1 \wedge rCounter = rC$ then
19:         $srvAck \leftarrow srvAck \cup \{(\langle \text{R-ACK}, t, rC \rangle, s)\}$

20:   **Output send**$(\langle \text{INFORM}, t, val, rC \rangle)_{r,s}$
21:     **Precondition:**
22:       $status = phase2$
23:       $s \in destSet$
24:       $(t, val, rC) = (maxTag, v, rCounter)$
25:     **Effect:**
26:       $destSet \leftarrow destSet \setminus \{s\}$

27:   **Input recv**$(\langle \text{I-ACK}, rC \rangle)_{s,r}$
28:     **Effect:**
29:       if $status = phase2 \wedge rCounter = rC$ then
30:         $srvAck \leftarrow srvAck \cup \{(\langle \text{I-ACK}, rC \rangle, s)\}$

31:   **Internal read-phase1-fix$_r$**
32:     **Precondition:**
33:       $status = phase1$
34:       $\exists Q \in \mathbb{Q} : Q \subseteq \{s : (*, s) \in srvAck\}$
35:     **Effect:**
36:       $replyQ \leftarrow Q$
37:       $maxTag \leftarrow$
38:         $\max_{s \in replyQ \wedge (m,s) \in srvAck}(m.t)$
39:       $maxAck \leftarrow$
40:         $\{(m, s) : (m, s) \in srvAck \wedge m.t = maxTag\}$
41:       $maxTagSrv \leftarrow$
42:         $\{s : s \in replyQ \wedge (s, m) \in maxAck\}$
43:       $v \leftarrow m.val$ s.t. $(m, s) \in maxAck$
44:       $status \leftarrow eval$

45:   **Internal read-qview-eval$_r$**
46:     **Precondition:**
47:       $status = eval$
48:       $replyQ \neq \emptyset$
49:     **Effect:**
50:       $tag \leftarrow \max_{s \in replyQ \wedge (s,m) \in srvAck}(m.t.tag)$
51:       $maxAck \leftarrow$
52:         $\{(m, s) : (m, s) \in srvAck \wedge m.t = tag\}$
53:       $maxTagSrv \leftarrow$
54:         $\{s : s \in replyQ \wedge (m, s) \in maxAck\}$
55:       $retvalue \leftarrow m.val$ s.t. $(m, *) \in maxAck$
56:       if $replyQ = maxTagSrv$ then   // QV1
57:         $status \leftarrow done$
58:       else
59:         if $\exists Q' \in \mathbb{Q}, Q' \neq replyQ$ s.t.
60:           $replyQ \cap Q' \subseteq maxTagSrv$
61:         then   // QV3
62:           $tag \leftarrow maxTag$
63:           $retvalue \leftarrow v$
64:           $status \leftarrow phase2$
65:           $srvAck \leftarrow \emptyset$
66:           $destSet \leftarrow S$
67:           $rCounter \leftarrow rCounter + 1$
68:         else   // QV2
69:           $replyQ \leftarrow replyQ \setminus \{s : s \in maxTagSrv\}$

70:   **Internal read-phase2-fix$_r$**
71:     **Precondition:**
72:       $status = phase2$
73:       $\exists Q \in \mathbb{Q} : Q \subseteq \{s : (s, m) \in srvAck\}$
74:     **Effect:**
75:       $status \leftarrow done$

76:   **Output read-ack**$(val)_r$
77:     **Precondition:**
78:       $status = done$
79:       $val = retvalue$
80:     **Effect:**
81:       $replyQ \leftarrow \emptyset$
82:       $srvAck \leftarrow \emptyset$
83:       $status \leftarrow idle$

84:   **Input fail$_r$**
85:     **Effect:**
86:       $failed \leftarrow true$

Quorum View analysis, this time for the second higher tag. If at some iteration, **QV1** holds on the remaining tag values (line 57), then a potentially completed write—that was overwritten by greater values in the rest of the servers—is discovered and that tag is returned (in a single round). If **QV3** is detected (line 61) on the remaining tags then we proceed to a second round. If **QV2** is

CwFr: Server Removal

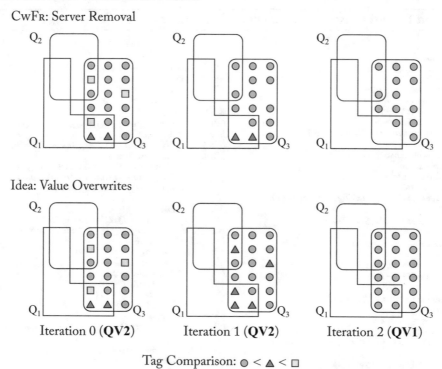

Idea: Value Overwrites

Iteration 0 (**QV2**)   Iteration 1 (**QV2**)   Iteration 2 (**QV1**)

Tag Comparison: ○ < ▲ < □

Figure 5.2: Server removal vs. value prediction within iterations performed when process i contacts Q_3.

detected again we remove the servers with the higher tag among the remaining servers and we repeat the analysis for the next higher tag (line 69) .

   If no iteration is interrupted because of **QV1** or **QV3**, then eventually **QV3** is observed, in the worst case when a single server remains in some intersection of Q. If a **QV3** is detected and a second round is necessary, the reader propagates $maxTag$ the highest tag observed in Q. At the end of the second round that tag is written to at least a single complete quorum and thus the reader can safely return it.

   Figure 5.2 presents an example where a process that contacts quorum Q_3 takes three iterations to reach a **QV1** for the smallest of the three values, the circle. The top row presents the quorum membership at each iteration due to server removals and the bottom row presents how the quorum would look like had we replace the tags of the servers. Observe that at each iteration the analysis of the tag distribution returns the same quorum view in both cases.

   Server Protocol (Specification 16, CwFr$_s$). Each server has relatively simple actions, very similar to those of the server automaton in algorithm MwABD. It receives *read* or *write*

Specification 16 CwFR_s Server Automaton: Signature, State, and Transitions

```
 1: Data Types:                                          21:    if status = active ∧ C > Counter(i) then
 2:    Msgs₁ ⊆ {WRITE,INFORM} × ⟨⟨N × W⟩ × V⟩ × N        22:       Counter(i) ← C
 3:    Msgs₂ ⊆ {READ,R-ACK} × ⟨⟨N × W⟩ × V⟩ × N          23:       if tag < t then
 4:    Msgs₃ ⊆ {W-ACK,I-ACK} × N                         24:          (tag.ts, tag.wid, v) ← (t.ts, t.wid, val)
 5:    Msgs = Msgs₁ ∪ Msgs₂ ∪ Msgs₃                      25:       if msgT = WRITE then
                                                         26:          m ← ⟨W-ACK, Counter(i)⟩
 6: Signature:                                           27:       if msgT = READ then
 7:    Input:                                            28:          m ← ⟨R-ACK, tag, v, Counter(i)⟩
 8:       recv(m)ᵢ,ₛ, m ∈ Msgs, s ∈ S, i ∈ R ∪ W         29:       if msgT = INFORM then
 9:       failₛ                                          30:          m ← ⟨I-ACK, Counter(i)⟩
10:    Output:                                           31:       replySet ← replySet ∪ {(m, i)}
11:       send(m)ₛ,ᵢ, m ∈ Msgs, s ∈ S, i ∈ R ∪ W
                                                         32: Output send(m)ₛ,ᵢ
12: State:                                               33:    Precondition:
13:    tag = ⟨ts, wid⟩ ∈ N × W init {0, min(W)}          34:       status = active
14:    v ∈ V init ⊥                                      35:       (m, i) ∈ replySet
15:    Counter(p) ∈ N⁺, p ∈ R ∪ W init 0                36:    Effect:
16:    status ∈ {active, failed} init active             37:       replySet ← replySet \ {(m, i)}
17:    replySet ⊆ Msgs × I init ∅
                                                         38: Input failₛ
18: Transitions:                                         39:    Effect:
19:    Input recv(⟨msgT, t, val, C⟩)ᵢ,ₛ                   40:       status ← failed
20:       Effect:
```

messages, updates its local object replica accordingly, and replies to the sender process. Upon receipt of a *read* or *write* message (lines 21–31), the server compares its local tag with the tag included in the message (line 23). If the tag of the message is higher than its local tag, the server adopts the higher tag along with its corresponding value (line 24). Once this is done the server replies to the invoking process (lines 34–37).

5.2.3 ALGORITHM CWFR CORRECTNESS

We need to show that any execution $\xi \in execs(\text{CwFR}, \mathbb{Q})$, for any quorum system $\mathbb{Q}$, satisfies liveness (i.e., termination) and safety (i.e., atomicity) properties. Termination is guaranteed given that at least a single quorum in $\mathbb{Q}$ remains correct. So we need to examine whether CwFR preserves atomicity.

Theorem 5.2 *Algorithm* CwFR *implements an atomic MWMR object.*

Proof. As in previous theorems, we order the operations based on the tags they write and return. More precisely, for each execution ξ of CwFR there must exist a partial order $\prec$ on the set of completed operations Π that satisfy conditions **A1**, **A2**, and **A3** of Definition 2.16. Let, for CwFR, tag_π be the value of the tag at the conclusion of write-phase2-fix when π is a write, and the tag computed as the maximum tag when the reader changes the *status* from *eval* to *done*, or *active* during read-qview-eval if π is a read. With this we define the partial order on operations as follows. For two operations π_1 and π_2 when π_1 is any operation and π_2 is a write we let $\pi_1 \prec \pi_2$ if $tag_{\pi_1} < tag_{\pi_2}$. For two operations π_1 and π_2 when π_1 is a write and π_2 is a read, we let $\pi_1 \prec \pi_2$ if $tag_{\pi_1} \leq tag_{\pi_2}$. The rest of the order is established by transitivity and reads with the same tags are not ordered.

A1 If for operations π_1 and π_2 in Π, $\pi_1 \rightarrow \pi_2$, then it cannot be the case that $\pi_2 \prec \pi_1$.

Let's assume by contradiction that $\pi_2 \prec \pi_1$ and let's examine the possible cases where π_1 and π_2 are writes or reads.

Suppose that both π_1 and π_2 are writes. Then, according to our model, $\pi_2 \prec \pi_1$ holds if $tag_{\pi_2} < tag_{\pi_1}$. Since $\pi_1 \rightarrow \pi_2$, then, by CwFr, the operation π_1 propagates tag_{π_1} to a quorum of servers before completing (during phase 2). When π_2 is invoked, it queries a quorum of servers during phase 1. Since by definition any two quorums intersect, then there should be at least a single server that reply to both the phase 2 of π_1 and phase 1 of π_2. This server, say s, receives the write message from π_1 before receiving the read message from π_2. Since the tag in each server monotonically increments, then s replies to π_2 with a tag $tag_s \geq tag_{\pi_1}$. So π_2 discovers a maximum tag $maxT \geq tag_s \geq tag_{\pi_1}$. Since π_2 generates a new tag $tag_{\pi_2} = \langle maxT.seq + 1, w \rangle$ then $tag_{\pi_2} > maxT$ and hence $tag_{\pi_2} > tag_{\pi_1}$, contradicting our initial assumption.

Suppose now that π_2 is a write and π_1 is a read. According to our model, $\pi_2 \prec \pi_1$ holds if $tag_{\pi_2} \leq tag_{\pi_1}$. There are two cases for π_1: (a) it proceeds in a phase 2 propagating the maximum tag it discovered in phase 1; or (b) it is fast. During phase 2, the read operation writes the maximum tag in a quorum of servers. So with similar reasoning as before, there will be a server s that will receive the write message from π_1 and will reply to phase 1 of π_2. Thus, π_2 will generate a larger tag and hence $tag_{\pi_2} > tag_{\pi_1}$, contradicting our assumption. If π_1 is fast, then it follows that it detected **QV1** for tag tag_{π_1} at some iteration. This means that neither **QV1** or **QV3** hold for any larger tag. It also means that every intersection contained a smaller tag in every iteration until π_1 reached tag_{π_1} (thus, **QV3** could not hold). Therefore, it follows that every intersection contained tag_{π_1}. So if we assume that Q_1 is the quorum that replied to π_1 and Q_2 the quorum that replied to π_2, then every server in $Q_1 \cap Q_2$ replies with a tag at least as large as tag_{π_1} to π_2. With the same reasoning as before π_2 will generate a new tag $tag_{\pi_2} > tag_{\pi_1}$, also leading to contradiction.

It remains to examine the cases where π_2 is a read. If π_1 is a write, then $\pi_2 \prec \pi_1$ if it holds that $tag_{\pi_2} < tag_{\pi_1}$. During phase 2, π_1 propagates tag_{π_1} to the servers of a quorum, say Q_1. Let the servers in quorum Q_2 be the ones to reply in phase 1 of π_2. Thus, every server in the intersection $Q_1 \cap Q_2$ replies with a tag at least as large as tag_{π_1}. If π_2 observes that $maxTag = tag_{\pi_1}$, then it is easy to see that π_2 witnesses either **QV1** (if $Q_1 = Q_2$) or **QV3** (every $s \in Q_1 \cap Q_2$ replies with $maxTag$). In any of these cases $tag_{\pi_2} = tag_{\pi_1}$. So it remains to investigate what tag the *read* returns had it detect a quorum view **QV2**. For this to happen it means that $maxTag$ is larger than tag_{π_1}. If at any iteration we detect **QV1** or **QV3** for a tag larger than tag_{π_1} then in any of these cases π_2 returns a tag $tag_{\pi_2} > tag_{\pi_1}$. Let every server with higher tag than tag_{π_1} be removed without detecting any of the terminating quorum views. By **QV2** it follows that any of those tags did not appear in all the servers of any intersection. We know, however, that all the servers in $Q_1 \cap Q_2$ have a tag at least as large as ts_{π_1}. Thus, if all the servers with a tag greater than ts_{π_1} are removed, all remaining servers in $Q_1 \cap Q_2$ reply to π_2 with tag_{π_1}. Hence, π_2 detects at least **QV3** on tag_{π_1} and so π_2 returns $tag_{\pi_2} \geq tag_{\pi_1}$ in this case as well. Therefore, in all cases $tag_{\pi_2} \geq tag_{\pi_1}$ when π_2 is a read and π_1 is a write, and thus it cannot hold that $\pi_2 \prec \pi_1$, contradicting again our assumption.

Finally, we need to examine the case where both π_2 and π_1 are reads. According to our model $\pi_2 \prec \pi_1$ holds if $tag_{\pi_2} < tag_{\pi_1}$. If $tag_{\pi_2} = tag_{\pi_1}$ then the two tags cannot be ordered. We need to examine two cases for π_1: (a) it performs two phases, or (b) it is fast. If it performs two phases then it propagates tag_{π_1} to a quorum of servers before completing. As shown before, op_2 will return $tag_{\pi_2} \geq tag_{\pi_1}$ in this case and hence either $\pi_1 \prec \pi_2$ or the reads cannot be ordered. If π_1 is fast then it must be the case that π_1 observed **QV1** for tag_{π_1}. Let π_1 receive replies from the servers in quorum **QV1** during its phase 1, and π_2 receive replies from the servers in Q_2 during the same phase. If π_1 observes **QV1** then all the servers in $Q_1 \cap Q_2$ will reply with a tag greater or equal to tag_{π_1} to π_2. So π_2 will return a tag $tag_{\pi_2} \geq tag_{\pi_1}$ in this case as well, since at the completion of iterations either will observe **QV1** with a tag greater or equal to tag_{π_1}, otherwise in the worst case will observe a **QV3** in $Q_1 \cap Q_2$ and will return the max tag it discovers which is also greater or equal to tag_{π_1}. So in any case $tag_{\pi_2} \geq tag_{\pi_1}$ and hence $\pi_1 \prec \pi_2$ or the two operations cannot be ordered, contradicting our initial assumption.

A2 If ω is a write operation and π is any operation, then either $\omega \prec \pi$ or $\pi \prec \omega$.

If $tag_\omega > tag_\pi$ then $\pi \prec \omega$ follows directly. If $tag_\omega = tag_\pi$ then it must be that π is a read that obtains its tag from a server written to by ω using the intersection property, and $\omega \prec \pi$ follows again from the definition of the order. It cannot be the case that π is a write operation, by defining tags as $\langle timestamp, wid \rangle$ pairs. In particular if ω and π retrieve the same tags, say $\langle ts, w_i \rangle$ during phase 1 then they generate $tag_\omega = \langle ts+1, w_1 \rangle$ and $tag_\pi = \langle ts+1, w_2 \rangle$, respectively, and assuming that w_1 invokes ω and w_2 invokes π. Assuming that the writer identifiers are comparable and unique, then if $w_1 > w_2$ then $tag_\omega > tag_\pi$ and $\pi \prec \omega$, otherwise $tag_\omega < tag_\pi$ and $\omega \prec \pi$. If $tag_\omega < tag_\pi$ then $\omega \prec \pi$ follows directly.

A3 The value returned by a read operation is the value written by the last preceding write operation according to $\prec$ (or the initial value if there is no such write).

Let ω be the last write operation preceding the read operation ρ. This means that $tag_\omega \leq tag_\rho$. Also, let the servers in Q_2 reply to phase 1 of ρ. Notice that $tag_\omega = tag_\rho$, and ρ returns the value written by ω, if during the *status* change at read-qview-eval: (a) $tag_\omega =$

$maxTag$ and there exists an intersection $Q_2 \cap Q$, for some quorum Q s.t. all servers in $Q_2 \cap Q$ reply with the same tag (i.e., **QV3** is satisfied), or (b) at some execution of read-qview-eval action, all the remaining servers in Q_2 reply with tag_ω (i.e., **QV1** is satisfied). These servers received tag_ω either from the ω directly or during the propagation phase (i.e., phase 2) of some read operation that returned tag_ω. If $tag_\omega < tag_\rho$, then it must be the case that ρ received a larger tag that satisfies some of the aforementioned quorum views. This tag can only be originated by a write that follows ω and hence ω is not the last preceding write, but this cannot be the case. Finally, if $tag_\rho = 0$, then there are no preceding writes, and ρ returns the initial value.

$\square$

5.3 LOWER BOUND: INHERENT LIMITATIONS OF MWMR ON FAST OPERATIONS

The algorithms presented in Sections 5.1 and 5.2 implement MWMR atomic read/write objects by requiring each *write* to perform two rounds to complete. A natural question arises whether it is possible to obtain solutions with single round *writes*. In this section, we present the implications that the MWMR setting has on the number of possible fast operations. We will show that the number of fast operations depends on the *intersection degree* (see Definition 2.7) of the quorum system that an algorithm uses. To obtain a general result we assume the use of an n-wise quorum system $\mathbb{Q}$ (see Definition 2.6), for $2 \leq n \leq |\mathbb{Q}|$. We begin with the definition of quorum switching operations.

Definition 5.3 Quorum Switching Operations. Two operations π and π' that contact quorums $Q', Q'' \in \mathbb{Q}$, respectively, are called **quorum switching** if $Q' \neq Q''$.

Recall that we seek write operations that complete in a single round. It is thus necessary for a write operation to propagate and write its indented value during its first and only round. Since we assume server failures, the writer may complete before communicating with all the servers. Moreover, by well-formedness (Definition 2.14), each process invokes a single operation at a time. Thus, in the Single-Writer (SW) setting the invocation of a write operation from the sole writer implies the completion of any previous write operation. This is not the case for the MW setting as multiple writers may invoke write operations concurrently. Dutta et al. [34] showed that it is not possible to construct MW implementations where all read and write operations complete in a single round, even when assuming a system with two writers, two readers, and a single server failure. Their proof relies on the existence of concurrent write operations, and it follows that read operations cannot order those writes in a consistent way. Here, we take a different approach: we examine how many fast writes may precede a single read operation, before that read is unable to safely (atomically) order those writes.

ξ_1^1

	Q1
S1	1
S2	1
S3	1
S4	1
S5	
	w1

ξ_1^2

	Q1	Q2
S1	1	
S2	1	2
S3	1	2
S4	1	2
S5		2
	w1	w2

$\Delta(\xi_1^2)$

	Q1	Q2
S1		
S2	1	2
S3	1	2
S4	1	2
S5		2
	w1	w2

ξ_1^3

	Q1	Q2	Q3
S1			3
S2	1	2	
S3	1	2	3
S4	1	2	3
S5		2	3
	w1	w2	w3

$\Delta(\xi_1^3)$

	Q1	Q2	Q3
S1			3
S2			
S3	1	2	3
S4	1	2	3
S5		2	3
	w1	w2	w3

ξ_1^4

	Q1	Q2	Q3	Q4
S1			3	4
S2				4
S3	1	2	3	4
S4	1	2	3	4
S5		2	3	4
	w1	w2	w3	w4

$\xi_1^{4,1}$

	Q1	Q2	Q3	Q4	
S1			3	4	1
S2				4	1
S3	1	2	3	4	
S4	1	2	3	4	
S5		2	3	4	1
	w1	w2	w3	w4	w1

$\xi_1^{4,2}$

	Q1	Q2	Q3	Q4		
S1			3	4	1	2
S2				4	1	2
S3	1	2	3	4		
S4	1	2	3	4		
S5		2	3	4	1	
	w1	w2	w3	w4	w1	w2

$\xi_1^{4,3}$

	Q1	Q2	Q3	Q4			
S1			3	4	1	2	
S2				4	1	2	3
S3	1	2	3	4			
S4	1	2	3	4			
S5		2	3	4	1		
	w1	w2	w3	w4	w1	w2	

ξ_1

	Q1	Q2	Q3	Q4				Q5
S1			3	4	1	2		
S2				4	1	2	3	
S3	1	2	3	4				
S4	1	2	3	4				
S5		2	3	4	1			
	w1	w2	w3	w4	w1	w2		ρ

Figure 5.3: Construction steps of execution ξ_1 in a *4-wise* quorum system.

We now proceed to the main result of this section and we show that atomicity cannot be preserved if n fast writes precede a read operation. In particular, it is shown that one cannot implement an atomic register using an *n-wise* quorum system and allowing more than $n - 1$ fast writes to precede a single read operation. In such a case, the reader may not be able to distinguish the real-time order of the writes, and thus return a value that violates that total order.

Execution ξ_1 (a)

	Q1	Q2	Q3	Q4				Q5
S1			3	4	1	2		
S2				4	1	2	3	
S3	1	2	3	4				
S4	1	2	3	4				
S5		2	3	4	1			
	w1	w2	w3	w4	w1	w2		ρ

Execution ξ_2 (b)

	Q2	Q3	Q4	Q1				Q5
S1		3	4	1	2			
S2			4	1	2	3		
S3				1	2	3	4	
S4	2	3	4	1				
S5	2	3	4	1				
	w2	w3	w4	w1	w2	w3		ρ

Execution ξ_3 (c)

	Q3	Q4	Q1	Q2				Q5
S1	3	4	1	2				
S2		4	1	2	3			
S3			1	2	3	4		
S4	3	4	1	2				
S5			2	3	4	1		
	w3	w4	w1	w2	w3	w4		ρ

Execution ξ_4 (d)

	Q4	Q1	Q2	Q3				Q5
S1				3	4	1	2	
S2	4	1	2	3				
S3		1	2	3	4			
S4	4	1	2	3				
S5		1	2	3	4	1		
	w4	w1	w2	w3	w4	w1		ρ

Figure 5.4: An example of the execution constructions for a *4-wise* quorum system. In execution ξ_1 the write operation ω_3 completes before ω_4 ($\omega_3 \to \omega_4$) and hence to preserve atomicity the read operation cannot return the value written by ω_3. It may return the value written from any other write as those are concurrent. Similarly, in ξ_2, ω_4 completes before ω_1 ($\omega_4 \to \omega_1$), in ξ_3, ω_1 completes before ω_2 ($\omega_1 \to \omega_2$) and in ξ_4, the write ω_2 completes before ω_3 ($\omega_2 \to \omega_3$). Thus, the read cannot return the value written by ω_4 in ξ_2, the value of ω_1 in ξ_3, or the value of ω_2 in ξ_4. Furthermore, the read operation cannot distinguish any of these executions as it receives the same messages from the same servers. So for the reader it must be the case that $\omega_3 \to \omega_4 \to \omega_1 \to \omega_2 \to \omega_3$. Hence, no matter what value the reader returns, it violates atomicity in some execution.

Operation Diagrams: To illustrate the execution constructions we use in the proof of the main theorem, we use the diagrams that appear in Figures 5.3 and 5.4. In the diagrams the quorum systems are such that each quorum has the same size, say $|\mathcal{S}| - f$, for some $f \leq |\mathcal{S}|$. Note that these quorum constructions are used explicitly for illustrative purposes; our execution constructions are general and hold for any n-wise quorum system (as per Definition 2.6). Assuming that no two quorums are identical, the following observation shows that such quorum systems have degree $\frac{|\mathcal{S}|}{f} - 1$.

Observation 5.4   The intersection degree of a quorum system $\mathbb{Q}$ where $\forall Q \in \mathbb{Q}, |Q| = |\mathcal{S}| - f$ is equal to $\frac{|\mathcal{S}|}{f} - 1$.

Proof. Since any $Q \in \mathbb{Q}$, $|Q| = |\mathcal{S}| - f$ then for $Q, Q' \in \mathbb{Q}$ it follows that $|Q \cap Q'| \geq |\mathcal{S}| - 2f$. For three quorums $Q, Q', Q'' \in \mathbb{Q}$ it then follows that $|Q \cap Q' \cap Q''| \geq |\mathcal{S}| - 3f$. Generalizing for n quorums we get:

$$\left| \bigcap_{i=0}^{n} Q_i \right| \geq |\mathcal{S}| - nf.$$

Since we want to find the biggest n such that the intersection is not empty, then it should be the case that

$$\bigcap_{i=0}^{n} Q_i \neq \emptyset \Rightarrow |\bigcap_{i=0}^{n} Q_i| > 0.$$

So, it follows that in the worst case $|\mathcal{S}| - nf > 0$ and thus $n \leq \frac{|\mathcal{S}|}{f} - 1$; this completes the proof. $\square$

By Observation 5.4, a *4-wise* quorum system (as in the diagrams) is possible when every quorum has a size $|\mathcal{S}| - f$, and $|\mathcal{S}| \geq 5f$. We split the servers into $\frac{|\mathcal{S}|}{f}$ sets, $S_1, S_2, \ldots, S_{\frac{|\mathcal{S}|}{f}}$, and each set contains f servers. Thus, each quorum contains all but one set. We list the sets of servers in the first column of each diagram. When notation Q_i appears at top of a column then a shaded block in the same row as a server set S_j denotes that all servers in S_j belong in Q_i, i.e., $S_j \subset Q_i$. Operations appear in the last row. An operation with a bordered identifier has completed, while a borderless identifier denotes an incomplete operation. The order in which the operations appear matches the order of the appearance of actions of those operations in the respective execution construction. In particular, if a block next to a set S_j contains a number k, then this indicates that all servers in S_j receive the messages of ω_k. If an operation ω_k does not appear below a number k then the operation completes before those messages are delivered (those are in-transit messages that are eventually delivered). For the read operation we only indicate the quorum (shaded blocks) that receives messages and reply to the read.

Theorem 5.5   *No MWMR implementation of a R/W atomic register that exploits an n–wise quorum $\mathbb{Q}$ s.t. $2 \leq n < |\mathbb{Q}|$ is possible, if it allows a set Π of fast write operations s.t. $|\Pi| \geq n$, and $\forall \omega \in \Pi$, ω precedes a (fast or slow) read operation ρ.*

Proof. It suffices to show that the claim holds for $|\Pi| = n$. We assume by contradiction that there exist executions that contain n fast write operations that precede a read, and do not violate atomicity. Let us begin by introducing execution constructions of *quorum-switching* write operations in an n-wise quorum system. In a nutshell, each execution construction contains $n - 2$ concurrent and two consecutive (i.e., two complete, non-concurrent operations originating at two distinct processors), quorum-switching write operations. Once all the writes are completed, each execution is extended by a single read operation. We examine the value returned by the read operation. Notice that by definition, an n-*wise* quorum system $\mathbb{Q}$ contains a subset $\mathbb{Q}^{[n+1]}$ of $n + 1$ quorums such that $\forall Q_1, Q_2 \in \mathbb{Q}^{[n+1]}$, s.t. $Q_1 \nsubseteq Q_2$. In the rest of the proof we will construct executions where operations communicate with such a set of $n + 1$ non-inclusive quorums.

Execution Constructions: We construct execution ξ_1 for an n-wise quorum system as follows. We begin from execution ξ_1^1 that contains a write operation ω_1 from w_1 that completes upon receiving replies from quorum Q_1. Execution ξ_1^1 is extended by a write operation from w_2 that receives replies from quorum Q_2 and we obtain execution ξ_1^2. Let $\Delta(\xi_1^2)$ be an execution similar to ξ_1^2 with the difference that the servers in $Q_1 \setminus Q_2$ do not receive the messages and do not reply to ω_1. Notice that only the servers in $Q_1 \setminus Q_2$ and the writer w_1 can distinguish ξ_1^2 from $\Delta(\xi_1^2)$. We extend $\Delta(\xi_1^2)$ by a write operation ω_3 that completes upon receiving replies from quorum Q_3 and we obtain execution ξ_1^3. Again, we obtain execution $\Delta(\xi_1^3)$ by removing all the messages received from the servers in $Q_2 \setminus Q_3$. In general, we obtain ξ_1^j, for $1 \leq j \leq n - 2$, by extending $\Delta(\xi_1^{j-1})$ with a write ω_j from writer w_j that receives messages from Q_j, and we obtain $\Delta(\xi_1^j)$ by removing any messages received by $Q_{j-1} \setminus Q_j$. Notice that by our construction, there exists at least a single server that receives the messages and replies to all the messages in $\Delta(\xi_1^{n-1})$. Those are all the servers in $\bigcap_{1 \leq k \leq n-2} Q_k$, which is not empty since we assume an n-wise quorum system. Finally, we extend $\Delta(\xi_1^{n-1})$ with a complete write operation ω_n that receives replies from Q_n. The messages from ω_n are received from all servers. We obtain execution ξ_1^n. Notice that in ξ_1^n, both writes ω_{n-1} and ω_n are complete, and in particular ω_{n-1} completes before ω_n is invoked. We now extend ξ_1^n by delivering the messages in transit and completing all the incomplete write operations. In particular, we extend ξ_1^n by delivering the messages sent by ω_1 to all the servers that did not received them and so ω_1 completes. This gives us execution $\xi_1^{n,1}$. In general, we obtain execution $\xi_1^{n,j}$, for $2 \leq j \leq n - 1$, by extending execution $\xi_1^{n,j-1}$ by delivering the messages of a write operation ω_j to all the servers that did not receive them, and completing ω_j. Lastly, we obtain execution ξ_1 by extending $\xi_1^{n,n-1}$ by a read operation ρ that receives replies from quorum Q_{n+1}. Notice that ρ is invoked after the completion of all write operations. Figure 5.3 illustrates the construction of execution ξ_1 for a *4-wise* quorum system.

In the same manner, we build a series of executions ξ_i, for $1 \leq i \leq n$, where the first write operation is ω_i, followed by the writes $\omega_{[(i+k) \bmod n]+1}$, for $0 \leq k \leq n - 2$. In particular, we start from ξ_i^1 that contains operation ω_i that receives replies from the quorum Q_i, and we obtain execution ξ_i^j by extending either ξ_i^i or $\Delta(\xi_i^{j-1})$ with a write ω_z, for $z = [(i + j - 1) \bmod n] + 1$ that receives replies from the servers in Q_z. Execution $\Delta(\xi_i^j)$ is derived from ξ_i^j when no messages are delivered to the servers in $Q_{z-1} \setminus Q_z$. Finally, the messages of ω_{i+k} that are in transit are delivered in the execution $\xi_i^{n,k+1}$, for $0 \leq k \leq n-2$, and after the completion of the write operations we obtain ξ_i by extending $\xi_i^{n,n-1}$ by a read operation that receives replies from Q_{n+1}. Figure 5.4, shows all the executions constructed for a *4-wise* quorum system.

Analysis: Let us now examine the order in which the write messages are received by the servers during execution ξ_i. We denote by m_k the message sent by the ω_k operation, for $1 \leq k \leq n$ and by $\mathbb{Q}^{[n]} = \{Q_1, Q_2, \ldots, Q_n\}$. It is easy to see that every server in $\left(\bigcap_{Q \in \mathbb{Q}^{[n]}} Q\right)$ first receives the message m_i, and then it receives the messages m_j, for $j = [(i+k) \mod n] + 1$ and $0 \leq k \leq n-2$. That is, in ξ_1 every $s \in \left(\bigcap_{Q \in \mathbb{Q}^{[n]}} Q\right)$ receives the messages in the order $m_1, m_2, \ldots, m_n$, in ξ_2 in the order $m_2, m_3, \ldots, m_n, m_1$, and so on. Thus, it is clear that the servers in $\left(\bigcap_{Q \in \mathbb{Q}^{[n]}} Q\right)$ can distinguish each execution ξ_i as they receive the messages in different order for each execution. Notice, however, that the read operation ρ receives replies from Q_{n+1}. By the definition of an n-wise quorum system, it follows that $\left(\bigcap_{Q \in \mathbb{Q}^{[n]}} Q\right) \cap Q_{n+1} = \emptyset$, thus the read operation does not receive any reply from the servers in $\left(\bigcap_{Q \in \mathbb{Q}^{[n]}} Q\right)$.

So for ρ to distinguish two executions ξ_i and ξ_j, for $i \neq j$ and $1 \leq i, j \leq n$, it must be the case that there is some server s in an intersection of Q_{n+1} with a subset of quorums in $\mathbb{Q}^{[n]}$, such that s receives the messages in the sequence seq_i in ξ_i and in the sequence seq_j in ξ_j, and $seq_i \neq seq_j$. W.l.o.g. let us focus on the servers in the intersection $\mathcal{S}_{n+1} = \left(\bigcap_{Q \in \mathbb{Q}^{[n]} \setminus \{Q_1\}} Q\right) \cap Q_{n+1}$ and examine the sequence of the messages received by these servers in the executions ξ_i and ξ_{i+1}, for $0 \leq i \leq n$.

Let's examine the messages received by the servers in $\mathcal{S}_{n+1}$ by the end of ξ_i^n and ξ_{i+1}^n, that is the last execution extensions before the delivery of the in-transit messages. According to our execution construction all servers in Q_1 receive message m_1 sent during ω_1. There are three cases for the position of ω_1, in both executions ξ_i^n and ξ_{i+1}^n: (a) either it is the first write and appears before ω_2; or (b) is the last write and appears after ω_n; or (c) it appears after ω_n and before ω_2. We examine the three cases separately.

Case a: In this case let ω_1 appear first in ξ_i^n, i.e., ξ_1^n. By our construction it follows that ω_1 appears last in ξ_{i+1}^n in this case, i.e., ξ_2^n. In ξ_1^n each server $s \in \mathcal{S}_{n+1}$ does not receive message m_1, but receives messages $m_2, \ldots, m_n$ in this order. Notice that the messages are not removed from s in any extension $\Delta(\xi_1^j)$ as $s \notin Q_j \setminus Q_{j+1}$, for $2 \leq j \leq n-1$. So the only message received after ξ_1^n at $s \in \mathcal{S}_{n+1}$ is m_1, and hence $seq_1 = m_2, \ldots, m_n, m_1$ in this case. On the other hand, since ω_1 appears last in ξ_2^n, then by our construction m_1 is delivered to all servers, including the ones in $\mathcal{S}_{n+1}$. Every server in $\mathcal{S}_{n+1}$ receives the messages $m_2, \ldots, m_n$ during executions ξ_2^1 to ξ_2^{n-1}. Moreover, those messages are not removed in any extension $\Delta(\xi_2^j)$ as $s \notin Q_{j+1} \setminus Q_{j+2}$, for $1 \leq j \leq n-3$. Hence, $seq_2 = m_2, \ldots, m_n, m_1$ and therefore $seq_1 = seq_2$ in this case.

Case b: In this case ω_1 appears last in ξ_i^n, and this is equivalent to execution ξ_2^n. By our construction ω_2 should be the last write in ξ_{i+1}^n, and ω_1 should appear between ω_n and ω_2 (similar to execution ξ_3^n). As explained in case (a), the sequence we get when ω_1 appears last is $seq_1 = m_2, \ldots, m_n, m_1$. It remains to examine the structure of seq_2. Notice that until execution ξ_3^{n-1} each server $s \in S_{n+1}$ received the messages $m_3, \ldots, m_n$ since for any extension $\Delta(\xi_3^j)$ as $s \notin Q_{j+2} \setminus Q_{j+3}$, for $1 \leq j \leq n-4$. We obtain $\Delta(\xi_3^{n-1})$ be removing all the messages from the servers in $Q_n \setminus Q_1$. Since $s \in Q_n$ and $s \notin Q_1$ then $s \in Q_n \setminus Q_1$. So every $s \in S_{n+1}$ does not contain any messages in $\Delta(\xi_3^{n-1})$. However, by construction we obtain ξ_3^n by extending $\Delta(\xi_3^{n-1})$ with write ω_2. The messages of ω_2 are received by all servers in Q_2 and hence every server $s \in S_{n+1}$. Thus, by the end of ξ_3^n, s receives only message m_2. Server s receives the message m_3 to obtain execution $\xi_3^{n,1}$, m_4 to obtain $\xi_3^{n,2}$, and finally, m_1 to obtain $\xi_3^{n,n-1}$. So $seq_2 = m_2, m_3, \ldots, m_n, m_1$ in execution ξ_3, and thus $seq_1 = seq_2$ in this case as well.

Case c: This is the last case where the ω_1 appears after ω_n and before ω_2 in ξ_i^n. In this case, ω_1 will also appear between ω_n and ω_2, or ω_1 will appear first in ξ_{i+1}^n. With similar arguments as in case (b), we can show that if ω_1 appears after ω_n, then all the messages $m_i, \ldots, m_n$ are removed from the servers in S_{n+1} once we obtain the execution $\Delta\xi_i^k$, for $k = n - i - 2$. Thus, each server $s \in S_{n+1}$ receives messages $m_2, \ldots, m_j$, for $j = [(i + n - 2) \mod n] + 1$. Notice that $j = i - 1$ except if $i = 1$ where $j = n$. When the in-transit messages are delivered then $seq_1 = m_2, \ldots, m_j, m_i, \ldots, m_n, m_1$. Similarly for ξ_{i+1}^n, $seq_2 = m_2, \ldots, m_j, m_i, \ldots, m_n, m_1$ when the write ω_1 is between ω_n and ω_2. According to case (a) $seq_2 = m_2, \ldots, m_n, m_1$ when ω_1 appears first. Hence, we showed that $seq_1 = seq_2$ in this case as well.

In a similar way we can show that the sequence of messages is the same for the servers of any other intersection between Q_{n+1} and $n-1$ quorums from $\mathbb{Q}^{[n]}$, for any pair of executions ξ_i, ξ_j. Therefore the read operation ρ receives the same messages from the servers in all of these executions and thus is unable to distinguish between them. However, by construction, ω_{n-1} completes before the invocation of ω_n in ξ_1 and thus by atomicity ω_{n-1} must be ordered before ω_n at ρ. In other words, ρ cannot return the value of ω_{n-1} in ξ_1. Similarly, ρ cannot return the value of ω_n in ξ_2 since $\omega_n \to \omega_1$. In general, ρ cannot return the value of ω_j in execution ξ_i, for $0 \leq i \leq n$ and $j = [(i + n - 3) \mod n] + 1$, as $\omega_j \to \omega_{[j \mod n]+1}$. Since ρ cannot distinguish between those executions, then ρ cannot return any of those values in any execution ξ_i. Thus, ρ does not return the value written even though all write operations precede ρ, violating this way atomicity and contradicting our initial assumption. $\qquad \square$

5.4   ALGORITHM SFW: EXPEDITING WRITE OPERATIONS

The result in Theorem 5.5 motivated the development of an algorithm that enables some write operations to be fast in the MWMR setting. We call it algorithm SFW. In contrast with the algorithms presented in Sections 5.1 and 5.2, algorithm SFW enables some *writes* and *reads* to be fast, and it is the first algorithm to allow fast write operations even during write concurrency. The algorithm adopts the approach of using tags associated with written values to impose an

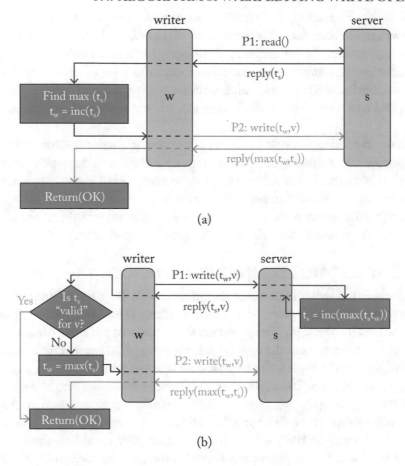

Figure 5.5: (a) Traditional writer side ordering and (b) server side ordering.

order on write operations. In contrast to previous implementations, SFW incorporates a new technique, called *Server Side Ordering* (SSO), that assigns to the servers (instead of the writers) the task of incrementing the tag associated with every value written on the object. At a first glance, SSO appears to be an intuitive and straightforward approach: servers are responsible to increment the tag associated with their local object replica whenever they receive a write request. Yet, fully developing the technique and reasoning about its correctness is challenging.

5.4.1   ALGORITHMIC TECHNIQUE: SERVER SIDE ORDERING (SSO)

Figure 5.5 presents the data flow between a writer and a server as it is implemented by the two techniques. In the algorithms presented so far, each write operation required two phases to complete as shown in Figure 5.5a. During the first phase a write operation was *querying* a set of object replicas for their latest tag. Each server s receiving such request was replying with its local tag tag_s. The writer was then detecting the maximum tag among those replies, was incrementing it (obtaining tag_w) and finally was assigning the new tag to the value to be written. In the second phase, the writer was sending tags and associated values to a set of object replica hosts. Such methodology established that each individual writer was responsible to decide a *single* and *unique* tag to be assigned to a written value. Following this technique a belief was shaped that *"writes must read."*

SSO allows the writer to avoid the query phase during a write operation. In particular, as shown in Figure 5.5b, the writer sends its local tag tag_w and the value to be written val during his first phase to a set of servers. Each server s that receives such a message generates a new tag tag_s by incrementing the maximum between its local and received tags ($inc(max(tag_s, tag_w))$), and replies back to the writer with the generated tag. If the writer collects the same tag from *"enough"* servers, then it completes without performing a second phase.

5.4.2   ALGORITHMIC TECHNIQUE: ENHANCED TAGGING

In approaches where the writer increments the timestamp each writer generates a *unique* timestamp for each of its writes. The writer identifier in that case is included in the tag to distinguish two write operations invoked by *different* writers that generated the *same* timestamp. However, allowing the servers to increment the tags introduces a complication: *multiple* and *different* tags may now be assigned to the same write request (and thus the same written value). For example, if a tag is a tuple of the form $\langle ts, wid \rangle$, then two server processes s and s' may associate two different tags $\langle ts_s, w \rangle$ and $\langle ts_{s'}, w \rangle$, respectively, to a single write operation ω. Any operation, however, that witnesses such tags is not able to distinguish whether the tags refer to a single or different write operations from w. For this purpose, SFW combines the server generated tags (*global ordering*) with writer generated operation counters (*local ordering*), introducing a tag that is a triple of the form $\langle ts, wid, wc \rangle \in \mathbb{N} \times \mathcal{W} \times \mathbb{N}$. The fields ts and wid are used as in common tags and represents the timestamp and writer identifier, respectively. Field wc represents the write operation counter and is used to distinguish the write operations originating from the writer with identifier wid. In other words, ts represents the *global* and wc the *local* value orderings, and are incremented by the servers and writers, respectively (as required by SSO).

So in the previous example, by including the writer's local ordering wc in each tag, the tags will become $\langle ts_s, w, wc \rangle$ and $\langle ts_{s'}, w, wc \rangle$. From the new tags it becomes apparent that the same write operation was assigned two different timestamps. The triples are compared lexicographically. We say that $tag_1 > tag_2$ if one of the following holds:

1. $tag_1.ts > tag_2.ts$,

2. $(tag_1.ts = tag_2.ts) \wedge (tag_1.wid > tag_2.wid)$, or

3. $(tag_1.ts = tag_2.ts) \wedge (tag_1.wid = tag_2.wid) \wedge (tag_1.wc > tag_2.wc)$.

5.4.3   ALGORITHM SFW SPECIFICATION

SFW is composed of four automata: SFW_w for every $w \in \mathcal{W}$; SFW_r for every $r \in \mathcal{R}$; SFW_s for every $s \in \mathcal{S}$ to handle the read and write requests on the shared object; and $Ch_{i,s}$ and $Ch_{s,i}$ that establish the reliable asynchronous process-to-process communication channels. The algorithm deploys quorum systems and relies on the assumption that a single quorum is non-faulty throughout the algorithm's execution. To enable fast operations, algorithm SFW involves two *predicates*: one for the read protocol and one for the write protocol. Both predicates evaluate the distribution of a tag within the quorum that replies to the read or write operation to establish the latest written value. The description that follows focus on tags written and returned. The association of values to those tags is straightforward.

Specification 17 SFW_s Server Automaton: Signature, State, and Transitions

---

```
 1:  Data Types:
 2:     Msgs₁ ⊆ {READ,WRITE,PROPAGATE}×
 3:              ⟨(ℕ × 𝒲 × ℕ⁺) × V⟩ × ℕ
 4:     Msgs₂ ⊆ {W-ACK,R-ACK} × 2^(ℕ×𝒲×ℕ×V) ×
 5:              ⟨(ℕ × 𝒲 × ℕ⁺) × V⟩ × ℕ
 6:     Msgs₃ ⊆ {P-ACK} × ℕ
 7:     Msgs = Msgs₁ ∪ Msgs₂ ∪ Msgs₃

 8:  Signature:
 9:    Input:
10:       recv(m)_{i,s}, m ∈ Msgs, s ∈ 𝒮, i ∈ ℛ ∪ 𝒲
11:       failₛ
12:    Output:
13:       send(m)_{s,i}, m ∈ Msgs, s ∈ 𝒮, i ∈ ℛ ∪ 𝒲

14:  State:
15:     tag = ⟨ts, wid, wc⟩ ∈ ℕ × 𝒲 × ℕ init {0, min(𝒲), 0}
16:     v ∈ V init ⊥
17:     inprogress ⊆ ℕ × 𝒲 × ℕ⁺ × V init ∅
18:     confirmed ∈
19:        ℕ × 𝒲 × ℕ⁺ × V init {0, min(𝒲), 0, ⊥}
20:     Counter(i) ∈ ℕ⁺, i ∈ ℛ ∪ 𝒲 init 0
21:     status ∈ {active, failed} init active
22:     replySet ⊆ Msgs × ℐ init ∅

23:  Transitions:
24:     Input recv(⟨msgT, t, val, opCount, C⟩)_{i,s}
25:        Effect:
26:           if status = active ∧ C > pCount(i) then
27:              Counter(i) ← count
28:              if tag < t then
29:                 (tag.ts, tag.wid, tag.wc, v) ←
```

```
30:                    (t.ts, t.wid, t.wc, val)
31:              if msgT = WRITE then
32:                 (tag.ts, tag.wid, tag.wc) ←
33:                    (tag.ts + 1, i, opCount)
34:              inprogress ←
35:                 (inprogress \ {⟨*, i, *⟩, *}) ∪ ⟨tag, val⟩
36:              if confirmed < t then
37:                 confirmed ← t
38:              if msgT = WRITE then
39:                 m ←
40:                    ⟨W-ACK, inprogress, confirmed,
                         Counter(i)⟩
41:              if msgT = READ then
42:                 m ←
43:                    ⟨R-ACK, inprogress, confirmed,
                         Counter(i)⟩
44:              if msgT = PROPAGATE then
45:                 m ← ⟨P-ACK, Counter(i)⟩
46:              replySet ← replySet ∪ {(m, i)}

47:     Output send(m)_{s,i}
48:        Precondition:
49:           status = active
50:           (m, i) ∈ replySet
51:        Effect:
52:           replySet ← replySet \ {(m, i)}

53:     Input failₛ
54:        Effect:
55:           status ← failed
```

Server Protocol (Specification 17, SFW_s). We begin with the description of the server as it plays a significant role in the system. In SFW, each server maintains the value of the replica and generates the tags associated with each value. As in the previous algorithms, the server waits to receive *read* and *write* requests. If any request is received, the server updates its local tag and value if the tag enclosed in the request is greater than the local tag of the server (lines 28–30). The server also updates the *confirmed* tag in case it is smaller than the tag enclosed in the received message (line 37). As we are going to see in the description of the read and write protocols, the tag for the associated value enclosed in a read or a write message is the latest returned tag by the invoking process. Thus, the *confirmed* tag maintains the largest tag returned by some process that is known to the server. Finally, the server generates a new tag if the message received is a write request from some writer w (lines 31–35). The new tag, *newTag*, contains the following fields:

- $tag_s.ts + 1$: the timestamp of the local tag incremented by 1,

- w: the identifier of the requesting writer, and

- *opCount*: the sequence number of the write operation at the requesting writer.

Note that the new tag is greater than both the server's local tag, tag_s, and the tag $t.tag$ enclosed in the message. Once the new tag is generated, the server updates its *inprogress$_s$* set (line 35). This set is constructed to hold one tag with its associated value per writer: the largest tag that the server generated for each writer as a result of a write request. Hence, in the worst case the *inprogress$_s$* contains a single tag and its associated value for each writer. The importance of using the *inprogress$_s$* is twofold.

1. Each write operation witnesses the tag assignments to the value to be written from all servers in the replying quorum (since even a concurrent write will not overwrite the tag of the specific write). Thus, the writer can establish if any of the tags was adopted by enough servers in the replying quorum or if it needs to proceed to a second round.

2. Each read operation obtains full knowledge on the tags reported to each writer, and is able to predict which tag each writer adopts for its latest write operation. By ordering the tags the reader is able to establish the write operation with the largest tag and hence, the latest written value.

The read and write predicates utilize the above observations to allow fast read and write operations. Once a server completes all the necessary actions, it acknowledges every message received by sending its *inprogress$_s$* set and *confirmed$_s$* variable to the requesting process i (lines 49–35).

Writer Protocol (Specification 18, S_FW_w). The write operation uses one or two rounds. A writer w maintains a local variable wc that is incremented each time w invokes a write operation ω (line 32). Using this variable any process can identify a write ω by the tuple $\langle w, wc \rangle$: ω is the wc^{th} write of w. Once the local counter is incremented, the writer w sends messages to all the servers and waits for a quorum of these to reply. When w receives replies from all the servers of some quorum Q (line 54), w inspects the *inprogress* sets enclosed in those replies to extract the tags assigned to ω ($\langle w, wc \rangle$) (line 57). Finally, w applies the following predicate on

Specification 18 SFW_w Writer Automaton: Signature, State, and Transitions

1: **Data Types:**
2:    *Msgs*, same as in Specification 17

3: **Signature:**
4:    **Input:**
5:       $\text{write}(val)_w,\ val \in V,\ w \in \mathcal{W}$
6:       $\text{recv}(m)_{s,w},\ m \in Msgs,\ s \in \mathcal{S},\ w \in \mathcal{W}$
7:       $\text{fail}_w,\ w \in \mathcal{W}$
8:    **Output:**
9:       $\text{send}(m)_{w,s},\ m \in Msgs,\ s \in \mathcal{S},\ w \in \mathcal{W}$
10:      $\text{write-ack}_w,\ w \in \mathcal{W}$
11:   **Internal:**
12:      $\text{write-phase1-fix}_w,\ w \in \mathcal{W}$
13:      $\text{write-phase2-fix}_w,\ w \in \mathcal{W}$

14: **State:**
15:   $tag = \langle ts, w, wc \rangle \in \mathbb{N} \times \{w\} \times \mathbb{N}\ \text{init}\ \{0, w, 0\}$
16:   $v \in V\ \text{init}\ \bot$
17:   $vp \in V\ \text{init}\ \bot$
18:   $wc \in \mathbb{N}^+\ \text{init}\ 0$
19:   $wCounter \in \mathbb{N}^+\ \text{init}\ 0$
20:   $status \in$
21:      $\{idle, phase1, phase2, done, failed\}\ \text{init}\ idle$
22:   $srvAck \subseteq Msgs \times \mathcal{S}\ \text{init}\ \emptyset$

23: **Transitions:**
24:   **Input** $\text{write}(val)_w$
25:      **Effect:**
26:         **if** $status = idle$ **then**
27:            $status \leftarrow phase1$
28:            $srvAck \leftarrow \emptyset$
29:            $vp \leftarrow v$
30:            $v \leftarrow val$
31:            $wCounter \leftarrow wCounter + 1$
32:            $wc \leftarrow wc + 1$

33:   **Output send**$(\langle \text{WRITE}, t, val, wc, C \rangle)_{w,s}$
34:      **Precondition:**
35:         $status = phase1$
36:         $(t, val, wc, C) = (tag, v, wc, wCounter)$
37:      **Effect:** none

38:   **Input** $\text{recv}(\langle \text{W-ACK}, inprogress, confirmed, C \rangle)_{s,w}$
39:      **Effect:**
40:         **if** $status = phase1$ and $wCounter = C$ **then**
41:            $srvAck \leftarrow srvAck \cup \{(m, s)\}$

42:   **Output send**$(\langle \text{PROPAGATE}, t, val, wc, C \rangle)_{w,s}$
43:      **Precondition:**
44:         $status = phase2$
45:         $(t, val, wc, C) = (tag, v, wc, wCounter)$
46:      **Effect:** none

47:   **Input** $\text{recv}(\langle \text{P-ACK}, C \rangle)_{s,w}$
48:      **Effect:**
49:         **if** $status = phase2$ and $wCounter = C$ **then**
50:            $srvAck \leftarrow srvAck \cup \{(m, s)\}$

51:   **Internal write-phase1-fix**$_w$
52:      **Precondition:**
53:         $status = phase1$
54:         $\exists Q \in \mathbb{Q} : Q \subseteq \{s : (m, s) \in srvAck\}$
55:      **Effect:**
56:         $T \leftarrow \{\langle ts, w, * \rangle :$
57:            $\langle ts, w, * \rangle \in \bigcup_{(m,s) \in srvAck} m.inprogress\}$
58:         **if** $\exists\ \tau, MS, \mathbb{Q}^{[\ell]}$ s.t.
59:            $\tau \in T$, and
60:            $MS = \{s : s \in Q \wedge (m, s) \in srvAck \wedge$
                  $\tau \in m.inprogress\}$, and
61:            $\mathbb{Q}^{[\ell]} \subseteq \mathbb{Q}$ s.t. $0 \le \ell \le \lfloor \frac{n}{2} - 1 \rfloor\ \wedge$
                  $(\bigcap_{Q' \in (\mathbb{Q}^{[\ell]} \cup \{Q\})} Q') \subseteq MS$
62:         **then**
63:            $\langle tag.ts, tag.wid, tag.wc \rangle \leftarrow \langle \tau.ts, w, wc \rangle$
64:            **if** $i \ge \max(0, \frac{n}{2} - 2)$ **then**
65:               $status \leftarrow phase2$
66:               $wCounter \leftarrow wCounter + 1$
67:               $srvAck \leftarrow \emptyset$
68:            **else**
69:               $status \leftarrow done$
70:         **else**
71:            $\langle tag.ts, tag.wid, tag.wc \rangle \leftarrow$
                  $\max_{\tau \in T}(\langle \tau.ts, w, wc \rangle)$
72:            $wCounter \leftarrow wCounter + 1$
73:            $status \leftarrow phase2$
74:            $srvAck \leftarrow \emptyset$

75:   **Internal write-phase2-fix**$_w$
76:      **Precondition:**
77:         $status = phase2$
78:         $\exists Q \in \mathbb{Q} : Q \subseteq \{s : (m, s) \in srvAck\}$
79:      **Effect:**
80:         $status \leftarrow done$

81:   **Output write-ack**$_w$
82:      **Precondition:**
83:         $status = done$
84:      **Effect:**
85:         $status \leftarrow idle$

86:   **Input fail**$_w$
87:      **Effect:**
88:         $status \leftarrow failed$
89:
90:

the set of collected tags, where $m(\omega, 1)_{s,w}.inprogress$ denotes the *inprogress* set enclosed in the first message sent from s to w for operation ω.

Writer predicate for a write ω (PW, lines 58–62):

$$\exists \tau, \mathbb{Q}^{[\ell]}, MS \text{ where: } \tau \in \{\langle *, \omega \rangle : \langle *, \omega \rangle \in m(\omega, 1)_{s,w}.inprogress \ \wedge \ s \in Q\},$$

$$MS = \{s : s \in Q \ \wedge \ \tau \in m(\omega, 1)_{s,w}.inprogress\}, \text{ and } \mathbb{Q}^{[\ell]} \subseteq \mathbb{Q}, 0 \le i \le \lfloor \tfrac{n}{2} - 1 \rfloor, \text{ s.t.}$$

$$\left(\bigcap_{\mathcal{Q} \in \mathbb{Q}^{[\ell]} \cup \{Q\}} \mathcal{Q} \right) \subseteq MS.$$

The predicate checks if any of the collected tags appears in some intersection of Q with at most $\tfrac{n}{2} - 1$ other quorums, where n the intersection degree of the deployed quorum system. The idea behind the predicate is quite intuitive: if all of the servers in the intersection of the *minority* $(< \tfrac{n}{2})$ of quorums assign ω to a tag τ, then the intersection of any other minority of quorums contains at least one server that assigns ω to a tag τ since we assume that every n quorums intersect. Thus, no process will discover a different tag τ' to be assigned to ω by all the servers in the intersection of any minority of quorums. Hence, τ will be the unique tag considered to be assigned to ω by any process. This is shown formally by Lemma 5.6. Given the validation of the predicate the writer proceeds as follows.

> **PW holds for a tag τ with $0 < \ell < \tfrac{n}{2} - 2$:** the writer associates the new value with τ and completes (lines 63, 69).

> **PW holds for a tag τ with $\ell = 0$ or $\ell \ge \tfrac{n}{2} - 2$:** the writer associates the new value with τ and performs a second round sending $\langle \tau, v \rangle$ to a quorum of servers (lines 63, 64–67).

> **PW does not hold:** the writer associates the new value with *the maximum received tag*, say τ_{max}, and performs a second round sending the $\langle \tau_{max}, v \rangle$ pair to a quorum of servers (lines 71–74).

The index i in the above cases refers to the number of quorums whose intersection only contains servers that replied with tag τ. If a second round is necessary, the writer terminates as soon as it receives replies from a quorum of servers (lines 77–80).

Reader Protocol (Specification 19, SFW_r). The reader protocol is similar to the writer protocol in the sense that it uses a predicate to decide the latest tag written on the shared object. When a read$_r$ request is received by a reader r (lines 26–28), the reader sends messages to all the servers and waits for the servers in some quorum Q to reply (line 52). The reader extracts the following from the collected replies:

- the maximum confirmed tag, *maxCT* (line 54) and

- the set *inPtag* of the tags contained in every $m(\rho)_{s,r}.inprogress$ set (line 56).

With the tags sorted in descending order the reader examines if any of the tags in *inPtag* that is higher than *maxCT* satisfies the reader predicate. The reader predicate for a read operation ρ from r that receives messages from a quorum Q, is the following (lines 57–61).

Reader predicate for a read ρ **(PR):** $\exists\ \tau, \mathbb{Q}^{[\ell]}, MS$, where: $\max(\tau) \in \bigcup_{s \in Q} m(\rho, 1)_{s,r}.inprogress$, $MS = \{s : s \in Q \ \wedge\ \tau \in m(\rho, 1)_{s,r}.inprogress\}$, and $\mathbb{Q}^{[\ell]} \subseteq \mathbb{Q}, 0 \leq \ell \leq \lfloor \frac{n}{2} - 2 \rfloor$, s.t. $\left(\bigcap_{\mathcal{Q} \in \mathbb{Q}^{[\ell]} \cup \{Q\}} \mathcal{Q} \right) \subseteq MS$.

The reader predicate shares a similar idea as the writer predicate. To ensure that subsequent operations do not return a smaller tag—and hence an older value—the reader must discover a tag τ in an intersection of Q with at most $\frac{n}{2} - 2$ (a minority) other quorums, where n the intersection degree of the quorum system. If there exists no tag in $inPtag$ that is greater than $maxCT$ and satisfies the predicate, then $maxCT$ is returned. In particular, given the validation of the predicate the reader proceeds as follows.

> **PR holds for a tag** τ **with** $0 < \ell < \frac{n}{2} - 2$: the reader returns the value associated with τ and completes in a single round (lines 62, 68).

> **PR holds for a tag** τ **with** $\ell = 0$ **or** $\ell = \frac{n}{2} - 2$: the reader returns the value v associated with τ and performs a second round sending $\langle \tau, v \rangle$ to a quorum of servers (lines 62, 63–66).

> **PR does not hold for any** $\tau > maxCT$: the reader returns the value v associated with $maxCT$ (lines 71–72). If the set of servers that replied with $maxCT$ (line 70) is a subset of the intersection of less than $n - 1$ quorums then the read is fast (line 76); otherwise the reader performs a second round sending $\langle maxCT, v \rangle$ to a quorum of servers (lines 78–80).

Again, the index i refers to the number of quorums whose intersection only contains servers that replied with tag τ. Notice that a read operation ρ cannot return any tag smaller than $maxCT$. Recall from the server description that $maxCT$ denotes a tag already decided by an operation π that precedes or is concurrent with ρ.

5.4.4   ALGORITHM SFW CORRECTNESS

To show the correctness of the algorithm we first proof a very important lemma showing that every process assigns a single tag to each write operation. The lemma shows that two tags can be found in the servers of an intersection among k quorums only if $k > \frac{n+1}{2}$.

Lemma 5.6   *In any execution* $\xi \in execs(\text{SFW}, \mathbb{Q})$, *if a read/write operation* π *invoked by* i *receives replies from a quorum* $Q \in \mathbb{Q}$ *and observes two tags* τ_1 *and* τ_2 *for a write operation* $\omega = \langle w, wc \rangle$, *s.t.* $\tau_1 = \langle ts_1, w, wc \rangle$, $\tau_2 = \langle ts_2, w, wc \rangle$, $ts_1 \neq ts_2$ *and* τ_1 *is propagated in a* k-*wise intersection, then* τ_2 *is propagated in at least* k-*wise intersection as well iff* $k > \frac{n+1}{2}$.

Proof. Let $\mathcal{S}_{\tau_1} \subseteq Q$ be a set of servers such that $\forall s \in \mathcal{S}_{\tau_1}$ replies with τ_1 for ω to π and $\mathcal{S}_{\tau_2} \subseteq Q$ the set of servers such that $\forall s' \in \mathcal{S}_{\tau_2}$ replies with τ_2 for ω to π. Since both τ_1 and τ_2 are propagated in a k-wise intersection and since every server maintains just a single copy in its *inprogress* set for ω, then there exists two sets of quorums $\mathbb{Q}_1^{[k]}$ and $\mathbb{Q}_2^{[k]}$ such that:

$$\left(\bigcap_{Q \in \mathbb{Q}_1^{[k]}} Q\right) \subseteq S_{\tau_1} \text{ and } \left(\bigcap_{Q \in \mathbb{Q}_2^{[k]}} Q\right) \subseteq S_{\tau_2} \text{ and } \left(\bigcap_{Q \in \mathbb{Q}_1^{[k]}} Q\right) \cap \left(\bigcap_{Q \in \mathbb{Q}_2^{[k]}} Q\right) = \emptyset.$$

From the fact that $S_{\tau_1}, S_{\tau_2} \subseteq Q$, it follows that $Q \in \mathbb{Q}_1^{[k]}$ and $Q \in \mathbb{Q}_2^{[k]}$. So we can write,

$$\left(\bigcap_{Q \in \mathbb{Q}_1^{[k]}} Q\right) = \left(\bigcap_{Q \in \mathbb{Q}_1^{[k-1]}} Q\right) \cap Q \text{ and } \left(\bigcap_{Q \in \mathbb{Q}_2^{[k]}} Q\right) = \left(\bigcap_{Q \in \mathbb{Q}_2^{[k-1]}} Q\right) \cap Q$$

and hence

$$\left(\bigcap_{Q \in \mathbb{Q}_1^{[k]}} Q\right) \cap \left(\bigcap_{Q \in \mathbb{Q}_2^{[k]}} Q\right) = \left(\bigcap_{Q \in \mathbb{Q}_1^{[k-1]}} Q\right) \cap \left(\bigcap_{Q \in \mathbb{Q}_2^{[k-1]}} Q\right) \cap Q = \emptyset.$$

By definition we know that $\mathbb{Q}^{[i]}$ is the quorum set that contains i quorums. So the intersection contains at most $k - 1 + k - 1 + 1 = 2k - 1$ quorums. Since we assume an n-wise intersection then the two sets of quorums have an empty intersection only if they consist of more than n quorums. Hence, it follows that the intersection is empty if and only if: $2k - 1 > n$ or $k > \frac{n+1}{2}$. This completes the proof. □

From the previous lemma we can derive that if a tag is found in the servers of an intersection of $k < \frac{n+1}{2}$ quorums, then any other tag can be found in an intersection of $z > \frac{n+2}{2}$ quorums. Since the predicate of any read/write operation π holds when some tag is found in the intersection of $k \leq \frac{n-1}{2} < \frac{n+1}{2}$ quorums then this is the only tag that may satisfy π's predicate.

Next, we sketch a proof of the correctness of the algorithm. We need to show that any execution $\xi \in \mathit{execs}(\textsc{SfW}, \mathbb{Q})$, for any quorum system $\mathbb{Q}$, satisfies liveness (i.e., termination) and safety (i.e., atomicity) properties. Termination is guaranteed since at least a single quorum in $\mathbb{Q}$ is correct. So it remains to address atomicity.

Theorem 5.7   *Algorithm* SfW *implements an atomic MWMR object.*

Proof. We order the operations based on the tags they write and return. Namely, for each execution ξ of SfW there must exist a partial order $\prec$ on the set of completed operations Π that satisfy conditions **A1**, **A2**, and **A3** of Definition 2.16. For SfW, we let tag_π be the value of the tag at the conclusion of write-phase1-fix when π is a write, and the tag at the conclusion of read-phase1-fix if π is a read. With this we define the partial order on operations as follows. For two operations π_1 and π_2 when π_1 is any operation and π_2 is a write we let $\pi_1 \prec \pi_2$ if $tag_{\pi_1} < tag_{\pi_2}$. For two operations π_1 and π_2 when π_1 is a write and π_2 is a read we let $\pi_1 \prec \pi_2$ if $tag_{\pi_1} \leq tag_{\pi_2}$. The rest of the order is established by transitivity and reads with the same tags are not ordered.

A1 If for operations π_1 and π_2 in Π, $\pi_1 \rightarrow \pi_2$, then it cannot be the case that $\pi_2 \prec \pi_1$.

Let's assume by contradiction that $\pi_2 \prec \pi_1$ and let's examine the possible cases where π_1 and π_2 are writes or reads. We also need to examine two subcases: (a) π_1 is fast, or (b) π_1 is slow, for both when π_1 is a read or a write.

Suppose that π_2 is a write and π_1 a read or a write. Then, according to our model, $\pi_2 \prec \pi_1$ holds if $tag_{\pi_2} < tag_{\pi_1}$.

If π_1 is fast, then it received tag_{π_1} from all the servers in some intersection of less than $\frac{n}{2} - 1$ (if π_1 is a write) or less than $\frac{n}{2} - 2$ (if π_1 is a read) quorums, not including the replying quorum. We use $\mathbb{Q}^{[r]}$ to denote this set of quorums. From Lemma 5.6 it follows that tag_{π_1} can be the only tag in the replying quorum, distributed in such an intersection. When π_2 is invoked it receives replies from a quorum of servers, say Q_2, during its first round. Since in an n-wise quorum system every n quorums intersect then:

$$\left(\bigcap_{Q \in \mathbb{Q}^{[r]}} Q\right) \cap Q_2 \neq \emptyset. \tag{5.4.4}$$

It is easy to see that every server in the intersection of 5.4.4 replies to π_1 before replying to π_2. Thus, π_2 receives a tag, say tag_s, larger than tag_{π_1} from each of these servers. If π_2 obtains the same tag $tag_s > tag_{\pi_1}$ from all the servers of the intersection then the predicate will hold for π_2 with a set $\mathbb{Q}^{[k]}$ for $k \leq \frac{n}{2}$ quorums (including Q_2). In this case π_2 completes in one (if $k < \frac{n}{2} - 2$) or two (if $\frac{n}{2} - 2 \leq k \leq \frac{n}{2}$) rounds and sets $tag_{\pi_2} = tag_s > tag_{\pi_1}$. Otherwise, π_2 sets $tag_{\pi_2} = maxTag$ and completes in two rounds. Since every server in the intersection in 5.4.4 replies with a tag higher than tag_{π_1} then $maxTag > tag_{\pi_1}$ and hence $tag_{\pi_2} > tag_{\pi_1}$ in this case as well. So it cannot be the case that $\pi_2 \prec \pi_1$.

If π_1 is slow, then it propagates the maximum tag it discovers during its first round (tag_{π_1}) to a quorum of servers, say Q_1. By definition, $Q_1 \cap Q_2 \neq \emptyset$ and every server $s \in Q_1 \cap Q_2$ replies to π_2 with some tag $tag_s > tag_{\pi_1}$ (due to the use of SSO). Operation π_2 examines the validation of the predicate starting from the maximum discovered tag in the *inprogress* set. If a tag larger than tag_{π_1} validates the predicate, then $tag_{\pi_2} > tag_{\pi_1}$. If no tag larger than tag_{π_1} validates the predicate for π_2, then all the servers in $Q_1 \cap Q_2$ reply with the same tag tag_s, and hence the predicate holds for tag_s with $k = 1$. Hence, $tag_{\pi_2} = tag_s$ and therefore $tag_{\pi_2} > tag_{\pi_1}$. As before if no tag validates the predicate then tag_{π_2} is set to the maximum discovered tag which is $maxTag \geq tag_s$ and thus $tag_{\pi_2} > tag_{\pi_1}$. So it cannot be the case that $\pi_2 \prec \pi_1$.

It remains to examine the case where π_2 is a read. If π_1 is a write, then $\pi_2 \prec \pi_1$ if it holds that $tag_{\pi_2} < tag_{\pi_1}$. If π_1 is slow, then it propagates tag_{π_1} to a quorum of servers Q_1 during phase 2. If π_2 receives replies from a quorum of servers Q_2 in phase 1, then all servers in $Q_1 \cap Q_2$ reply with a confirmed tag, $confirmed$, such that $confirmed \geq tag_{\pi_1}$. It is easy to see from the algorithm that a read returns a tag greater or equal to the maximum confirmed tag ($maxCT$) discovered. Thus, in this case $tag_{\pi_2} \geq maxCT \geq tag_{\pi_1}$ and cannot be the case that $\pi_2 \prec \pi_1$.

If the write π_1 is fast, it means that it observed tag_{π_1} in an intersection of $k < \frac{n}{2} - 1$ quorums. Thus, the read will either: (i) observe tag_{π_1} in an intersection of $k \leq \frac{n}{2} - 2$ quorums and hence the predicate will be valid for π_2 and will return $tag_{\pi_2} = tag_{\pi_1}$ in one (if $k < \frac{n}{2} - 2$) or two (if $k = \frac{n}{2} - 2$) rounds; or (ii) the predicate will be valid for a larger tag than tag_{π_1}, and hence $tag_{\pi_2} > tag_{\pi_1}$. There is one more case where the writer that invoked π_1 will invoke a new write causing the predicate to be invalid for π_2. In that case, it follows that some servers in the intersection of the $k \le \frac{n}{2} - 2$ quorums received the new message from that writer for some write π'. However, by well-formedness each writer may invoke a single write at a time, then $\pi_1 \to \pi'$. Hence, the tag enclosed in the writer message will be greater or equal to $tag_{\pi_1}!$ and each server that receives the message updates its $confirmed_s \ge tag_{\pi_1}$. By SFW, π_2 returns $tag_{\pi_2} \ge maxCT$ and hence $tag_{\pi_2} \ge tag_{\pi_1}$. Thus, $\pi_2 \prec \pi_1$ does not hold in this case either.

With similar arguments we can show that if π_1 is a read then $tag_{\pi_2} \ge tag_{\pi_1}$. In particular, if π_1 is slow, then by the intersection property of the quorums, there exists a server that replies to the second phase of π_1 and the first phase of π_2. This server replies with a $confirmed \ge tag_{\pi_1}$ to π_2, and thus by SfW, $tag_{\pi_2} \ge tag_{\pi_1}$. If π_1 is fast, then it observed tag_{π_1} in an intersection of $k < \frac{n}{2} - 2$ quorums (not including the replying quorum). When π_2 receives replies from a quorum of servers during its first phase, will iterate all the candidate tags to find the largest tag that satisfies its predicate or picks the largest confirmed tag. If a larger tag satisfies the predicate then $tag_{\pi_2} > tag_{\pi_1}$. If no tag larger than tag_{π_1} is detected then π_2 evaluates the distribution of tag_{π_1}. Note that since tag_{π_1} is propagated in at least the servers of an intersection $\left(\bigcap_{\mathcal{Q} \in \mathbb{Q}^{[\frac{n}{2}-2]}} \mathcal{Q} \right)$ of a set of $\mathbb{Q}^{[\frac{n}{2}-2]}$ of quorums then π_2 observes tag_{π_1} from the servers in:

$$\left(\bigcap_{\mathcal{Q} \in \mathbb{Q}^{[\frac{n}{2}-2]}} \mathcal{Q} \right) \cap Q_2 \neq \emptyset.$$

That holds since we assume n-wise quorum system and the above intersection contains at most $\frac{n}{2} - 1$ quorums. So the predicate in π_2 holds for $k \le \frac{n}{2} - 2$ not including Q_2. Hence in this case π_2 returns $tag_{\pi_2} = tag_{\pi_1}$ in one (if $k < \frac{n}{2} - 2$) or two (if $k = \frac{n}{2} - 2$) rounds. According to our model $\pi_2 \prec \pi_1$ holds if $tag_{\pi_2} < tag_{\pi_1}$. If $tag_{\pi_2} = tag_{\pi_1}$ then the two operations cannot be ordered. Since $tag_{\pi_2} \ge tag_{\pi_1}$ in every case, then it cannot hold that $\pi_2 \prec \pi_1$.

A2 If ω is a write operation and π is any operation, then either $\omega \prec \pi$ or $\pi \prec \omega$.

If $tag_\omega > tag_\pi$ then $\pi \prec \omega$ follows directly. If $tag_\omega = tag_\pi$ then it must be that π is a read that satisfies its predicate with tag_w or tag_ω is confirmed in some servers. When $tag_\omega = tag_\pi$ it cannot be the case that π is a write operation. Each server generates a new tag by assigning the writer identifier to the incremented timestamp. Assuming that the writer identifiers are comparable and unique, then tags can be ordered lexicographically and either $tag_\omega > tag_\pi$ and $\pi \prec \omega$, or $tag_\omega < tag_\pi$ and $\omega \prec \pi$. If $tag_\omega < tag_\pi$ then $\omega \prec \pi$ follows directly.

A3 The value returned by a read operation is the value written by the last preceding write operation according to $\prec$ (or the initial value if there is no such write).

Let ω be the last write operation preceding the read operation ρ. This means that $tag_\omega \le tag_\rho$. Also, let the servers in Q_2 reply to phase 1 of ρ. Notice that $tag_\omega = tag_\rho$, and ρ returns the value written by ω, if: (a) the predicate holds for tag_w and there is not a larger tag that satisfies the predicate or is confirmed; and (b) tag_ω is the largest confirmed tag. For a server to set $confirmed = tag_\omega$, either it receives tag_ω from the ω directly or during the propagation phase (i.e., phase 2) of some read operation that returned tag_ω. If $tag_\omega < tag_\rho$, then it must be the case that ρ received a larger tag that satisfies its predicate or is confirmed. This tag can only be originated by a write that follows ω and hence ω is not the last preceding write, but this cannot be the case. Finally, if $tag_\rho = 0$, then there are no preceding writes, and ρ returns the initial value.

This completes the proof.   □

5.5   BIBLIOGRAPHIC NOTES

Following the advances in algorithms for the SWMR setting researchers turned to the question of the existence of MWMR atomic read and write shared object implementations in the asynchronous, message-passing environment. Lynch and Shvartsman were the first to present a generalization of the ABD algorithm for the MWMR setting in [83]. Following this development, a series of algorithms were introduced for the dynamic environment, some of which we present in the next part of the book. With the introduction of the *fast* implementation in 2004, Dutta et al. [34] showed that implementations with single round operations are not possible in the MWMR setting. This was also shown by Georgiou, Nicolaou, and Shvartsman [43], in a more relaxed setting that allowed some operations to perform two rounds before completing. Some attempts by Dolev et al. [30], Chockler et al. [24], allowed some read operations to be *fast* in the MWMR setting. The same was achieved by algorithm CwFr (see Section 5.2) that was presented by Georgiou, et al. [42]. A more refined and in-depth study of the implications of the MWMR setting was presented by Englert et al. [36] (see also Section 5.3). This study specified the exact relation of the number of *fast* operations to the replica access policy followed by any algorithm. In the same paper, the authors presented SfW the *first* algorithm to allow single round *writes* in the MWMR setting (see Section 5.4). A follow-up paper by Georgiou et al. [42] proved that the first algorithm is computationally hard and they presented an approximation algorithm with polynomial time complexity without sacrificing atomic correctness in all executions. More recently, Georgiou et al. [39] established algorithms performing one-and-a-half rounds for every read and write operation. To achieve this performance the authors utilized the idea of quorum views along with a communication between the servers.

Specification 19 SFW_r Reader Automaton: Signature, State, and Transitions

1: **Data Types:**
2:   $Msgs$, same as in Specification 17
3: **Signature:**
4:   **Input:**
5:    $read_r$, $r \in \mathcal{R}$
6:    $recv(m)_{s,r}$, $m \in Msgs$, $r \in \mathcal{R}$, $s \in \mathcal{S}$
7:    $fail_r$, $r \in \mathcal{R}$
8:   **Output:**
9:    $send(m)_{r,s}$, $m \in Msgs$, $r \in \mathcal{R}$, $s \in \mathcal{S}$
10:   $read\text{-}ack(val)_r$, $val \in V$, $r \in \mathcal{R}$
11: **Internal:**
12:   $read\text{-}phase1\text{-}fix_r$, $r \in \mathcal{R}$
13:   $read\text{-}phase2\text{-}fix_r$, $r \in \mathcal{R}$

14: **State:**
15: $tag = \langle ts, wid, wc \rangle \in \mathbb{N} \times \mathcal{W} \times \mathbb{N}$ **init** $\{0, min(\mathcal{W}), 0\}$
16: $v \in V$ **init** $\bot$
17: $rCounter \in \mathbb{N}^+$ **init** 0
18: $status \in$
19:   $\{idle, phase1, phase2, done, failed\}$ **init** $idle$
20: $srvAck \subseteq Msgs \times \mathcal{S}$ **init** $\emptyset$
21: $maxCT \in \mathbb{N} \times \mathcal{W} \times \mathbb{N} \times V$ **init** $\{\langle 0, min(\mathcal{W}), 0 \rangle, \bot\}$
22: $inPtag \subseteq \mathbb{N} \times \mathcal{W} \times \mathbb{N} \times V$ **init** $\emptyset$

23: **Transitions:**
24: **Input read$_r$**
25:   **Effect:**
26:    **if** $status = idle$ **then**
27:     $status \leftarrow phase1$
28:     $rCounter \leftarrow rCounter + 1$

29: **Output send$(\langle \text{READ}, t, val, wc, C \rangle)_{r,s}$**
30:   **Precondition:**
31:    $status = phase1$
32:    $(t, val, wc, C) = (tag, v, tag.wc, rCounter)$
33:   **Effect:** none

34: **Input recv$(\langle \text{R-ACK}, inprogress, confirmed, C \rangle)_{s,r}$**
35:   **Effect:**
36:    **if** $status = phase1$ **then**
37:     **if** $rCounter = C$ **then**
38:      $srvAck \leftarrow srvAck \cup \{(m, s)\}$

39: **Output send$(\langle \text{PROPAGATE}, t, val, wc, C \rangle)_{r,s}$**
40:   **Precondition:**
41:    $status = phase2$
42:    $(t, val, wc, C) = (tag, v, tag.wc, rCounter)$
43:   **Effect:** none

44: **Input recv$(\langle \text{P-ACK}, C \rangle)_{s,r}$**
45:   **Effect:**
46:    **if** $status = phase2$ **then**
47:     **if** $rCounter = C$ **then**
48:      $srvAck \leftarrow srvAck \cup \{(m, s)\}$

49: **Internal read-phase1-fix$_r$**
50: **Precondition:**
51:   $status = phase1$
52:   $\exists Q \in \mathbb{Q} : Q \subseteq \{s : (m, s) \in srvAck\}$
53: **Effect:**
54:   $maxCT \leftarrow \max(\{m.confirmed :$
55:      $(s, m) \in srvAck \wedge s \in Q\})$
56:   $inPtag \leftarrow$
     $\{\tau : \tau \in \bigcup_{(s,m) \in srvAck \wedge s \in Q} m.inprogress\}$
57:   **if** $\exists \tau, MS, \mathbb{Q}^{[\ell]} :$
58:    $\tau = \max_{\tau' \in inPtag}(\tau')$ s.t. $\tau > maxCT$, and
59:    $MS = \{s : s \in Q \wedge (m, s) \in srvAck$
        $\wedge \tau \in m.inprogress\}$, and
60:    $\mathbb{Q}^{[\ell]} \subseteq \mathbb{Q}$ s.t. $0 \leq \ell \leq \lfloor \frac{n}{2} - 2 \rfloor \wedge$
        $(\bigcap_{Q' \in (\mathbb{Q}^{[\ell]} \cup \{Q\})} Q') \subseteq MS$
61:   **then**
62:    $\langle \langle tag.ts, tag.wid, tag.wc \rangle, v \rangle \leftarrow$
        $\langle \langle \tau.ts, \tau.w, \tau.wc \rangle, \tau.val \rangle$
63:    **if** $\ell = \max(0, \frac{n}{2} - 2)$ **then**
64:     $status \leftarrow phase2$
65:     $srvAck \leftarrow \emptyset$
66:     $rCounter \leftarrow rCounter + 1$
67:    **else**
68:     $status \leftarrow done$
69:   **else**
70:    $MC \leftarrow \{s : s \in Q \wedge$
       $(m, s) \in srvAck \wedge m.confirmed = maxCT\}$
71:    $\langle tag.ts, tag.wid, tag.wc \rangle \leftarrow$
       $\langle maxCT.ts, maxCT.w, maxCT.wc \rangle$
72:    $v \leftarrow maxCT.val$
73:    **if** $\exists C : C \subseteq \mathbb{Q} \wedge |C| \leq n - 2 \wedge$
74:      $(\bigcap_{Q' \in C} Q') \cap Q \subseteq MC$
75:    **then**
76:     $status \leftarrow done$
77:    **else**
78:     $status \leftarrow phase2$
79:     $srvAck \leftarrow \emptyset$
80:     $rCounter \leftarrow rCounter + 1$

81: **Internal read-phase2-fix$_r$**
82: **Precondition:**
83:   $status = phase2$
84:   $\exists Q \in \mathbb{Q} : Q \subseteq \{s : (m, s) \in srvAck\}$
85: **Effect:**
86:   $status \leftarrow done$

87: **Output read-ack$(val)_r$**
88: **Precondition:**
89:   $status = done$
90:   $val = v$
91: **Effect:**
92:   $replyQ \leftarrow \emptyset$
93:   $srvAck \leftarrow \emptyset$
94:   $status \leftarrow idle$

95: **Input fail$_r$**
96: **Effect:**
97:   $status \leftarrow failed$

CHAPTER 6

The Dynamic Environment

We now consider a more dynamic distributed setting where the participants, including the set of replica servers, can change over time. In the previously considered static setting the set of servers is fixed at the outset, and while the servers may fail or leave during an execution, no new servers can be introduced to replace the lost ones. To cope with an increasing number of server failures, or to allow the replacement of old with upgraded machines, one needs a more dynamic system where new servers can be introduced. In the remaining chapters we present several approaches for providing consistent shared memory in such dynamic systems, viz., where nodes may not only crash or depart voluntarily, but where new nodes may join the service. In general, the set of object replicas can substantially evolve over time, ultimately migrating to a completely different set of replica hosts.

We observe that the approach taken by algorithm ABD cannot be used directly in such settings because it relies on the majority of original replica hosts to always be available. In order to use an ABD-like approach in dynamic settings, one must provide some means for managing the collections of replica hosts, and to ensure that readers and writers contact suitable such collections.

It is noteworthy that dealing with dynamic settings and managing collections of nodes does not directly address the provision of consistency in memory services. Instead, these issues are representative of the broader challenges present in the realm of dynamic distributed computing. It is illustrative that implementations of consistent shared memory services can sometimes be constructed using distributed building blocks, such as those designed for managing collections of participating nodes, for providing suitable communication primitives, and for reaching agreement (consensus) in dynamic distributed settings. A tutorial covering several of these topics is given by Aguilera et al. [2]. A brief survey of consistent storage for dynamic systems is given by Musial et al. [93].

We start here by briefly presenting the consensus problem because it provides a natural basis for implementing an atomic memory service by establishing an agreed-upon order of operations, and because consensus is used in other ways in atomic memory implementations.

Next we take a quick tour of group communication services (GCS) solutions that use strong communication primitives, such as totally ordered broadcast, to order operations.

Finally, the rest of this part, we focus on approaches that extend the ideas of the ABD algorithm to dynamic settings with explicit management of the evolving collections of replica hosts.

6.1 CONSENSUS

Reaching agreement in distributed settings is a fundamental problem of computer science. The agreement problem in distributed settings is called *consensus*. In this problem a collection of cooperating processor nodes must agree on a common value. The decision value at each process must be among the values proposed by the participants. All deciding processes must decide on the same value. The decision procedure must terminate under the failure model for which the procedure is developed. More formally, the solutions to the consensus problem must satisfy the three properties given below.

Definition 6.1 Consensus. The *consensus problem* is for a set of processes to agree on a value, with processes proposing their local values for consideration. Any solution must have the following properties.

> *Agreement:* no two processes decide on different values.

> *Validity:* the value decided was proposed by some process.

> *Termination:* all correct (non-faulty) processes reach a decision.

Consensus is a powerful tool in designing distributed services [80], however, consensus is a notoriously difficult problem in asynchronous systems where termination cannot be guaranteed in the presence of even a single process crash [38]; thus, consensus must be used with care. Note that this impossibility result does not state that consensus can never be reached: it states that under the model's assumptions, no algorithm can always reach consensus in bounded time. (One approach to solving consensus is based on introducing "failure detectors" that provide, possibly limited, information about the nodes in the system [22].)

Consensus algorithms can be used directly to implement an atomic data service by letting the participants use consensus to agree on a global total ordering of all operations [73]. The correctness (atomicity) in this approach is guaranteed regardless of the choice of a specific consensus implementation, but the understanding of the underlying platform characteristics can guide the choice of the implementation for the benefit of system performance (for a *tour de force* of implementations see [80]). Nevertheless, using consensus for each operation is a heavy-handed approach, especially given that perturbations may delay or even prevent termination. Thus, when using consensus, one must avoid invoking it in conjunction with individual memory operations, and make operations independent of the termination of consensus.

We note that achieving consensus is a more difficult problem than implementing atomic read/write objects in static settings, in particular, consensus cannot be solved for two or more processes by using atomic read/write registers [88]. We will revisit consensus in more detail in Chapters 7 and 8 when we present algorithms for dynamic systems.

6.2   GROUP COMMUNICATION SERVICES

Among the most important building blocks for distributed systems are *group communication services* (GCSs) [13]. GCSs enable processes located at different nodes of a network to operate collectively as a group. The processes do this by using a GCS multicast service to send messages to all members of the group. GCSs offer various guarantees about the order and reliability of message delivery.

The basis of a GCS is a *group membership service*. Each process, at each time, has a unique *view* of the group that includes a list of the processes that are members of the group. Views can change over time, and may become different at different processes. Another important concept introduced by the GCS approach is *virtual synchrony*, where an essential requirement is that processes that proceed together through two consecutive views deliver the same set of messages between these views. This allows the recipients to take coordinated action based on the message, the membership set, and the rules prescribed by the application [13].

GCSs provide one approach for implementing shared memory in dynamic networks. This can be done, for example, by implementing a global totally ordered multicast service on top of a view-synchronous GCS [37] (where there is a total order on the messages associated with each view, and each participant receives a prefix of this order). The ordered multicast is used to impose an order on the memory access operations, yielding atomic memory. The main disadvantage in such solutions is that in most GCS implementations, forming a new view takes a substantial amount of time, and client memory operations are delayed (or aborted) during the view-formation period. New view formation normally involves several rounds of communication, and in typical GCS implementations performance is degraded even if only one node crashes. In memory services it is desirable to make sure that read and write operations make progress during reconfiguration, and it is important to tolerate a modest number of failures without imposing a performance penalty.

Another approach is to integrate a GCS with algorithm ABD. For example, the dynamic primary configuration GCS of [27] implements atomic memory by using techniques of [5] within each configuration. Here a *configuration* combines a group view with a quorum system. Configurations can change either due to the dynamic nature of the system or because a different quorum system is desired, and like other solutions based on GCSs, reads and writes are delayed during reconfiguration. Last, any new configuration must satisfy certain intersection properties with respect to the previous configurations. This impacts the flexibility of reconfiguration and requires intermediate configuration changes in reaching the desired configuration.

A general methodology for dynamic service replication is presented in [15]. This reconfiguration model unifies the virtual synchrony approach with state machine replication, as used in consensus solutions, in particular, Paxos [73].

6.3 USING RECONFIGURATION FOR DIRECT IMPLEMENTATIONS.

As we just discussed, dynamic memory systems can be readily constructed with the help of consensus implementations and group communication services. However, using consensus for each memory access operation is a heavy-handed approach that typically carries a substantial communication overhead. Using GCS also has its disadvantages. In most GCS implementations, forming a new view takes a substantial amount of time, and client-level operations are delayed during the view-formation period. Also, in some GCS implementations, this performance degradation occurs even if only one server crash is detected.

Some of these observations motivated the development of new approach that directly focus on atomic memory implementations and that incorporate certain types of reconfiguration. To deal with the dynamically changing collection of servers we introduce the notion of a *configuration*. A configuration is comprised of the set of servers, and possibly some additional information used to provide the shared memory service. Configurations are changed by means of the process called *reconfiguration*. In the cases where a quorum system (e.g., majorities) needs to be defined over the set of servers, the configuration also includes the definition of the quorum system. In such cases, reconfiguration also transitions the service from using one quorum system to another quorum system.

The ability to reconfigure a distributed storage system on-the-fly, that is, concurrently with processing read and write operations, has several benefits. The first is that reconfiguring the system can enhanced its fault-tolerance. When a system experiences failures that come "too close" to invalidating the assumptions of the failure model for which the system was developed, the system can be reconfigured to introduce new server resources, to take out failed servers, and to take some long-running servers down for maintenance. Another benefit is elasticity: reconfiguration can help adapting the resources depending on the changing service demand to avoid over-provisioning or to help balancing the load. Yet another is software update: reconfiguration can be used to upgrading a storage server from one version to the next, or to roll back a server to a previous stable version. Of course these benefits depend on the system being available for use during reconfiguration, and this is a major challenge in designing such systems.

In the sequel, we present three approaches to implementing consistent shared storage for dynamic systems. Chapter 7 presents an approach that implements reconfiguration as an external service that relies on consensus. We also discuss a specialization of this approach that eliminates the need for consensus when there is a known finite set of configurations. Chapter 8 presents another design that integrates more tightly reconfiguration with the memory service, allowing for efficiency gains in target settings; this chapter builds on the definitions given in Chapter 7. Chapter 9 presents an optimistic approach to reconfiguration, allowing individual servers to be added and removed without coordination, but ensuring that ultimately memory access operations involve a collection of servers sufficient to guarantee atomic consistency.

CHAPTER 7

RAMBO: Reconfigurable Dynamic Memory

We present a reconfigurable atomic memory service, called RAMBO, that uses a loosely coupled approach to reconfiguration that relies on an external consensus service. RAMBO is a dynamic memory service supporting multi-reader/multi-writer objects. RAMBO stands for Reconfigurable Atomic Memory for Basic Objects. We first give a high level overview, then delve into the details.

This service uses *configurations*, each consisting of a set of replica hosts plus a quorum system defined over these hosts. The service supports *reconfiguration*, by which configurations can be replaced. Notably, any quorum configuration may be installed at any time, and quorums from distinct configurations are not required to have non-empty intersections. The algorithm tolerates crash failures and message losses. The algorithm ensures atomicity in all executions and without any additional assumptions about failures or delays.

During quiescent periods when there are no reconfigurations, the algorithm operates similarly to the static two-phase ABD algorithm [5] extended for multi-writer registers. Each of the two phases involves interaction with one complete quorum in the current configuration. New participants *join* the service by means of message handshakes with at least one existing participant (this involves no reconfiguration).

Since participants may crash, quorum configurations can be reconfigured at any time to enable long-term operation of the service in dynamic networks. Reconfigurations are performed concurrently with any read and write operations, and are transparent to the clients invoking operations. Multiple reconfigurations may be in progress concurrently. Reconfiguration involves two decoupled protocols: (1) introduction of a new configuration by the component called *Recon* and (2) upgrade to the new configuration and garbage collection of obsolete configurations. Thus, it is helpful to think of *Recon* as *recon*, that is *reconnaissance* (and not as reconfiguration) because its purpose is to explore any proposed new configurations and identify the unique next configuration. Then the garbage-collection procedure performs the upgrade to remove obsolete configurations, with the purpose of leaving only one most recent configuration, thus accomplishing reconfiguration.

In slightly more detail, the main data structure maintained by each participant is the *configuration map*, or *cmap*, that stores a sequence of configurations, where for node i, $cmap_i(k)$ is the configuration number k. This sequence evolves as new configurations are scouted out by *Recon* and as old configurations are garbage-collected. It is possible for participants to have differing views on what is in each *cmap*, and have different proposals for new configurations, however once *Recon* performs reconnaissance of the proposals it always emits a unique new configuration k to be stored in every $cmap_i(k)$. This is done as follows. Any node i that is a member of its latest known configuration $c = cmap_i(k-1)$ can propose a new configuration at any time. Different proposals are reconciled by executing consensus among the members of configuration c (here consensus can be implemented, e.g., using Paxos [73]). Although a consensus execution may be slow—in fact, in some situations, it may not even terminate—this does *not* delay read and write operations (provided at least one quorum is intact for the configurations used by the operations). Note that the members of the new configuration may or may not know the latest value of the object.

It is the duty of a decoupled *garbage collection* (or *upgrade*) protocol to remove old configurations and propagate the information about the object to the latest locally-known configuration. Here, a two-phase algorithm first tells a quorum of each older configuration about the new one and obtains the latest object information, then propagates this information to a quorum of the new configuration and removes the obsolete configurations.

It is possible for the participants to have multiple active (non-garbage-collected) configurations in their *cmap* if reconfigurations occur rapidly, or if configuration upgrade lags behind. If this is the case the two-phases of read and write operations behave as follows. The first phase gathers information from the quorums of active configurations, then the second phase propagates information to the quorums of active configurations. If new configurations are discovered within a phase, the phase continues until a *fixed point* condition is reached that involves a quorum from each active configuration.

7.1   MODELS AND DEFINITIONS

Here we adapt the model of Chapter 2 to the now dynamic setting. For simplicity, we let the set of server processes S, the set of read processes R and the set of write processes W be equal to I.

Similar to static storage, dynamic storage uses quorum systems. Any type of a quorum system is sufficient, but for clarity we use biquorum systems (cf. Definition 2.11), consisting of read quorums and write quorums due to the role they play in read and write operations. A configuration thus consists of the set of process identifiers, and a biquorum system defined over this set. The two sets of quorums are called *read-quorums* and *write-quorums*, respectively.

We denote by C the set of configuration identifiers. We use the trivial partial order on C, in which all elements are incomparable. For each object $x \in X$, we denote by $(c_0)_x \in C$ the *initial configuration id* for x. For each $c \in C$: *members(c)*, a finite subset of I, *read-quorums(c)* and *write-quorums(c)*, two sets of finite subsets of *members(c)*. We assume that *members($(c_0)_x$)* = $\{(i_0)_x\}$, that is, the initial configuration for x has one member, the creator of x. For every c, every $R \in$ *read-quorums(c)*, and every $W \in$ *write-quorums(c)*, their intersection is non-empty: $R \cap W \neq \emptyset$.

Figure 7.1: A configuration map $cm \in Truncated$.

For simplicity of notation we omit the subscript x when the considered object is clear from the context.

Definition 7.1   Configuration.   A *configuration* $c \in C$ consists of its members, *members*(c), and a biquorum system $\langle read\text{-}quorum(c), write\text{-}quorum(c) \rangle$ defined over its members.

We assume distinguished elements $\bot$ and $\pm$, which are not in C. We define types $C_\bot = C \cup \{\bot\}$. and $C_\pm = C \cup \{\bot, \pm\}$. We augment the ordering on $C_\pm$ by assuming that $\bot < c < \pm$ for every $c \in C$. We will use the $\pm$ value to denote a configuration that was garbage collected, and the $\bot$ to denote an undefined configuration.

We define the following functions on configurations.

- Function *update* is a binary function on $C_\pm$, defined by $update(c, c') = \max(c, c')$ if c and c' are comparable, else $update(c, c') = c$.

- Function *extend* is a binary function on $C_\pm$, defined by $extend(c, c') = c'$ if $c = \bot$ and $c' \in C$, and $extend(c, c') = c$ otherwise.

We define the set of *configuration maps*, *CMap*, as the set of mappings $\mathbb{N} \to C_\pm$. We extend the *update* and *extend* operators elementwise to binary operations on *CMap*.

We also define the following.

- *truncate*, a unary function on *CMap*, defined by $truncate(cm)(\ell) = \bot$ if there exists $k \leq \ell$ such that $cm(k) = \bot$, $truncate(cm)(\ell) = cm(\ell)$ otherwise. Truncation removes all the configuration ids that follow a $\bot$.

- *Truncated*, the subset of *CMap* such that $cm \in Truncated$ if and only if $truncate(cm) = cm$.

- *Usable*, the subset of *CMap* such that $cm \in Usable$ iff the pattern occurring in cm consists of a prefix of finitely many $\pm$s, followed by an element of C, followed by an infinite sequence of elements of $C_\bot$ in which all but finitely many elements are $\bot$.

The example in Figure 7.1 illustrates a configuration map cm in the set *Truncated*. The configuration map is depicted as an infinite array, where $cm(i)$ is the ith entry. Interpreting $\pm$ as a garbage-collected configuration, and $\bot$ as an undefined configuration, the figure shows that a prefix of garbage-collected configurations $\pm$ is followed by a contiguous segment of configurations $c_k, ..., c_\ell$ in C, followed by an infinite sequence of undefined configurations $\bot$.

7.2 RAMBO SERVICE SPECIFICATIONS

Here we specify the behavior of a read/write distributed shared memory. The specification of the RAMBO atomic memory service is in Section 7.2.1 (the algorithm that satisfies this specification is then presented in Section 7.3). A key subcomponent of RAMBO is a *Recon* service that deals with reconfiguration requests. This service is specified in Section 7.2.2.

7.2.1 RAMBO SERVICE SPECIFICATION

Here we give a specification for a reconfigurable atomic memory service. This specification consists of an external signature (i.e., an interface) plus a set of traces that embody the safety properties. No liveness properties are included in the specification; these are replaced with conditional latency bounds, which are discussed in Section 7.5.

The external signature of the service appears in Specification 20. It includes of four basic actions: join, read, write, and recon, each of which has an acknowledgment. It also produces a report output and accepts a fail input.

Specification 20 External Signature of RAMBO

```
1:  Input:                                                   8:  Output:
2:      join(rambo, J)_{x,i},  J a finite subset of I − {i},  9:      join-ack(rambo)_{x,i}, x ∈ X, i ∈ I
3:          x ∈ X, i ∈ I such that if i = (i_0)_x then J = ∅  10:     read-ack(v)_{x,i}, x ∈ X, i ∈ I
4:      read_{x,i}, x ∈ X, i ∈ I                              11:     write-ack_{x,i}, x ∈ X, i ∈ I
5:      write(v)_{x,i}, x ∈ X, i ∈ I                          12:     recon-ack()_{x,i}, x ∈ X, i ∈ I
6:      recon(c, c')_{x,i}, c, c' ∈ C, x ∈ X, i ∈ members(c)  13:     report(c)_{x,i}, c ∈ C, x ∈ X, i ∈ I
7:      fail_i, i ∈ I
```

Node i issues a request to join the system for a particular object x by performing a join(rambo, J)$_{x,i}$ input action. The set J represents the client's best guess at a set of processes that have already joined the system for x. We refer to this set J as the *initial world view* of i. If the join attempt is successful, the RAMBO service responds with a join-ack(rambo)$_{x,i}$ response.

Node i initiates a read or write operation by requesting a read or a write (respectively), which the RAMBO service acknowledges with a read-ack response or a write-ack response (respectively).

Node i initiates a reconfiguration by requesting a recon, which is acknowledged with a recon-ack response. Notice that when a recon is acknowledged, this does not imply that the configuration was installed; it simply means that the request has been processed. New configurations are reported by RAMBO via report outputs. Thus, a node can determine whether its reconfiguration request was successful by observing whether the proposed configuration is reported.

Finally, a crash at node i is modeled using a fail$_i$ input action. We do not explicitly model graceful process "leaves," but instead we model process departures as failures.

RAMBO **Safety properties.** We now define the safety guarantees, i.e., the properties that are to be guaranteed by every execution. Under the assumption that the client requests are well-formed, a reconfigurable atomic memory service guarantees that the responses are also well-formed, and that the read and write operations satisfy atomic consistency. In order to define these guarantees, we specify a set of traces that capture exactly the guaranteed behavior. We first specify what it means for requests to be well-formed. In particular, we require that a node i issues no further requests after it fails, that a node i issues a join request before initiating read and write operations, that node i does not begin a new operation until it has received acknowledgments from all previous operations, and that configurations are unique.

Definition 7.2 Reconfigurable Atomic Memory Request Well-Formedness. For every object $x \in X$, node $i \in I$, configurations $c, c' \in C$.

1. *Failures:* After a fail_i event, there are no further $\text{join}(\text{rambo}, *)_{x,i}$, $\text{read}_{x,i}$, $\text{write}(*)_{x,i}$, or $\text{recon}(*, *)_{x,i}$ requests.

2. *Joining:* The client at i issues at most one $\text{join}(\text{rambo}, *)_{x,i}$ request. Any $\text{read}_{x,i}$, $\text{write}(*)_{x,i}$, or $\text{recon}(*, *)_{x,i}$ event is preceded by a $\text{join-ack}(\text{rambo})_{x,i}$ event.

3. *Acknowledgments:* The client at i does not issue a new $\text{read}_{x,i}$ request or $\text{write}_{x,i}$ request until there has been a read-ack or write-ack for any previous read or write request. The client at i does not issue a new $\text{recon}_{x,i}$ request until there has been a recon-ack for any previous reconfiguration request.

4. *Configuration Uniqueness:* The client at i issues at most one $\text{recon}(*, c)_{x,*}$ request. This says that configuration identifiers are unique. It does not say that the membership and/or quorum sets are unique—just the identifiers. The same membership and quorum sets may be associated with different configuration identifiers.

5. *Configuration Validity:* If a $\text{recon}(c, c')_{x,i}$ request occurs, then it is preceded by: (i) a $\text{report}(c)_{x,i}$ event, and (ii) a $\text{join-ack}(\text{rambo})_{x,j}$ event for every $j \in \text{members}(c')$. This says that the client at i can request reconfiguration from c to c' only if i has previously received a report confirming that configuration c has been installed, and only if all the members of c' have already joined. Notice that i may have to communicate with the members of c' to ascertain that they are ready to participate in a new configuration.

When the requests are well-formed, we require that the responses also be well-formed.

Definition 7.3 Reconfigurable Atomic Memory Response Well-Formedness. For every object $x \in X$, and node $i \in I$.

1. *Failures:* After a fail_i event, there are no further $\text{join-ack}(\text{rambo})_{x,i}$, $\text{read-ack}(*)_{x,i}$, $\text{write-ack}_{x,i}$, $\text{recon-ack}()_{x,i}$, or $\text{report}(*)_{x,i}$ outputs.

2. *Acknowledgments:* Any join-ack(rambo)$_{x,i}$, read-ack($*$)$_{x,i}$, write-ack$_{x,i}$, or recon-ack()$_{x,i}$ outputs has a preceding join(rambo, $*$)$_{x,i}$, read$_{x,i}$, write($*$)$_{x,i}$, or recon($*$, $*$)$_{x,i}$ request (respectively) with no intervening request or response for x and i.

We also require that the read and write operations satisfy *atomicity* (this mirrors Definition 2.16 of atomicity given earlier).

Definition 7.4   Atomicity.   For every object $x \in X$: If all read and write operations complete in an execution, then the read and write operations for object x can be partially ordered by an ordering $\prec$, so that the following conditions are satisfied.

1. No operation has infinitely many other operations ordered before it.

2. The partial order is consistent with the external order of requests and responses, that is, there do not exist read or write operations π_1 and π_2 such that π_1 completes before π_2 starts, yet $\pi_2 \prec \pi_1$.

3. All write operations are totally ordered and every read operation is ordered with respect to all the writes.

4. Every read operation ordered after any writes returns the value of the last write preceding it in the partial order; any read operation ordered before all writes returns $(v_0)_x$.

We now specify precisely what it means for an algorithm to implement a reconfigurable atomic memory.

Definition 7.5   Reconfigurable Atomic Memory.   We say that an algorithm A implements a reconfigurable atomic memory if it has the external signature found in Specification 20 and if every trace β of A satisfies the following:

> If requests in β are well-formed (Definition 7.2), then responses are well-formed (Definition 7.3) and operations in β are atomic (Definition 7.4).

In the rest of this chapter we will be dealing with a particular x, and for simplicity we suppress explicit mention of x. Thus, we write V, v_0, c_0, and i_0 from now on as shorthand for V_x, $(v_0)_x$, $(c_0)_x$, and $(i_0)_x$, respectively. Similarly, we suppress x in signatures and action specifications.

7.2.2   RECON SERVICE SPECIFICATION

In this section, we present the specification for a generic *Recon* service. Recall that *Recon* is not a complete reconfiguration service, but it is the initial "reconnaissance" part. The main goal of the service is to respond to reconfiguration requests and produce a (totally ordered) sequence of configurations. Reconfiguration completes with the garbage collection of obsolete configurations that will be described later. The *Recon* service will be used as part of the RAMBO protocol (and we discuss in Section 7.3.4 how to implement it). We proceed by describing its external signature, along with a set of traces that define its safety guarantees. The *Recon* external signature is given in Specification 21, and its service specification can be found in Definition 7.9.

Specification 21 External Signature of Recon

1: **Input:**
2:     join(recon)$_i$, $i \in I$,
3:     recon$(c, c')_i$, $c, c' \in C$, $i \in members(c)$
4:     fail$_i$, $i \in I$
5: **Output:**

6:     join-ack(recon)$_i$, $i \in I$
7:     recon-ack$_i$, $i \in I$
8:     report$(c)_i$, $c \in C$, $i \in I$
9:     new-config$(c, k)_i$, $c \in C$, $k \in \mathbb{N}^+$, $i \in I$

Let node $i \in I$ be a node in the system. Node i requests to join the reconfiguration service by performing a join(recon)$_i$ request. The service acknowledges this with a corresponding join-ack$_i$ response. The client initiates a reconfiguration using a recon$_i$ request, which is acknowledged with a recon-ack$_i$ response.

When the kth configuration becomes available, the reconfiguration service performs out action new-config$(c, k)_i$, announcing configuration c at node i.

The service also announces new configurations to the client, producing a report$(c)_i$ output to provide an update when a new configuration is installed. Notice that the report output differs from new-config in that it is externally observable by clients outside of the RAMBO; by contrast, new-config is an output from the *Recon* service, but is hidden from clients. In particular, the new-config output includes a sequence number k that would be meaningless to an external client.

Lastly, crashes are modeled using fail input actions.

Recon safety properties. Now we define the set of traces describing *Recon*'s safety properties. Again, these are defined in terms of environment well-formedness requirements and service guarantees. The well-formedness requirements are as follows.

Definition 7.6   Recon Request Well-Formedness. For every node $i \in I$, configuration $c, c' \in C$.

1. *Failures:* After a fail$_i$ event, there are no further join(recon)$_i$ or recon$(*, *)_i$ requests.

2. *Joining:* At most one join(*recon*)$_i$ request occurs. Any recon$(*, *)_i$ request is preceded by a join-ack(recon)$_i$ response.

3. *Acknowledgments:* Any recon$(*, *)_i$ request is preceded by an recon-ack response for any preceding recon$(*, *)_i$ event.

4. *Configuration Uniqueness:* For every c, at most one recon$(*, c)_*$ event occurs.

5. *Configuration Validity:* For every c, c', and i, if a recon$(c, c')_i$ request occurs, then it is preceded by: (i) a report$(c)_i$ output and (ii) a join-ack(recon)$_j$ for every $j \in members(c')$.

We next describe the well-formedness guarantees of the reconfiguration service.

Definition 7.7　Recon Response Well-Formedness.　For every node $i \in I$:

1. *Failures:* After a fail$_i$ event, there are no further join-ack($recon$)$_i$, recon-ack$(*)_i$, report$(*)_i$, or new-config$(*, *)_i$ responses.

2. *Acknowledgments:* Any join-ack($recon$)$_i$ or recon-ack$(c)_i$ response has a preceding join($recon$)$_i$ or recon$_i$ request (respectively) with no intervening request or response action for i.

The *Recon* service also guarantees that configurations are produced consistently. That is, for every node i, the service outputs an ordered set of configurations; the configurations must be among those proposed, and every node is notified about an identical sequence of configurations.

Definition 7.8　Configuration Consistency.　For every node $i \in I$, configurations $c, c' \in C$, and index k.

1. *Agreement:* If new-config$(c, k)_i$ and new-config$(c', k)_j$ both occur, then $c = c'$. Thus, no disagreement arises about the kth configuration identifier, for any k.

2. *Validity:* If new-config$(c, k)_i$ occurs, then it is preceded by a recon$(*, c)_{i'}$ request for some i'. Thus, any configuration identifier that is announced was previously requested.

3. *No duplication:* If new-config$(c, k)_i$ and new-config$(c, k')_{i'}$ both occur, then $k = k'$. Thus, the same configuration identifier cannot be assigned to two different positions in the sequence of configuration identifiers.

We can now specify precisely what it means to implement a reconfiguration service.

Definition 7.9　Recon Service.　We say that an algorithm A implements a reconfiguration service if it has the external signature described in Figure 7.2 and if every trace β of A satisfies the following:

> If β satisfies *Recon* Request Well-Formedness (Definition 7.6), then it satisfies *Recon* Response Well-Formedness (Definition 7.7) and Configuration Consistency (Definition 7.8).

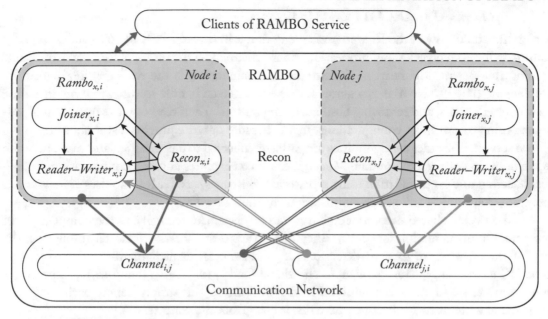

Figure 7.2: RAMBO architecture depicting the main components at nodes i and j: *Joiner*, *Reader-Writer*, *Recon*, and their interactions, and the *Channel* automata showing interactions over a communication network, where solid arrows are the send actions and double-line arrows are the receive actions.

We discuss the implementation of *Recon* in Section 7.3.4.

Remark 7.10 *Recon* **service implementation:**   At this point, the reader should note that Configuration Consistency given in Definition 7.8 has two safety provisions, *agreement* and *validity*, that closely correspond to the safety provisions of Consensus, given in Definition 6.1. Indeed, the implementation of *Recon* takes advantage of an arbitrary external consensus service, and we discuss this in more detail in Section 7.3.4.   **End remark**

7.3   IMPLEMENTATION OF RAMBO

We now present the algorithms comprising the RAMBO implementation. Section 7.3.1 gives a high level overview of the implementation. Section 7.3.2 provides the details on the implementation of *Joiner* and Section 7.3.3 of *Reader-Writer* component. We discuss the *Recon* implementation in Section 7.3.4.

7.3.1   OVERALL ARCHITECTURE

An architectural view of the RAMBO implementation is in Figure 7.2. RAMBO includes $Joiner_{x,i}$ automata for each object x and process identifier i that handle the protocol for new participants joining the system. The heart of the RAMBO implementation is the reader-writer algorithm, implemented by $Reader\text{-}Writer_{x,i}$ automata. These automata handle reading, writing, installing new configurations, and removing obsolete configurations. Each read or write operation is processed using one or more configurations, that the reader or write process learns about from the *Recon* service. The older configurations are garbage-collected to ensures that later read and write operations do not need to use them. $Recon_{x,i}$ automata explores any new configuration proposals, selecting one for installation using an external consensus service. RAMBO uses asynchronous point-to-point unidirectional communication channels $Channel_{i,j}$.

The overall shared memory emulation can be described, formally, as the composition of a separate implementation for each x. Therefore, to avoid the notational clutter throughout the rest of the chapter, we fix a particular $x \in X$, and suppress explicit mention of x. Thus, we write V, v_0, c_0, and i_0 from now on as shorthand for V_x, $(v_0)_x$, $(c_0)_x$, and $(i_0)_x$, respectively. Furthermore, we suppress the subscript x in specifications and simply denote each service by their name without that subscript where this is clear from the context.

7.3.2   IMPLEMENTATION OF JOINER

The signature, state, and transitions of $Joiner_i$ appear in Specification 22. The automaton is simple, when a request is made to join, it informs *Reader-Writer* and *Recon* at node i, and when this is acknowledged it replies to the requester. In more detail, when $Joiner_i$ receives a join(rambo, J) request from its environment, it sends join messages to the processes in J with the hope that they are already participating, and so can help in the attempt to join. Also, it submits join requests to the local *Reader-Writer* and *Recon* components and waits for associated acknowledgments. The join messages that are sent by *Joiner* automata are handled by *Reader-Writer* automata at other locations as we discuss in the next section. Once input actions join-ack take place for both *Reader-Writer* and *Recon* and recorded in *child-status*, process i outputs a join-ack(rambo).

7.3.3   IMPLEMENTATION OF READER-WRITER

The main part of the RAMBO algorithm is the reader-writer algorithm, which handles read and write requests. Each read or write operation takes place in the context of one or more configurations. The reader-writer protocol also participates in the join protocol and handles the garbage-collection of older configurations, which ensures that later read and write operations need not use them.

Signature and State
The signature and state of $Reader\text{-}Writer_i$ appear in Specification 23.

Specification 22 *Joiner$_i$* – Joiner of RAMBO

1: **Signature:**
2: **Input:**
3:     *join*(rambo, J)$_i$, J a finite subset of $I - \{i\}$
4:     *join-ack*(r)$_i$, $r \in \{$recon, rw$\}$
5:     *fail$_i$*, $i \in I$

6: **Output:**
7:     *send*(join)$_{i,j}$, $j \in I - \{i\}$
8:     *join*(r)$_i$, $r \in \{$recon, rw$\}$
9:     *join-ack*(rambo)$_i$

10: **State:**
11:     *status* $\in \{$idle, joining, active, failed$\}$, initially idle
12:     *child-status*, a mapping from $\{$recon, rw$\}$ to $\{$idle, joining, active$\}$, initially everywhere idle
13:     *hints* $\subseteq I$, initially $\emptyset$

14: **Transitions:**

15: **Input join**(rambo, J)$_i$
16:   **Effect:**
17:     if ¬*failed* **then**
18:       if *status* = idle **then**
19:         *status* ← joining
20:         *hints* ← J

21: **Input join-ack**(r)$_i$
22:   **Effect:**
23:     if ¬*failed* **then**
24:       if *status* = joining **then**
25:         *child-status*(r) ← active

26: **Input fail$_i$**
27:   **Effect:**
28:     *failed* ← true
29: **Output join-ack**(rambo)$_i$

30:   **Precondition:**
31:     ¬*failed* ∧ *status* = joining
32:     $\forall r \in \{$recon, rw$\}$: *child-status*(r) = active
33:   **Effect:**
34:     *status* ← active

35: **Output join**(r)$_i$
36:   **Precondition:**
37:     ¬*failed* ∧ *status* = joining
38:     *child-status*(r) = idle
39:   **Effect:**
40:     *child-status*(r) ← joining

41: **Output send**(join)$_{i,j}$
42:   **Precondition:**
43:     ¬*failed* ∧ *status* = joining
44:     $j \in$ *hints*
45:   **Effect:**
46:     None

The *Reader-Writer* signature contains an interface to process read and write requests: read, read-ack, write, and write-ack. It also includes an interface for communicating with the *Joiner* automaton, from which it receives a join(rw) request and returns a join-ack(rw) response. And it includes an interface for communicating with the *Recon* service, from which it receives new-config reports whenever a new configuration is selected. Finally, it includes send and recv actions for communicating with other nodes. Notice that one of the recv actions is dedicated to receiving join-related messages. The internal actions of *Reader-Writer* deal with garbage collection of obsolete configurations.

We now describe the state maintained by *Reader-Writer*. The *status* variable keeps track of the progress as the node joins the protocol. When *status* = idle, *Reader-Writer$_i$* does not respond to any input except a join input, and it does not perform any local actions. When *status* = joining, *Reader-Writer$_i$* is receptive to inputs but does not perform any local actions just yet. When *status* = active, the automaton participates fully in the protocol.

The *world* variable is the set of all processes that are known to have attempted to join the system. The current value of x at node i is stored in variable *value*, and variable *tag* stores the tag

Specification 23 Signature and State of Reader-Writer

1: **Input:**
2:    $read_i$, $i \in I$
3:    $write(v)_i$, $i \in I$
4:    $new\text{-}config(c, c')_i$, $c, c' \in C$,
         $i \in members(c)$
5:    $recv(join)_i$, $i \in I$
6:    $recv(m)_i$, $i \in I$

7:    $join(rw)_i$
8:    $fail_i$, $i \in I$
9: **Output:**
10:    $join\text{-}ack(rw)_i$, $i \in I$
11:    $read\text{-}ack(v)_i$, $i \in I$
12:    $write\text{-}ack_i$, $i \in I$
13:    $send(m)_{i,j}$, $m \in M$, $j \in I$

14: **Internal:**
15:    $query\text{-}fix(rw)_i$,
16:    $prop\text{-}fix(v)_i$,
17:    $gc(k)_i$, $k \in \mathbb{N}$
18:    $gc\text{-}query\text{-}fix(k)_i$, $k \in \mathbb{N}$
19:    $gc\text{-}prop\text{-}fix(k)_i$, $k \in \mathbb{N}$
20:    $gc\text{-}ack(k)_i$, $k \in \mathbb{N}$

21: **State:**
22:    $status \in \{idle, joining, active\}$, initially idle
23:    $world$, a finite subset of I, initially $\emptyset$
24:    $value \in V$, initially v_0
25:    $tag \in T$, initially $\langle 0, i_0 \rangle$
26:    $cmap \in CMap$, initially
27:        $cmap(0) = c_0$,
28:        $cmap(k) = \perp$ for $k \geq 1$,
29:    $pnum1 \in \mathbb{N}$, initially 0
30:    $pnum2 \in I \to \mathbb{N}$, initially everywhere 0
31:    $failed$, a Boolean, initially false
32:    op, a record with fields:
33:        $type \in \{read, write\}$, initially $\perp$

34:        $phase \in \{idle, query, prop, done\}$ initially idle
35:        $pnum \in \mathbb{N}$, initially 0
36:        $cmap \in CMap$ initially c_0 at index 0 and $\perp$
37:        elsewhere
38:        acc, a finite subset of I, initially $\emptyset$
39:        $value \in V$, initially 0

40:    gc, a record with fields:
41:        $phase \in \{idle, query, prop\}$, initially idle
42:        $pnum \in \mathbb{N}$, initially 0
43:        acc, a finite subset of I, initially $\emptyset$
44:        $index \in \mathbb{N}$, initially 0

associated with this value. The information about the configurations is stored in the configuration map *cmap* and updated once *Reader-Writer$_i$* learns it either directly, from the *Recon* service, or indirectly, from other *Reader-Writer* processes. *Reader-Writer$_i$* has not yet learned what the kth configuration identifier is, when we have $cmap(k) = \perp$ indicating that the configuration at index k is unknown. *Reader-Writer$_i$* has learned that the kth configuration identifier is c and has not yet been garbage collected, when we have $cmap(k) = c \in C$. *Reader-Writer$_i$* has garbage-collected the kth configuration identifier when $cmap(k) = \pm$. The configuration map *cmap* always starts with a potentially empty finite prefix of $\pm$, followed by an element of C, followed by elements of $C_\perp$ with finitely many elements of C, meaning that *cmap* is *Usable*. When *Reader/Writer$_i$* processes a read or write operation, it has to use all the configurations whose identifiers appear in *cmap*. By garbage collecting eagerly the configurations whose identifiers appear in *cmap*, one can thus reduce the complexity of these operations, as we will see in Chapter 8.

The phase numbers *pnum1* and *pnum2* are used to implement a handshake that identifies recent messages as part of query or propagate phases. *Reader-Writer$_i$* uses *pnum1* to count the total number of operation phases it has initiated, including phases occurring in read or write and garbage collection operations. For every j, including $j = i$, *Reader-Writer$_i$* uses *pnum2(j)* to record the largest number of a phase that i has learned that j has started, via a direct message from j. Finally, two records, *op* and *gc*, are used to maintain information about a locally initiated read, write, or garbage-collection operation in progress.

Specification 24 *ReaderWriter$_i$* – Join-Related and Failure Transitions

---

1: **Input** join(rw)$_i$
2:    **Effect:**
3:      **if** ¬*failed* ∧ *status* = idle **then**
4:        **if** $i = i_0$ **then** *status* ← active
5:        **else** *status* ← joining
6:      *world* ← *world* ∪ {i}

7: **Input** fail$_i$
8:    **Effect:**
9:      *failed* ← true

10: **Output** join-ack(rw)$_i$
11:    **Precondition:**
12:      ¬*failed* ∧ *status* = active
13:    **Effect:**
14:      None

15: **Input** recv(join)$_{j,i}$
16:    **Effect:**
17:      **if** ¬*failed* ∧ *status* = idle **then**
18:        *world* ← *world* ∪ {j}

Joining Transitions

When a join(rw)$_i$ input occurs and *status* = idle and if i is the object's creator i_0, then *status* becomes active, which means that *Reader-Writer$_i$* is ready to participate in the protocol. Otherwise, *status* becomes joining, which means that *Reader-Writer$_i$* is receptive to inputs but not ready to perform any local actions. In either case, *Reader-Writer$_i$* records itself as a member of its own *world*. From this point on, *Reader-Writer$_i$* also adds to its *world* any process from which it receives a join message.

If *status* = joining, then *status* becomes active when *Reader-Writer$_i$* receives a message from another process (the code for this is at line 16 of the recv transition in Specification 25). At this point, process i has acquired enough information to begin participating fully, and action join-ack(rw) can take place.

The fail action results in *status* = failed, and the process carries out no further activity. (A process may fail in this way at any time.)

Information Propagation Transitions

Information is propagated between *Reader-Writer* processes in the background, via point-to-point channels that are accessed using send and recv actions. The algorithm uses only one kind of message, which contains a tuple including the sender's *world*, its latest known *value* and *tag*, its *cmap*, and two phase numbers—the current phase number of the sender, *pnum1*, and the latest known phase number of the receiver, from the *pnum2* array. Once the sender is active these background messages may be sent at any time to processes in the sender's *world* set, i.e., to processes that are locally known to have tried to join the system.

When *Reader-Writer$_i$* receives a message in a recv action, it sets its *status* to active, if it has not already done so (line 16). It adds incoming information about the world, in W, to its local *world* set (line 17). It compares the incoming tag t to its own *tag* (line 18). Like in the multi-writer ABD described in Section 5.1, if t is strictly greater, it represents a more recent version of the object; in this case, *Reader-Writer$_i$* sets its *tag* to t and its *value* to the incoming value v (line 19). *Reader-Writer$_i$* also updates its *cmap* with the information in the incoming configuration map, cm, using the *update* operator defined in Section 7.1. More precisely, for each k, if $cmap(k) = \perp$ and $cm(k)$ is a configuration identifier $c \in C$, then process i sets its $cmap(k)$ to c. Also, if $cmap(k) \in C_\perp$, and $cm(k) = \pm$, indicating that the sender knows that configuration k has already been garbage-collected, then *Reader-Writer$_i$* sets its $cmap(k)$ to $\pm$. The automaton also updates its $pnum2(j)$ component (line 21) for the sender j to reflect new information about the phase number of the sender, which appears in the *pns* component of the message.

If *Reader-Writer$_i$* is currently conducting a phase of a read, write, or garbage-collection operation, it verifies that the incoming message is "recent," in the sense that the sender j sent it after j received a message from i that was sent after i began the current phase. *Reader-Writer$_i$* uses the phase numbers to perform this check (line 23): if the incoming phase number *pnr* is at least as large as the current operation phase number (*op.pnum* or *gc.pnum*), then process i knows that the message is recent. If the message is recent, then it is used to update the records for current read, write or garbage-collection operations. We describe the operation processing in more detail in the next section.

Remark 7.11 Message size and incremental communication: The astute reader may note that the information exchange messages may grow in size because of the variables *world* and *cmap*. The amount of information in these variables does grow monotonically, but this is so mainly in the name of specification simplicity. In particular, Georgiou et al. [41] and Gramoli et al. [54] show how to reduce message size, sending gossip "incrementally", and to reduce gossip frequency. **End remark**

Read and Write Operation Transitions

The read or write operation of RAMBO are performed in two phases: a query phase and a propagation phase. In each phase, *Reader-Writer$_i$* updates its *value*, *tag*, and *cmap* information from "enough" processes. This information is obtained as the result of message exchange in the background, as we described earlier. While the purpose of each phase is similar to the case of the multi-writer register in static distributed storage (Section 5.1), the protocol is more involved. The transitions of the read and write operations are given in Specification 25.

When *Reader-Writer$_i$* starts either a query phase or a propagation phase of a read or write operation, it sets *op.cmap* to a *CMap* whose configurations are intended to be used to conduct the phase. More specifically, *Reader-Writer$_i$* chooses the *CMap truncate(cmap)*, which includes all the configuration identifiers in the local *cmap* up to the first $\perp$ as defined in Section 7.1. When a new *CMap*, *cm*, is received during the phase, *op.cmap* gets extended by adding all newly discovered configuration identifiers, up to the first $\perp$ in *cm*. Doing so may create a "gap" as shown in Figure 7.3, that is, *cm* $\notin$ *Truncated*.

If adding these new configuration identifiers does not create a gap, that is, if *cm* $\in$ *Truncated* (line 25), then the phase continues using the extended *op.cmap*. Otherwise (line 27),

Specification 25 *ReaderWriter$_i$* – Read and Write Transitions

1:   **Output send**$(W, v, t, cm, pns, pnr)_{i,j}$
2:       **Precondition:**
3:           $\neg failed \wedge status \neq$ idle
4:           $j \in world$
5:           $W = world$
6:           $v = value$
7:           $t = tag$
8:           $cm = cmap$
9:           $pns = pnum1$
10:          $pnr = pnum2(j)$
11:      **Effect:**
12:          None

13: **Input recv**$(W, v, t, cm, pns, pnr)_{j,i}$
14:      **Effect:**
15:          **if** $\neg failed \wedge status \neq$ idle **then**
16:              $status \leftarrow$ active
                                        // *becomes active upon reception*
17:              $world \leftarrow world \cup W$
18:              **if** $t > tag$ **then**
19:                  $\langle value, tag \rangle \leftarrow \langle v, t \rangle$
20:              $cmap \leftarrow$ update$(cmap, cm)$
21:              $pnum2(j) \leftarrow$ max$(pnum2(j), pns)$
22:              **if** $op.phase \in \{$query, prop$\} \wedge$
23:                  $pnr \geq op.pnum$ **then**
24:                  $op.cmap \leftarrow$ extend$(op.cmap,$ truncate$(cm))$
25:                  **if** $op.cmap \in Truncated$ **then**
26:                      $op.acc \leftarrow op.acc \cup \{j\}$
27:                  **else**
28:                      $op.acc \leftarrow \emptyset$
29:                      $op.cmap \leftarrow$ truncate(cm)
30:              **if** $(gc.phase \in \{$query, prop$\} \wedge$
31:                  $pnr \geq gc.pnum)$ **then**
32:                  $gc.acc \leftarrow gc.acc \cup \{j\}$

33: **Input read**$_i$
34:      **Effect:**
35:          **if** $\neg failed \wedge status \neq$ idle **then**
36:              $pnum1 \leftarrow pnum1 + 1$
37:              $op.pnum \leftarrow pnum1$
38:              $op.type \leftarrow$ read
39:              $op.phase \leftarrow$ query
40:              $op.cmap \leftarrow$ truncate$(cmap)$
41:              $op.acc \leftarrow \emptyset$

42: **Input write**$(v)_i$
43:      **Effect:**
44:          **if** $\neg failed \wedge status \neq$ idle **then**
45:              $pnum1 \leftarrow pnum1 + 1$
46:              $op.pnum \leftarrow pnum1$
47:              $op.type \leftarrow$ write
48:              $op.phase \leftarrow$ query
49:              $op.cmap \leftarrow$ truncate$(cmap)$
50:              $op.acc \leftarrow \emptyset$

51:              $op.value \leftarrow v$
52: **Internal query-fix**$_i$
53:      **Precondition:**
54:          $\neg failed \wedge status =$ active
55:          $op.type \in \{$read, write$\}$
56:          $op.phase =$ query
57:          $\forall k \in \mathbb{N}, c \in C : op.cmap(k) = c \implies$
58:              $(\exists R \in$ read-quorums$(c) : R \subseteq op.acc$
59:      **Effect:**
60:          **if** $op.type =$ read **then**
61:              $op.value \leftarrow value$
62:              $op.tag \leftarrow tag$
63:          **else**
64:              $value \leftarrow op.value$
65:              $tag \leftarrow \langle tag.counter + 1, i \rangle$
66:              $op.tag \leftarrow tag$
67:          $pnum1 \leftarrow pnum1 + 1$
68:          $op.pnum \leftarrow pnum1$
69:          $op.phase \leftarrow$ prop
70:          $op.cmap \leftarrow cmap$
71:          $op.acc \leftarrow \emptyset$

72: **Internal prop-fix**$_i$
73:      **Precondition:**
74:          $\neg failed \wedge status =$ active
75:          $op.type \in \{$read, write$\}$
76:          $op.phase =$ prop
77:          $\forall k \in \mathbb{N}, c \in C : op.cmap(k) = c \implies$
78:              $(\exists W \in$ write-quorums$(c) : W \subseteq op.acc$
79:      **Effect:**
80:          $op.phase \leftarrow$ done

81: **Output read-ack**$_i$
82:      **Precondition:**
83:          $\neg failed \wedge status =$ active
84:          $op.type =$ read
85:          $op.phase =$ done
86:          $v = op.value$
87:      **Effect:**
88:          $op.phase \leftarrow$ idle

89: **Output write-ack**$_i$
90:      **Precondition:**
91:          $\neg failed \wedge status =$ active
92:          $op.type \leftarrow$ write
93:          $op.phase \leftarrow$ done
94:      **Effect:**
95:          $op.phase \leftarrow$ idle

96: **Input new-config**$(k)_i$
97:      **Effect:**
98:          **if** $\neg failed \wedge status \neq$ idle **then**
99:              $cmap(k) \leftarrow$ update$(cmap(k), c)$

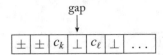

Figure 7.3: A configuration map *cm* ∈ *Usable* whose gap indicates that *cm* is out-of-date.

it restarts the phase by emptying the *op.acc* field (line 28) and using the best currently known *CMap* information, which is obtained by computing *truncate(cmap)* for the latest local *cmap* (line 29).

In between restarts, while process i is engaged in a single attempt to complete a phase, it never removes a configuration identifier from *op.cmap*. In fact, the set of configuration identifiers being used for the phase is only increased. In particular, if process i learns during a phase that a configuration identifier in *op.cmap(k)* has been garbage-collected, it does not remove it from *op.cmap*, but continues to include it in conducting the phase.

As mentioned before, the query phase of a read or write operation terminates when a *query fixed point* is reached in action query-fix. This happens when *Reader-Writer$_i$* determines that it has received recent responses from some read-quorum of each configuration in its current *op.cmap*. Let t denote the *tag* of process i at the query fixed point. Then we know that t is at least as large as the *tag* value that each process in each of these read-quorums had at the start of the query phase.

If the operation is a read operation, then process i determines at this point that its current value is the value to be returned to its client. However, before returning this value, process i starts the propagation phase of the read operation, whose purpose is to make sure that "enough" *Reader-Writer* processes have acquired tags that are larger or equal to t and the associated values. Again, the information is propagated in the background, and *op.cmap* is managed as described above. The propagation phase ends once a *propagation fixed point* is reached in action prop-fix, when *Reader-Writer$_i$* has received recent responses from some write-quorum of each configuration in the current *op.cmap*. When this occurs, we know that the *tag* of each process in each of these write-quorums is larger or equal to t.

A write operation starting with a write$(v)_i$ event is similar to a read operation. The query phase is conducted exactly as for a read, but processing after the query fixed point is reached in the effects of query-fix is different. Let t, the *tag* of process i at the query fixed point, be of the form $\langle n, j \rangle$. Then *Reader-Writer$_i$* defines the tag for its write operation to be the pair $\langle n + 1, i \rangle$. *Reader-Writer$_i$* sets its local *tag* to $\langle n + 1, i \rangle$ and its *value* to v, the value it is to write. Then it performs its propagation phase. The purpose of the propagation phase is to ensure that "enough" processes acquire tags that are at least as large as the new tag $\langle n + 1, i \rangle$. The propagation phase is conducted exactly as for a read operation: information is propagated in the background, and *op.cmap* is managed as described above. The propagation phase is over when the same propagation fixed point condition is satisfied in action prop-fix as for the read operation.

Remark 7.12 On the gossip communication paradigm and optimization: As we mentioned earlier, the communication strategy for reads and writes is different from what is done in other similar algorithms where messages are explicitly sent to appropriate subsets of processors. In RAMBO, communication occurs in the background, and process i just checks a fixed point condition, which ensures that enough processes have received recent messages, implying in turn that they must have tags at least as large as the one that process i is trying to propagate. This can be used for subsequent optimization without impacting the correctness of the algorithms because RAMBO safety does not depend on when and how messages are sent around.   **End remark**

New Configurations and Garbage Collection

When *Reader-Writer$_i$* learns about a new configuration identifier via a new-config input action, it simply records it in its *cmap*. From time to time, configuration identifiers get garbage-collected at i, in numerical order. The configuration identifiers used in performing query and propagation phases of reads and writes are those in *truncate(cmap)*, that is, all configurations that have not been garbage-collected and that appear before the first $\perp$.

There are two situations in which *Reader-Writer$_i$* may garbage-collect a configuration identifier, say, the one in *cmap(k)*. The *Reader-Writer$_i$* can garbage-collect *cmap(k)* if it learns that another process has already garbage-collected it. This happens when a recv$_{*,i}$ event occurs in which $cm(k) = \pm$. The second, more interesting situation, is where *Reader-Writer$_i$* acquires enough information to garbage-collect configuration k on its own. The relevant transitions are shown in Specification 26. *Reader-Writer$_i$* acquires this information by carrying out a garbage-collection operation, which is a two-phase operation with a structure similar to the read and write operations. *Reader-Writer$_i$* may initiate a garbage-collection of configuration k when its $cmap(k)$ and $cmap(k + 1)$ are both in C, and when any configurations with indices smaller than $k - 1$ have already been garbage-collected. Garbage-collection operations may proceed concurrently with read or write operations at the same process.

In the query phase of a garbage-collection operation, *Reader-Writer$_i$* communicates with both a read-quorum and a write-quorum of configuration k. The query phase accomplishes two tasks.

1. The *Reader-Writer$_i$* ensures that certain information is conveyed to the processes in a read-quorum and a write-quorum of k. In particular, all these processes learn about both configurations k and $k + 1$, and also learn that all configurations smaller than k have been garbage-collected. We refer loosely to the fact that they know about configuration $k + 1$ as the "forwarding pointer" condition—if such a process j, is contacted later by someone who is trying to access a quorum of configuration k, j is able to tell that process about the existence of configuration $k + 1$.

2. In the query phase, *Reader-Writer$_i$* collects *tag* and *value* information from the read-quorum and write-quorum that it accesses. This ensures that, by the end of the query

---

Specification 26 *ReaderWriter$_i$* – Garbage-Collection Transitions

1: Internal gc$(k)_i$
2:    **Precondition:**
3:      ¬*failed* ∧ *status* = active
4:      *gc.phase* = idle
5:      *cmap(k)* ∈ C
6:      *cmap(k + 1)* ∈ C
7:      $k = 0 ∨ cmap(k - 1) = ±$
8:    **Effect:**
9:      *pnum1* ← *pnum1* + 1
10:     *gc.pnum* ← *pnum1*
11:     *gc.phase* ← query
12:     *gc.acc* ← ∅
13:     *gc.index* ← k

14: Internal gc-ack$(k)_i$
15:   **Precondition:**
16:     ¬*failed* ∧ *status* = active
17:     *gc.index* = k
18:     *cmap(k)* = ±
19:   **Effect:**
20:     *gc.phase* ← idle
21: Internal gc-query-fix$(k)_i$

22:   **Precondition:**
23:     ¬*failed* ∧ *status* = active
24:     *gc.phase* = query
25:     *gc.index* = k
26:     ∃R ∈ *read-quorums(cmap(k))* :
27:       ∃W *write-quorums(cmap(k))* : $R ∪ W ⊆ gc.acc$
28:   **Effect:**
29:     *pnum1* ← *plum1* + 1
30:     *gc.pnum* ← *pnum1*
31:     *gc.phase* ← prop
32:     *gc.acc* ← ∅

33: Internal gc-prop-fix$(k)_i$
34:   **Precondition:**
35:     ¬*failed* ∧ *status* = active
36:     *gc.phase* = prop
37:     *gc.index* = k
38:     ∃W ∈ *write-quorums(cmap(k + 1))* :
39:       $W ⊆ gc.acc$
40:   **Effect:**
41:     *cmap(k)* ← ±

---

phase, *Reader-Writer$_i$*'s *tag* is equal to some t that is at least as great as the *tag* that each of the quorum members had when it sent a message to *Reader-Writer$_i$* for the query phase.

In the propagation phase, *Reader-Writer$_i$* ensures that all the processes in a write-quorum of the new configuration, $k + 1$, have acquired the values with *tag*s that are larger or equal to t.

Note that, unlike a read or write operation, a garbage-collection for k uses only two configurations—k in the query phase and $k + 1$ in the propagation phase. Thus, each phase consists of exactly one communication round.

At any time when *Reader-Writer$_i$* is carrying out a garbage-collection operation for configuration k, it may discover that someone else has already garbage-collected k; it learns this by observing that $cmap(k) = ±$ (line 18). When this happens, *Reader-Writer$_i$* simply terminates its garbage-collection operation.

7.3.4   IMPLEMENTATION OF THE RECON SERVICE

The *Recon* algorithm is considerably simpler than the *Reader-Writer* algorithm and we discuss it here at a high level. Recall the specification of the *Recon* service given in Section 7.2.2 and its external signature that appears in Specification 21. The algorithm consists of a *Recon$_i$* automaton for each location i, which interacts with a collection of global consensus services *Cons(k, c)*, one for each $k ≥ 1$ and each $c ∈ C$, and with a point-to-point communication service. The external signature of *Cons* appears in Specification 27.

Cons(k, c) accepts inputs from members of configuration c, which it assumes to be the $k - 1$st configuration. These inputs are of the form init$(c')_{k,c,i}$, where c' is a proposed new config-

Specification 27 External Signature of *Cons*

1: **Input:**
2:      $\text{init}(c')_{k,c,i}, c, c' \in C, i \in members(c), k \in \mathbb{N}$
3:      $\text{fail}_i, i \in members(c)$

4: **Output:**
5:      $\text{decide}(c')_{k,c,i}, c, c' \in C, i \in members(c), k \in \mathbb{N}$

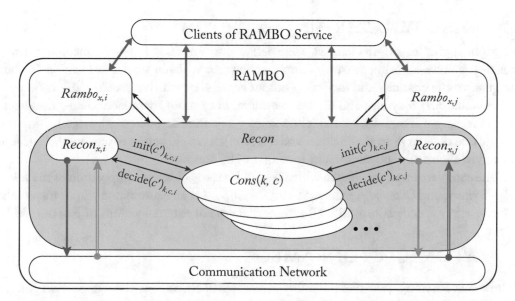

Figure 7.4: *Recon* architecture within RAMBO depicting the main components and their interactions.

uration. The configuration that $Cons(k, c)$ decides upon, (using $\text{decide}(c')_{k,c,i}$ outputs, is deemed to be the kth configuration. The validity property of consensus implies that this decision is one of the proposed configurations.

$Recon_i$ is activated by a $\text{join}(\text{recon})_i$ action, which is an output of $Joiner_i$. $Recon_i$ accepts reconfiguration requests from clients, and initiates consensus to help determine new configurations. It records the new configurations that the consensus services determine. $Recon_i$ also informs $Reader\text{-}Writer_i$ about newly determined configurations, and disseminates information about newly-determined configurations to the members of those configurations. It returns acknowledgments and configuration reports to its client.

While any consensus implementation can be used with *Recon*, one natural choice is to implement $Cons(k, c)$ using the Paxos consensus algorithm [72], as described formally in [28]. The complete implementation of *Recon*, $Recon_{impl}$, consists of the $Recon_i$ automata, channels connecting all the $Recon_i$ automata (the same channels as the rest of RAMBO), and the implementations of the *Cons* services. (A detailed presentation can be found in any of [46, 49, 81].)

Remark 7.13   Consensus service: Here we presented one example of how *Recon* is implemented with the help of an external service. In Chapter 8 we present another approach to implementing reconfiguration, and we give a detailed description of a particular consensus service used by the participants to agree on a unique configuration.   **End remark**

7.3.5   THE COMPLETE RAMBO ALGORITHM

We assume point to point channels *Channel*$_{i,j}$, one for each $i, j \in I$ (including $i = j$). *Channel*$_{i,j}$ is accessed using send$(m)_{i,j}$ input actions, by which a sender at location i submits message m to the channel, and recv$(m)_{i,j}$ output actions, by which a receiver at location j receives m. Channels may lose and reorder messages, but cannot manufacture new messages or duplicate messages. Formally, we model *Channel*$_{i,j}$ as a multiset, where a send$(m)_{i,j}$ input action adds one copy of m to the multiset and a recv$(m)_{i,j}$ output removes one copy of m. A lose input action allows any sub-multiset of messages to be removed.

The complete implementation, which we call RAMBO$_{impl}$, is the composition of the *Joiner*$_i$, *Reader-Writer*$_i$, and *Channel*$_{i,j}$ automata, and *Recon*$_{impl}$ (or any automaton whose traces satisfy the *Recon* safety specification), with all actions that are not external actions of RAMBO hidden.

7.4   ATOMICITY OF RAMBO

We show that RAMBO$_{impl}$ satisfies the safety guarantees of RAMBO, as given in Section 7.2.1, assuming the environment safety assumptions. An *operation* can be of type read, write, or garbage-collection. An operation is uniquely identified by its starting event: read$_i$, write$(v)_i$, or gc$(*)_i$ event.

We introduce the following history variables. (1) For every $k \in \mathbb{N}$: $c(k) \in C$. This is set when the first new-config$(*, k)_*$ occurs, to the configuration id that appears as the first parameter of this action. (2) For every operation π: $tag(\pi) \in T$. This is set just after π's query-fix or gc-query-fix event, to the *tag* of the process running π. (3) For every read or write operation π: (a) *query-cmap*(π), a *CMap*. This is set in the query-fix step of π, to the value of *op.cmap* in the pre-state. (b) *prop-cmap*(π), a *CMap*. This is set in the prop-fix step of π, to the value of *op.cmap* in the pre-state.

For any read or write operation π, we designate the following events. (1) query-phase-start(π). This is defined in the query-fix step of π, to be the unique earlier event at which the collection of query results was started and not subsequently restarted (that is, *op.acc* is set to $\emptyset$ in the effects of the corresponding step, and *op.acc* is not later reset to $\emptyset$ following that event and prior to the query-fix step). This is either a read, write, or recv event. (2) prop-phase-start(π). This is defined in the prop-fix step of π, to be the unique earlier event at which the collection of propagation results was started and not subsequently restarted. This is either a query-fix or recv event.

Now we present several lemmas describing information flow between operations. All are stated for any execution α satisfying the environment assumptions. The first lemma describes information flow between garbage-collection operations. We say that a gc-prop-fix$(k)_i$ event is *initial* if it is the first gc-prop-fix$(k)_*$ event in α, and a garbage-collection operation is *initial* if its gc-prop-fix event is initial. The algorithm ensures that garbage-collection of successive configurations is sequential: for each k, the initial gc-prop-fix(k) event precedes garbage-collection of $k + 1$. This implies that tags of garbage-collection operations are monotone with respect to the configuration indices.

Lemma 7.14   *For an execution α, suppose γ_k and γ_ℓ are garbage-collection operations for k and ℓ, respectively, where $k \leq \ell$ and γ_k is initial. If a gc-query-fix(ℓ) event for γ_ℓ occurs, then $tag(\gamma_k) \leq tag(\gamma_\ell)$.*

Proof. By induction on ℓ, for fixed k. For the inductive step, assume that $\ell \geq k + 1$ and the result is true for $\ell - 1$. A write-quorum of $c(\ell)$ is used in the propagation phase of $\gamma_{\ell-1}$ and a read-quorum of $c(\ell)$ is used in the query phase of γ_ℓ. The quorum intersection property for $c(\ell)$ guarantees propagation of tag information. $\square$

The following lemma describes situations in which certain configurations must appear in the *query-cmap* of a read or write operation π. First, if no garbage-collection operation for k completes before the query-phase-start event of π, then some configuration with index $\leq k$ must be included in *query-cmap*(π). Second, if some garbage-collection for k completes before the query-phase-start event of π, then some configuration with index $\geq k + 1$ must be included in the *query-cmap*(π). The proof is straightforward.

Lemma 7.15   *Let π be a read or write operation whose query-fix event occurs in α. (1) If no gc-prop-fix(k) event precedes the query-phase-start(π) event, then query-cmap$(\pi)(\ell) \in C$ for some $\ell \leq k$. (2) If some gc-prop-fix(k) event precedes the query-phase-start(π) event, then query-cmap$(\pi)(\ell) \in C$ for some $\ell \geq k + 1$.*

Next, we show propagation of *tag* information from a garbage-collection operation to a following read or write operation. The proof follows by observing that tags are monotone.

Lemma 7.16   *Let γ be an initial garbage-collection operation for k. Let π be a read or write operation whose query-fix event occurs in α. Suppose that the gc-prop-fix(k) event of γ precedes the query-phase-start(π) event. Then $tag(\gamma) \leq tag(\pi)$, and if π is a write operation then $tag(\gamma) < tag(\pi)$.*

Now we describe relationships between reads and writes that execute sequentially. The first lemma says that the smallest configuration index used in the propagation phase of the first operation π_1 is less than or equal to the largest index used in the query phase of the second operation π_2. In other words, the query phase of π_2 cannot use only configurations with indices that are less than any used in the propagation phase of π_1.

Lemma 7.17   *Assume π_1 and π_2 are two read or write operations such that the* prop-fix *event of π_1 precedes the* query-phase-start(π_2) *event in execution α. Then* $\min(\{\ell : prop\text{-}cmap(\pi_1)(\ell) \in C\}) \leq \max(\{\ell : query\text{-}cmap(\pi_2)(\ell) \in C\})$.

Proof. Suppose not. Let $k = \max(\{\ell : query\text{-}cmap(\pi_2)(\ell) \in C\})$. Then some gc-prop-fix($k$) event occurs before the prop-fix of π_1, and so before the query-phase-start(π_2) event. Lemma 7.15, Part 2, then implies that $query\text{-}cmap(\pi_2)(\ell) \in C$ for some $\ell \geq k + 1$, which contradicts the choice of k.   □

Next, we describe propagation of *tag* information between sequential reads and writes.

Lemma 7.18   *Suppose π_1 and π_2 are two read or write operations, such that the* prop-fix *event of π_1 precedes the* query-phase-start(π_2) *event in α. Then* $tag(\pi_1) \leq tag(\pi_2)$, *and if π_2 is a write then* $tag(\pi_1) < tag(\pi_2)$.

Proof. Let i_1 and i_2 be the processes that run operations π_1 and π_2, respectively. Let $cm_1 = prop\text{-}cmap(\pi_1)$ and $cm_2 = query\text{-}cmap(\pi_2)$. If there exists k such that $cm_1(k) \in C$ and $cm_2(k) \in C$, then the quorum intersection property for configuration k implies the conclusions of the lemma. So we assume that no such k exists. Lemma 7.17 implies that $\min(\{\ell : cm_1(\ell) \in C\}) \leq \max(\{\ell : cm_2(\ell) \in C\})$. Since the set of indices used in each phase consists of consecutive integers and the intervals have no indices in common, it follows that $k_1 < k_2$, where $k_1 = \max(\{\ell : cm_1(\ell) \in C\})$ and $k_2 = \min(\{\ell : cm_2(\ell) \in C\})$.

Since, for every $k \leq k_2 - 1$, $query.cmap(\pi_2)(k) \notin C$, Lemma 7.15, Part 1, implies that, for every such k, a gc-prop-fix(k) event occurs before the query-phase-start(π_2) event. For each such k, define γ_k to be the initial garbage-collection operation for k.

The propagation phase of π_1 accesses a write-quorum of $c(k_1)$, and the query phase of γ_{k_1} accesses a read-quorum of $c(k_1)$. By the quorum intersection property, there is some j in the intersection of these quorums. Let message m be the message sent from j to i_1 in the propagation phase of π_1, and let m' be the message sent from j to the process running γ_{k_1} in its query phase. We claim that j sends m before it sends m'. For if not, then information about configuration $k_1 + 1$ would be conveyed by j to i_1, who would include it in cm_1, contradicting the choice of k_1. Since j sends m before it sends m', j conveys *tag* information from π_1 to γ_{k_1}, ensuring that $tag(\pi_1) \leq tag(\gamma_{k_1})$.

Since $k_1 \leq k_2 - 1$, Lemma 7.14 implies that $tag(\gamma_{k_1}) \leq tag(\gamma_{k_2-1})$. Lemma 7.16 implies that $tag(\gamma_{k_2-1}) \leq tag(\pi_2)$, and if π_2 is a write then $tag(\gamma_{k_2-1}) < tag(\pi_2)$. Combining all the inequalities then yields both conclusions.   □

Theorem 7.19   *Let β be a trace of S. If β satisfy the* RAMBO *environment assumptions, then β satisfies the* RAMBO *service guarantees (well-formedness and atomicity).*

Proof. Let β be a trace of S that satisfies the RAMBO environment assumptions. We argue that β satisfies the RAMBO service guarantees. The proof that β satisfies the RAMBO well-formedness guarantees is straightforward from the code. To show that β satisfies atomicity (as defined in Section 7.2.1), assume that all read and write operations complete in β. Let α be an execution of S that satisfies the environment assumptions and whose trace is β. Define a partial order $\prec$ on read and write operations in α: totally order the writes in order of their tags, and order each read with respect to all the writes so that a read with tag t is ordered after all writes with tags $\leq t$ and before all writes with tags $> t$. Then we claim that $\prec$ satisfies the four conditions in the definition of atomicity. The interesting condition is Condition 2; the other three are straightforward.

For Condition 2, suppose for the sake of contradiction that π_1 and π_2 are read or write operations, π completes before π_2 starts, and $\pi_2 \prec \pi_1$. If π_2 is a write operation, then since π_1 completes before π_2 starts, Lemma 7.18 implies that $tag(\pi_2) > tag(\pi_1)$. But the fact that $\pi_2 \prec \pi_1$ implies that $tag(\pi_2) \leq tag(\pi_1)$, yielding a contradiction. On the other hand, if π_2 is a read operation, then since π_1 completes before π_2 starts, Lemma 7.18 implies that $tag(\pi_2) \geq tag(\pi_1)$. But the fact that $\pi_2 \prec \pi_1$ implies that $tag(\pi_2) < tag(\pi_1)$, again yielding a contradiction. This completes the proof. □

7.5   CONDITIONAL PERFORMANCE ANALYSIS: LATENCY BOUNDS

We now show latency bounds for the complete RAMBO system.[1] We fix $d > 0$, the *normal message delay*, and some $\epsilon > 0$. RAMBO allows sending of messages at arbitrary times. For the purpose of latency analysis, we restrict RAMBO's sending pattern: we assume that each automaton has a local real-valued clock, and sends messages at the first possible time and at regular intervals of d thereafter, as measured on the local clock. Also, non-send locally controlled events occur just once, within time 0 on the local clock.

The results also require restrictions on timing and failure behavior: We define an admissible timed execution to be *normal* provided that all local clocks progress at rate exactly 1, all messages that are sent are delivered within time d. Additionally, the normal timing and failure behavior[2] for all consensus services is that all messages are delivered within time d, local processing time is 0, and information is gossiped at intervals of d.

Next, we define a reliability property for configurations. In general, in quorum-based systems, operations that use quorums are guaranteed to terminate only if some quorums do not fail. Because we use many configurations, we attempt to take into account which configurations

---

[1]Strictly speaking, to handle timing formally, we convert all the input/output automata of RAMBO*impl* to general timed automata (GTAs) as defined in [80], by allowing arbitrary amounts of time to pass in any state.

[2]This timing and failure behavior is defined as "normal" in [28].

might be in use. We say that k is *installed* in a timed execution α provided that either $k = 0$ or there exists $c \in C$ such that (1) some $\mathsf{init}(*)_{k,c,*}$ event occurs, and (2) for every $i \in members(c)$, either $\mathsf{decide}(*)_{k,c,i}$ or fail_i occurs (thus, configuration $k - 1$ is c, and every non-failed member of c has learned about configuration k). We say that α is *e-configuration-viable*, $e \geq 0$, provided that for every c and k such that some *rec-cmap*$(k)_* = c$ in some state there exist $R \in$ *read-quorums*(c) and $W \in$ *write-quorums*(c) such that either (1) no process in $R \cup W$ ever fails in α, or (2) $k + 1$ is installed in a finite prefix α' of α and no process in $R \cup W$ fails in α by time $\ell time(\alpha') + e$ (where $\ell time(\alpha')$ is the limit time of α'). Thus, quorums remain non-failed for at least time e after the next configuration is installed. This condition is called *e-configuration-viability*.

The e-configuration-viability assumption is useful in situations where a configuration is no longer needed for performing operations after time e after the next configuration is installed. This condition holds in RAMBO executions in which certain timing assumptions hold; the strength of those assumptions determines the value of e that must be considered. We believe that such an assumption is reasonable for a reconfigurable system, because it can be reconfigured when quorums appear to be in danger of failing.

A variety of conditional latency bounds can be shown. It is straightforward to prove a bound of $2d$ on the time to join. The bound on time for a configuration to be installed through *Recon* depends on the time for *Cons* to decide on the configuration. If s is a bound on the time for *Cons*, then the bound on installation can be shown to be $d + s$. For the specific implementation of *Cons* given in [28] it is shown that $s = 10d + \epsilon$, and thus with this implementation the time to install a configuration is $11d + \epsilon$. A bound of $4d$ can be shown on the time for garbage-collection, assuming that enough of the relevant processes remain non-failed, by observing that garbage-collection takes exactly two communication rounds. It is not difficult to prove a bound of $4d$ on the latency for read and write operations in a "quiescent" situation, in which all joins and configuration management events have stopped, and the configuration map of the operation's initiator includes the latest configuration and has value $\pm$ for all earlier configurations. This is because under these assumptions RAMBO behaves from the performance standpoint exactly as algorithm ABD. More generally, this bound holds even if this map contains more than one configuration: multiple configurations in the map are used concurrently, and this does not slow the operation down.

What "prods" various operations along is the fact that all participants exchange information about configurations within a short time: if i and j have joined and do not fail, then any information that i has about configurations is conveyed to j within time $2d$. Using this result, it can be shown that, if reconfiguration requests are spaced sufficiently far apart, and if quorums of configurations remain alive for sufficiently long, then garbage collection keeps up with reconfiguration.

The main latency theorem presented here examines the latency of the service under certain reasonable assumptions and establishes that read and write operations terminate in time $8d$. The theorem bounds the time for operations in the "steady-state" case, where reconfigurations do not stop, but are spaced sufficiently far apart. Fix $e \geq 0$.

Theorem 7.20   *Let α be a normal admissible timed execution of* RAMBO$_{impl}$ *such that:*
(1) If a recon$(*, c)_i$ *event occurs at time t then for every $j \in$ members(c),* join-ack(rambo)$_j$ *occurs by time $t - e$. (2) If* join-ack(rambo)$_i$ *and* join-ack(rambo)$_j$ *both occur by time t, and neither i nor j fails by time $t + e$, then by time $t + e$, $i \in$ world$_j$. (3) For any* recon$(c, *)_i$ *that occurs in α, the time since the corresponding* report$(c)_i$ *event is $\geq 12d + \varepsilon$. (4) α satisfies $11d$–configuration–viability. (5) α contains* decide *events for infinitely many configurations.*
Suppose that a read$_i$ *(resp.,* write$(*)_i$*) event occurs at time t, and* join-ack$_i$ *occurs strictly before time $t - (e + 8d)$. Then the corresponding* read-ack$_i$ *(resp.,* write-ack$(*)_i$*) event occurs by time $t + 8d$.*

Proof. The various spacing properties and bounds on time to disseminate information imply that each phase of the read or write completes with at most one restart for learning about a new configuration. Therefore, each phase takes time at most $4d$, for a total of $8d$. □

Note again that the theorem considers infinite executions and assumes that reconfigurations never stop (Premise 5), but where recon requests are not issued too often (Premise 4). Then during each phase of an operation at most one new configuration becomes known. In practical systems, one would expect that reconfigurations are much less frequent than read and write operations, and so even under the pessimistic assumptions of the theorem the latency of read and write operations is very reasonable.

The full exposition [46, 81] also presents latency results analogous to those described above, for executions that have normal timing and failure characteristics after some point in the execution. These results are similar to the previous results, but include dependence on the time when normal behavior begins. It can also be observed that the system exhibits other pleasing performance characteristics. For example, consider a process that learns about configuration k is delayed for a long time. Suppose the process again becomes active when the most recent configuration is configuration ℓ, with $k < \ell$. Then this process is able to "catch up" to configuration ℓ in $O(\log(\ell - k))$ gossip rounds, provided only one process (or more) in each of configurations $k + 1$ to ℓ is active. This is easy to see by observing that the gossip protocol in effect implements a pointer-doubling algorithm on the sequence of configurations.

Remark 7.21   Reconfiguration and concurrency: In a static storage system at least one quorum (or a majority) of servers must remain correct forever to guarantee operation termination. In a dynamic storage one only needs to assume that some quorums in a configuration remain correct for a finite period of time that is sufficiently long to replace a configuration with another configuration (using a different quorum system). Thus, in general faster reconfiguration results in better fault tolerance.

In RAMBO, the reconfiguration is a two step process. First, the members of the current configuration agree upon the next configuration; then obsolete configurations are garbage-collected using the configuration upgrade process. Thus, multiple configurations may co-exist in the system. This leads to an interesting dilemma. (a) On the one hand, decoupling the choice of new configurations from the removal of old configurations allows better concurrency, simplifies operation, and improves modularity. (b) On the other hand, the delay between the installation of a new configuration and the removal of obsolete configurations depends on the expeditiousness of the latter. Delaying the removal of obsolete configurations may require stronger fault-tolerance assumptions because of multiple co-existing configurations.   **End remark**

Remark 7.22   Reconfiguration and memory access operation performance: The overall reconfiguration process in RAMBO involving two separate activities that proceed independently of any concurrent read and operations can indeed be of benefit. First, in RAMBO memory access operations are not only decoupled from reconfiguration, they are able to terminate even when *Recon* may be slow due to frequent reconfiguration or its use of consensus. In fact, read and write operations can still terminate if *Recon* does not terminate.

An experimental study [64] of several reconfigurable atomic memory implementations yielded some interesting observations. For example, in the WAN setting under constant reconfiguration (unoptimized) RAMBO implementation had on average the highest reconfiguration latency, yet it had the lowest latency of read and write operations. Another broad observation in the study is that separating reconfiguration activities from read and write operations helps improve reconfiguration performance.   **End remark**

Another study evaluated several algorithms for reconfigurable atomic storage, both with and without consensus. The study encompassed several algorithm implementations, including DynaStore, RAMBO, an optimized version of RAMBO, and two other specialized implementations [64].

Our experiments suggest that if read and write operations do not help concurrent reconfigurations to complete, that significantly reduces the overhead.

7.6   EXTENSIONS OF RAMBO

As can be seen from the presentation of RAMBO, it is described in an abstract and non-deterministic manner, which allows RAMBO to be easily adapted for use in a given system. In fact, one can see RAMBO as an architectural template for other and future systems.

Indeed, following its introduction, RAMBO has formed the basis for much research. Some of this research has focused on tailoring RAMBO to specific distributed platforms, ranging from networks-of-workstations to mobile networks. Other research has used RAMBO as a building block for higher-level applications, and it has been optimized for improved performance in certain domains.

In many ways, it is the highly non-deterministic and modular nature of RAMBO that makes it so adaptable to various optimizations. A given implementation of RAMBO has significant flexibility in when to send messages, to whom messages are sent, how many messages to send, what to include in messages, whether to combine messages, how nodes join the system, and how reconfiguration is implemented, etc. This flexibility, along with the unrestricted choice of configurations, has led to several extensions and implementations of RAMBO. An implementation can substitute a more involved *Joiner* protocol, or a different *Recon* service. In this way, we see the RAMBO algorithm presented in this chapter as a template for implementing a reconfigurable service in a highly dynamic environment.

A number of results are either motivated by RAMBO or directly use RAMBO as a point of departure for optimizations and practical implementations. We now survey selected additional results.

Aggressive garbage collection.   The work of Gilbert et al. [48, 49] improves the garbage collection mechanism of RAMBO by aggressively collecting obsolete configurations. The resulting algorithm (called RAMBO II) speeds up the configuration upgrade (i.e., garbage collection) process by garbage-collecting multiple configurations at the same time. If one or more obsolete configurations are present in the system, then a single configuration upgrade operation removes a maximal contiguous sequence of obsolete configurations up to the most current (at the time of the start of the upgrade) configuration. The upgrade proceeds in two phases. Each phase corresponds to the delay of one message exchange. In phase 1, a process contacts a read quorum and a write quorum of each obsolete configuration. By doing so, the process tells the members of obsolete configurations about the new configuration, and members of a read quorum of each obsolete configuration inform the process about the state of their object. In phase 2, the process propagates the most recent information to a read quorum and a write quorum of the new configuration, and marks obsolete configurations as garbage-collected before concluding.

Long-lived operation of RAMBO service.   To make the RAMBO service practical for long-lived settings where the size and the number of the messages needs to be controlled, Georgiou et al. [41] develop two algorithmic refinements. The first introduces a *leave* protocol that allows nodes to gracefully depart from the RAMBO service, hence reducing the number of, or completely eliminating, messages sent to the departed nodes. The second reduces the size of messages by introducing an incremental communication protocol. The two combined modifications are proved correct by showing that the resulting algorithm implements RAMBO. Musial [92, 94] implemented the algorithms on a network-of-workstations, experimentally showing the value of these modifications.

Restricting gossiping patterns and enabling operation restarts.   To further reduce the volume of gossip messages in RAMBO, Gramoli et al. [54] constrain the gossip pattern so that gossip messages are sent only by the nodes that (locally) believe that they have the most recent configuration. To address the side-effect of some nodes potentially becoming out-of-date due to reduced gossip (nodes may become out-of-date in RAMBO as well), the modified algorithm allows for non-deterministic operation restarts. The modified algorithm is shown to implement

RAMBO, and the experimental implementation [92, 94] is used to illustrate the advantages of this approach. In practice, non-deterministic operation restarts are most effectively replaced by a heuristic decision based on local observations, such as the duration of an operation in progress. Of course, any such heuristic preserves correctness.

Implementing a complete shared memory service.   The RAMBO service is specified for a single object, with complete shared memory implemented by composing multiple instances of the algorithm. In practical system implementations this may result in significant communication overhead. Georgiou et al. [40] developed a variation of RAMBO that introduces the notion of *domains*, collections of related objects that share configurations, thus eliminating much of the overhead incurred by the shared memory obtained through composition of RAMBO instances. A networks-of-workstations experimental implementation is also provided. Since the specification of the new service includes domains, the proof of correctness is achieved by adapting the correctness proof of RAMBO to that service.

Indirect learning in the absence of all-to-all connectivity.   The RAMBO algorithm assumes that either all nodes are connected by direct links or that an underlying network layer provides transparent all-to-all connectivity. Assuming this may be unfeasible or prohibitively expensive to implement in dynamic networks, such as ad hoc mobile settings. Konwar et al. [68] develop an approach to implementing RAMBO service where all-to-all gossip is replaced by an *indirect learning* protocol for information dissemination. The indirect learning scheme is used to improve the liveness of the service in the settings with uncertain connectivity. The algorithm is proved to implement RAMBO service. The authors examine deployment strategies for which indirect learning leads to an improvement in communication costs.

Dynamic atomic memory in sensor networks.   Beal et al. [9] developed an implementation of the RAMBO framework in the context of a wireless ad hoc sensor network. In this context, configurations are defined with respect to a specific geographic region: every sensor within the geographic region is a member of the configuration, and each quorum consists of a majority of the members. Sensors can store and retrieve data via RAMBO read and write operations, and the geographic region can migrate via reconfiguration. In addition, reconfiguration can be used to incorporate newly deployed sensors, and to retire failed sensors. An additional challenge was to *efficiently* implement the necessary communication (presented in this paper as point-to-point channels) in the context of a wireless network that supports one-to-many communication.

Dynamic atomic memory in a peer-to-peer network.   Muthitacharoen et al. [95] developed an implementation of the RAMBO framework, known as Etna, in the context of a peer-to-peer network. Etna guaranteed fault-tolerant, mutable data in a distributed hash table (DHT), using an optimized variant of RAMBO to maintain the data consistently despite continual changes in the underlying network.

Distributed enterprise disk arrays.   Another variation of RAMBO was used by researchers at Hewlett-Packard to implement a "federated array of bricks" (FAB), a distributed enterprise disk array [3, 103].

Integrated reconfiguration and garbage collection.   Earlier we noted that in RAMBO the decoupling of configuration introduction and removal of obsolete configurations may create delays during which old configurations must not fail until they are garbage collected. To address this, Gramoli [50] and Chockler et al. [24] developed an integrated approach to reconfiguration and garbage collection that reduces such delays. In Chapter 8, we present the RDS algorithm that implements this approach, thus improving fault tolerance. The idea is to overlay the configuration introduction algorithm that is based on an optimized version of the Paxos [73] protocol with the protocol used to remove obsolete configurations. The result is that there is never more than one old configuration at a time, which increases fault tolerance. On the other hand, using this approach new configurations cannot be introduced until the obsolete configuration is removed.

7.7   GEOQUORUMS—ADAPTATION OF RAMBO FOR MOBILE SETTINGS

We close this chapter with a more detailed example of how RAMBO can be viewed as a framework for refinements and optimizations. Specifically, here we describe a reformulation of the RAMBO framework for ad hoc mobile networks.

Dolev et al. [31] developed a new approach for implementing atomic read/write shared memory in mobile ad hoc networks where the individual stationary locations constituting the members of a fixed number of quorum configurations are implemented by mobile devices. This work specializes RAMBO algorithms in two ways. (1) In RAMBO the first (query) phase of write operations serves to establish a time stamp that is higher than any time stamps of the previously completed writes. If a global time service is available, then taking a snapshot of the global time value obviates the need for the first phase in write operations. (2) The full-fledged consensus service is necessary for reconfiguration in RAMBO only when the universe of possible configurations is unknown. When the set of possible configurations is small and known in advance, a much simpler algorithm suffices. The resulting approach, called *GeoQuorums*, yields an algorithm that efficiently implements read and write operations in a highly dynamic, mobile network.

In more detail, *GeoQuorums* implements atomic shared memory on top of a physical platform that is based on mobile nodes moving in arbitrary patterns. An ad hoc network uses no pre-existing infrastructure, instead, the network is formed by the mobile nodes who cooperate to route communication from sources to destinations. *GeoQuorums* can be viewed as a system of two layers, where the top layer implements a dynamic replicated storage system, and the bottom layer provides object replicas in terms of stationary *focal points* that are implemented by the mobile nodes.

The *focal points* are geographic areas of interest that are normally "populated" by mobile nodes. This may be a road junction, a scenic observation point, or a water resource in the desert. Mobile nodes in the vicinity of a focal point participate in implementing a stationary virtual object, called the focal point object. The implementation at each focal point supports a local broadcast service, *LBcast*, that provides reliable, totally ordered broadcast. *LBcast* is used to implement a type of replicated state machine, one that tolerates joins and leaves of mobile nodes. If every mobile node leaves the focal point, the focal point object fails.

Next, this approach defines a collection of quorum systems over the focal points. Each quorum system involves two sets, called get-quorums and put-quorums, with the property that every get-quorum intersects every put-quorum. The use of quorums enables the service to tolerate the failure of a limited number of focal point objects. For reasons of performance, or in response to periodic migration of mobile nodes, different quorum systems can be installed.

To facilitate communication with the focal point objects, *GeoQuorums* assumes the availability of a GeoCast service (as in [63]) that enables message delivery to the geographic area of a focal point. With this setting, one can use the RAMBO framework as the top layer to implement an atomic memory system with focal points serving as replica hosts. Motivated by simplicity and efficiency considerations, *GeoQuorums* approach makes additional modifications. The first deals with reconfiguration, and the second affects how read and write operations are processed.

GeoQuorums introduced the first general reconfiguration capability that does not rely on consensus. The algorithm reconfigures among a finite number of predetermined configurations, and instead of consensus it uses a two-phase protocol that is similar to the upgrade protocol in RAMBO. Here in the first phase the invoker contacts any complete get-quorum and put-quorum of all preceding configurations (note that at most one pair of messages per focal point is needed even if the finite number of possible configurations is large), then in the second phase information is conveyed to any complete put-quorum of the next configuration.

GeoQuorums implements a modified approach to read and write operations that allows some operations to complete in just one phase. This is accomplished for the case of writes with the help of a global positioning system (GPS) clock to generate tags for the written values, thus ordering writes. This obviates the need for the phase that in other implementations determines the highest tag, and the write protocol here performs just a single *put* phase that interacts with any put-quorum in the current configuration. If the write detects a concurrent reconfiguration, it also awaits response from put-quorums in every configuration (this involves at most one contact with each focal point). Once the write completes, the tag becomes *confirmed*. For the case of reads, this protocol involves one or two phases. The first, *get*, phase proceeds as a typical query phase to obtain the value with the maximum tag from some complete get-quorum; if a concurrent reconfiguration is detected, then the phase also awaits responses from one get-quorum from each configuration (again, at most one message exchange per focal point). Once the *get* phase completes, and it is determined that the maximum obtained tag is *confirmed*, the read terminates. Otherwise, the read performs the *put* phase that propagates the maximum tag-value pair to some put-quorum. The information about the *confirmed* tags is propagated through the system to enable single-phase read operations.

The use of separate get-quorums and put-quorums allows one to tune the system performance depending on the balance between reads and writes. When there are more writes than reads, the system can reconfigure to use larger get-quorums and smaller put-quorums because writes access only the put-quorums. When reads are more prevalent, the system can use smaller get-quorums and larger put-quorums because some reads access just the get-quorums.

GeoQuorums uses real-time timestamps (provided through GPS) to expedite read and write operations, allowing the writes and some reads to complete in a single round. Lastly, the assumption that there is a fixed set of focal points limits the system's evolvability, but allows the algorithm to reconfigure without the use of consensus.

7.8   BIBLIOGRAPHIC NOTES

Object reconfiguration was originally proposed as a four step process by Herlihy [60]: (1) get the current state of the object, (2) store this state, (3) initialize a new configuration, and (4) update configurations to remove obsolete ones.

The original RAMBO protocol is due to Lynch and Shvartsman [82]. An HP Labs technical report provides a concise pedagogic presentation of the system for "dummies" [3]. A complete implementation can be derived from the full specification of RAMBO [49] and the input/output automata specification [28] of the Paxos consensus algorithm [73]. RAMBO II improves the garbage collection mechanism of RAMBO by aggressively collecting obsolete configurations [48, 49].

RAMBO III [50] improves fault-tolerance by combining RAMBO with Paxos [73] with the goal of maintaining only two active configurations at any time. RAMBO III couples the garbage collection process with the installation process hence upper-bounding the number of simultaneously active configurations to 2. During a reconfiguration, the old configuration gets upgraded into a new one, reaching a transient state that has exactly two active configurations. By minimizing the number of active configurations, RAMBO III minimizes the number of quorum members that have to remain active, hence improving the fault tolerance of the previous versions of RAMBO. The RDS algorithm, presented in Chapter 8, exploits a similar coupling mechanism to improve fault tolerance and propose additional performance improvements.

Gramoli et al. [54] introduced refinements that: (a) reduce the communication cost by restricting the all-to-all gossip pattern to replica owners, based on the local decisions of the participating nodes; and (b) allows certain blocked (or delayed) operations to resume processing and complete successfully. Georgiou et al. [41] considers long-lived objects and present improvements that: (a) Provide an incremental communication protocol that takes advantage of the local knowledge, and manages the size of messages by removing redundant information. (b) Implement a leave service allows the nodes to depart gracefully, which results in reduced communication burden. The implementation of Georgiou et al. [40] extends the abstract RAMBO algorithm that supports individual atomic objects by introducing the notion of *domains* that allow the users to group related atomic objects. This implementation manages configurations on the basis of domains, resulting in practical improvements to the utility and the performance of the resulting service. RAMBO and several refinements and variations were implemented by Musial [92] in a research system that was used to evaluate optimizations and compare performance of different versions of the distributed memory services.

GeoQuorums [31] presented in Section 7.7 gives an implementation of atomic shared memory on top of a platform consisting of mobile nodes moving in arbitrary patterns. It is the first implementation of atomic memory that does not rely on consensus.

CHAPTER 8

RDS: Integrated Reconfigurations

The RAMBO framework presented in the previous chapter decouples the new configuration installation service from the garbage collection of obsolete configurations, thus offering concurrency and modularity. In some settings, however, it is beneficial to tightly integrate reconfiguration with garbage collection. Doing so reduces the latency of removing old configurations, thus improving robustness when configurations may fail rapidly. In this chapter we present an algorithm that integrates reconfiguration with garbage collection by "opening" the external consensus service and combining it with the removal of the old configuration. This is accomplished by combining an optimized version of the Paxos algorithm [72] and the RAMBO garbage-collection protocol. The resulting reconfiguration protocol reduces the latency of the configuration installation service and the garbage collection as compared to RAMBO.

Some consensus algorithms that tolerate failures of participants, like Paxos, require a candidate leader to exchange messages with an active quorum of servers. This is similar to the previous distributed storage that also require a process to exchange messages with a quorum of replicas. This observation indicates that the same communication pattern is common to both reconfiguration and distributed storage algorithms, which is the motivation behind integrating reconfiguration within the distributed storage service. Let us first have a closer look at a high level description of the Paxos consensus algorithm to identify similarities with a distributed storage implementation. We then present the Reconfigurable Distributed Storage (RDS) that integrates the installation of new configuration that builds upon an optimized version of Paxos with the removal of obsolete configuration.

8.1 PRELIMINARIES

Similarly to RAMBO in Chapter 7, we need to ensure that the client requests to RDS are well-formed in order to ensure that a reconfigurable atomic memory service guarantees that the responses are well-formed, and that the read and write operations satisfy atomic consistency.

We consider *good* executions of RDS, whose traces satisfy the following environmental assumptions that form the *well-formedness* conditions.

- For every x and i:

  - No join$(*)_i$, read$_i$, write$(*)_i$, or recon$(*, *)_i$ event is preceded by a fail$_i$ event.

- At most one join$(*)_i$ event occurs.

- Any read$_i$, write$(*)_i$, or recon$(*, *)_i$ is preceded by a join-ack(rds)$_i$ event.

- Any read$_i$, write$(*)_i$, or recon$(*, *)_i$ is preceded by a -ack event for any preceding event of any of these kind.

• For every c, at most one recon$(*, c)_i$ event occurs. Uniqueness of configuration identifier is achievable using local process identifier and sequence numbers.

• For every c, c', and i, if a recon$(c, c')_i$ event occurs, then it is preceded by:

- A recon-ack$(c)_i$ event and

- A join-ack$_j$ event for every $j \in members(c')$.

8.2 THE PAXOS CONSENSUS ALGORITHM

In RAMBO, the reconfiguration assumed the presence of an external consensus algorithm to ensure that new configurations are installed one after the other such that there is a totally ordered sequence of configurations in time in the system. Here we describe a reconfigurable distributed storage, called RDS, that combines Paxos with RAMBO. RDS improves on RAMBO by coupling the configuration installation—consensus instance—with the configuration removal. This coupling speeds up the reconfiguration process for better fault-tolerance. To strengthen this result, RDS specifies a fast version of Paxos.

The Paxos algorithm is a famous consensus algorithm that achieves optimal delay in practical circumstances.[1] Paxos uses quorums to ensure agreement among participants.

The key idea of Paxos is as follows. The participants of Paxos share three roles: *proposers* that propose values, *acceptors* that choose a value, and *learners* that learn the chosen value. A single process can play multiple roles. One Paxos instance is divided into ballots each representing a new attempt to reach consensus. (Ballots can occur concurrently, are not necessarily ordered, and may interfere with each other, delaying Paxos termination but not violating safety.) Paxos is a leader-based algorithm in the sense that a single *leader* is responsible of one ballot.

8.2.1 THE PART-TIME PARLIAMENT

This presentation describes the functioning of an ancient Part-Time Parliament of a Greek island named Paxos. More precisely, this paper explains how decrees can be passed while legislators may not be present in the Chamber at the same time and may experience difficulties to communicate. Interestingly, this part-time parliament boils down to an algorithm providing consistency despite any number of failures and resuming properly after more than half of the processes recover.

---

[1]Traditional consensus algorithms save one message delay in comparison with Paxos by assuming that the set of participants that propose a value is the same as the set of participants that decide upon a value. In practice, it might not be the case.

Phase 1a. A leader sends a new ballot to a quorum of proposers.

Phase 1b. Upon reception of the message, any proposer responds by sending the value of the highest ballot (if any) they have already voted for. Each proposer that learns about a more up-to-date ballot abstained from any earlier ballot.

Phase 2a. After having received the response of at least a quorum of proposers, the leader chooses a new value for its ballot and informs a quorum of acceptors of the value it has chosen for its ballot.

Phase 2b. Any acceptor, that learns about this value and that did not abstain from that ballot, may vote for it and tells the learners (and the leader) about this vote. When the learners (and the leader) hear that a quorum of acceptors has voted for it, they decide this value.

Figure 8.1: Informal description of Paxos.

Figure 8.1 describes the normal sequence of messages sent in a ballot of Paxos, where a message exchange is called a phase. Acceptors abstain from a ballot b if they discover another ballot b' with a larger identifier (**Phase 1b**). Acceptors may vote for a ballot if they did not abstain from it earlier. A ballot succeed only if a quorum of acceptors vote for its value, however, acceptors of a single quorum may vote for concurrent ballots. If this happens, a new ballot with a larger identifier must be started to try reaching consensus again. The consensus is reached when learners receive a message informing them of the chosen value; this reception (**Phase 2b**) terminates the ballot.

8.2.2   FAST PAXOS

A fast consensus algorithm is an algorithm in which a process learns the chosen value two message delays of when the value has been proposed. Fast Paxos is a fast consensus algorithm that is a variant of Paxos. That is, in Fast Paxos, a process may learn about the decided value at the latest 2δ after the value has been proposed, where δ is an upper bound on the transmission delay of messages. This result is achieved when no collisions (also called *split votes*) occur between concurrent distinct ballots. A collision occurs when all quorums of acceptors vote for distinct values of concurrent ballots.

The main improvement over classic Paxos is to avoid the two first message delays of Paxos in case no collision occurs. The first phase of the original algorithm aims at renewing the ballot number. This renewal might be avoided under specific circumstances.

- At the beginning of the first ballot execution: since no value has been proposed yet, the leader might first send message **2a** proposing any value.

- If the same leader runs multiple consensus instances: the leader who successfully led the ballot of the previous consensus instance may reuse the same ballot number for the following consensus instance proposing directly any value in message **2a**.

- If the leader sends a message to acceptors for them to treat any proposer message like if it were a **2a** message. In this specific case an additional collision recovery must be implemented to ensure progress.

Avoiding the first phase speeds up Paxos. Without this phase, the algorithm becomes a fast consensus algorithm, i.e., a value is chosen two message delays after it has been proposed. In some cases, where Fast Paxos can avoid the first phase (e.g., because the leader did not change in two consecutive instances), Fast Paxos lasts two message delays less than Classic Paxos. The time taken to solve the consensus, i.e., the time taken for a proposed value to be accepted takes three message delays in Fast Paxos while it takes four message delays in Classic Paxos.

8.2.3 DECIDING UPON A NEW CONFIGURATION

In our context, consensus is used to decide upon a configuration, hence the value proposed and decided in the previous Paxos example is actually a "configuration" in our context. The RDS algorithm involves lots of actions to be taken in many corner cases induced by concurrency.

- The first one is the split-vote issue. As there may be multiple candidate leaders, they may conflict in the configuration they proposed. Although no two configurations can be voted upon by distinct quorums, thanks to the intersection property of quorums, a split vote problem may occur.

- The second issue is when the messages get lost so that a phase cannot terminate because quorum members are not answering. It is desirable for the algorithm to exit such a blocking situation when for example the blocked process received another reconfiguration request.

But in a simple situation where none of these concurrency issues arise, the algorithm simply executes in three phases.

1. The candidate leader prepares a new ballot number and configuration and sends it to some read quorums of the current configuration and waits for an acknowledgment of all members of one read quorum. (Note that sending this message to only one read quorum does not guarantee fault tolerance as a particular quorum member may fail but tentatively sending this message to all read quorums may unnecessarily consume the available bandwidth.) If the leader receives a larger ballot number from one of these quorum members, it sets both its ballot number and its associated configuration to the ones of this quorum member.

2. The candidate leader proposes the ballot number and the associated configuration to some read and write quorums of the current configuration. The quorum members either abstain (by sending the largest ballot number they have already voted for) or vote (if they have not yet voted for a larger ballot).

3. Once a server receives the votes of every member of at least one read and one write quorum of the current configuration, it decides the new configuration and simply propagates this configuration information to a read and a write quorum of the current configuration (that is now considered old) and some read and some write quorum of the newly decided configuration. (While the leader may get informed here as well, this is not required.)

8.3   RECONFIGURABLE DISTRIBUTED STORAGE

8.3.1   SIGNATURE AND STATE

The external specification of the algorithm appears in Specification 28. Similarly to the protocol described in Chapter 7, before issuing any operation, a client instructs the process to join the system, providing the algorithm with a set of "seed" processes already in the system. When the algorithm succeeds in contacting processes already in the system, it returns a join-ack. A client can then choose to initiate a read or write operation, which result, respectively, in read-ack and write-ack responses. A client can initiate a reconfiguration, recon, resulting in a recon-ack. The network sends and recvs messages, and each process may fail. Finally, a leader election service may occasionally notify a process as to whether it is currently the leader.

Specification 28 Signature of RDS

```
 1:  Input:                              11:     read-ack(v)_i, v ∈ V, i ∈ I,      21:        i ∈ I,
 2:      join(W)_i, W ⊆ I, i ∈ I,        12:     write-ack_i, i ∈ I,             22:     prepare-done(b)_i, b ∈ T × N × C,
 3:      read_i, i ∈ I,                  13:     recon-ack(r)_i, r ∈ {ok, failed},  23:        i ∈ I,
 4:      write(v)_i, v ∈ V, i ∈ I,       14:        i ∈ I,                        24:     init-propose(k)_i, k ∈ N, i ∈ I,
 5:      recon(c, c')_i, c, c' ∈ C, i ∈ I,  15:     send(m)_i, m ∈ M, i ∈ I,      25:     propose(k)_i, k ∈ N, i ∈ I,
 6:      recv(m)_i, i ∈ I,               16:  Internal:                          26:     propose-done(k)_i, k ∈ N, i ∈ I,
 7:      fail_i, i ∈ I,                  17:     query-fix_i, i ∈ I,             27:     propagate(k)_i, k ∈ N, i ∈ I,
 8:      leader(b)_i, b ∈ N, i ∈ I,      18:     prop-fix(v)_i, v ∈ V, i ∈ I,    28:     propagate-done(k)_i, k ∈ N, i ∈ I,
 9:  Output:                             19:     init_i, i ∈ I,
10:      join-ack_i, i ∈ I,              20:     prepare(b)_i, b ∈ T × N × C,
```

The state of the algorithm is described in Specification 29 and shares similarities with the state of Specification 23 in Chapter 7. The *value* $\in V$ of process i indicates the value of the object from the standpoint of i. A *tag* $\in T$ is maintained by each process as a unique pair of *counter* and *id*. The *counter* denotes the version of the value of the object from a local point-of-view, while the *id* is the process identifier and serves as a tie-breaker, when two processes have the same counter for two different values. The value and the tag are simultaneously sent and updated when a larger tag is discovered, or when a write operation occurs.

Specification 29 State of RDS

```
 1:  State:
 2:      value ∈ V, initially 0
 3:      tag ∈ T, a tag containing
 4:          counter ∈ ℕ, initially 0
 5:          id ∈ I, initially i
 6:      status ∈ {idle, joining, active, failed}, initially
 7:          idle
 8:      world, a finite subset of I, initially ∅
 9:      cmap ∈ CMap, initially c₀ at index 0 and ⊥
10:          elsewhere
11:      pnum1 ∈ ℕ, initially 0
12:      pnum2, a mapping from I → ℕ, initially mapping
13:          all to 0
14:      isLeader ∈ {true, false}, initially false

15:      confirmed, a set of tags, initially ∅
16:      failed ∈ {true, false}, initially false
17:      op, a record with fields:
18:          type ∈ {read, write}, initially ⊥
19:          phase ∈ {idle, query, prop, done} initially idle
20:          pnum ∈ ℕ, initially 0
```

```
21:      cmap ∈ CMap initially c₀ at index 0 and ⊥
22:          elsewhere
23:      acc, a finite subset of I, initially ∅
24:      tag ∈ T, initially ⟨0, i⟩
25:      value ∈ V, initially 0

26:  pxs, a record with fields:
27:      pnum ∈ ℕ, initially 0
28:      phase ∈ {idle, prepare, propose, propagate},
29:          initially idle
30:      conf-index ∈ ℕ, initially 0
31:      old-conf ∈ C, initially ⊥
32:      conf ∈ C, initially ⊥
33:      acc, a finite subset of I, initially ∅
34:      prepared-id ∈ I, the id of the lastly prepared ballot
35:  ballot, a record with fields:
36:      id ∈ T, a tag initially ⟨0, i⟩
37:      conf-index ∈ ℕ, initially 0
38:      conf ∈ C, initially ⊥
39:  voted-ballots, a set of ballots, initially ∅.
```

The *status* of process i expresses the current state of i. A process may participate fully in the algorithm only if its status is active. The set of identifiers of processes known to i to have joined the service is maintained locally in a set called *world*. Each process maintains a list of configurations in a configuration map. A configuration map is denoted *cmap* $\in$ *CMap*, a mapping from integer indices to $C \cup \{\perp, \pm\}$, and initially maps every integer, except 0, to $\perp$. The index 0 is mapped to the default configuration c_0 that is used at the beginning of the algorithm. This default configuration can be arbitrarily set by the designer of the application depending on its needs, e.g., since the system is reconfigurable, the default configuration can be chosen as a single process known to be reliable a sufficiently long period of time for the system to bootstrap. The configuration map tracks which configurations are active, which have not yet been created, indicated by $\perp$, and which have already been removed, indicated by $\pm$. The total ordering on configurations determined by the reconfiguration ensures that all processes agree on which configuration is stored in each position in *cmap*. As before, we define $c(k)$ to be the configuration associated with index k.

Read and write operations are divided into phases; in each phase a process exchanges information with all the replicas in some set of quorums. Each phase is initiated by some process that we refer to as the *phase initiator*. When a new phase starts, the *pnum1* field records the corresponding phase number, allowing the client to determine which responses correspond to its phase. The *pnum2* field maps an identifier j to an integer $pnum2(j)_i$ indicating that i has heard about the $pnum2(j)_i^{th}$ phase of process j. The three records *op*, *pxs*, and *ballot* store the information about read/write operations, reconfiguration, and ballots used in reconfiguration, respectively. We describe their subfields in the following.

- The record *op* is used to store information about the current phase of an ongoing read or write operation. The *op.cmap* $\in$ *CMap* subfield records the configuration map associated with a read/write operation. This consists of the process's *cmap* when a phase begins. It is augmented by any new configuration discovered during the phase in the case of a read or write operation. A phase completes when the initiator has exchanged information with quorums from every valid configuration in *op.cmap*. The *op.pnum* subfield records the read or write phase number when the phase begins, allowing the initiator to determine which responses correspond to the phase. The *op.acc* subfield records which processes from which quorums have responded during the current phase.

- The record *pxs* stores information about the paxos subprotocol. It is used as soon as a reconfiguration request is received. The *pxs.pnum* subfield records the reconfiguration phase number, the *pxs.phase* indicates if the current phase is idle, prepare, propose, or propagate. The *pxs.conf-index* subfield is the index of *cmap* for the last installed configuration, while the *pxs.old-conf* subfield is the last installed configuration. Therefore, *pxs.conf-index* $+ 1$ represents the index of *cmap* where the new configuration, denoted by the subfield *pxs.conf*, will be installed (in case reconfiguration succeeds). The *pxs.acc* subfield records which processes from which quorums have responded during the current phase.

- Record *ballot* stores the information about the current ballot. This is used once the reconfiguration is initiated. The *ballot.id* subfield records the unique ballot identifier. The *ballot.conf-index* and the *ballot.conf* subfields record *pxs.conf-index* and *pxs.conf*, respectively, when the reconfiguration is initiated.

Finally, the *voted-ballot* set records the set of ballots that have been voted by the participants of a read quorum of the last installed configuration. In the remaining, a state field indexed by i indicates a field of the state of process i, e.g., tag_i refers to field *tag* of process i.

8.3.2   READ AND WRITE OPERATIONS

The pseudocode for read and write operations appears in Specification 30. Read and write operations proceed by accessing quorums of the currently active configurations. Each replica maintains a *tag* and a *value* for the data being replicated. Each read or write operation potentially requires two phases: one to *query* the replicas, learning the most up-to-date tag and value, and a second to *propagate* the tag and value to the replicas. First, the *query* phase starts when a read (Specification 30, line 2) or a write (Specification 30, line 11) event occurs and ends when a query-fix event occurs (Specification 30, line 21). In a *query* phase, the initiator contacts one read quorum from each active configuration, and remembers the largest tag and its associated value by possibly updating its own tag and associated value, as detailed in Section 8.3.3. Second, the *propagate* phase starts when the aforementioned query-fix event occurs and ends when a prop-fix (Specification 30, line 41) event occurs. In a *propagate* phase, read operations and write operations behave differently: a write operation chooses a new tag (Specification 30, line 33) that is strictly larger than the one discovered in the query phase, and sends the new tag and new value to a write quorum; a read operation sends the tag and value discovered in the query phase to a write quorum.

Sometimes, a read operation can avoid performing the propagation phase, if some prior read or write operation has already propagated that particular tag and value. Similarly to the optimization used in Chapter 5, once a tag and value has been propagated, be it by a read or a write operation, it is marked *confirmed* (Specification 30, line 49). If a read operation discovers that a tag has been confirmed, it can skip the second phase (Specification 30, line 55).

One complication arises when during a phase, a new configuration becomes active. In this case, the read or write operation must access the new configuration as well as the old one. In order to accomplish this, read or write operations save the set of currently active configurations, *op.cmap*, when a phase begins (Specification 30, lines 17, 38); a reconfiguration can only add configurations to this set—none are removed during the phase. Even if a reconfiguration finishes, the read or write phase must continue to use the same configuration.

8.3.3   COMMUNICATION AND INDEPENDENT TRANSITIONS

In this section, we describe the transitions that propagate information between processes. Those appear in Specification 31. Information is propagated in the background via point-to-point channels that are accessed using send and recv actions. The join and join-ack actions are identical to the ones of the previous chapter. The join input sets the current process into the joining status and indicates a set of processes denoted W that it can contact to start being active. Finally, a leader election service informs a process that it is currently the leader, through a leader action, and the fail action models a disconnection.

The communication transitions treat many different cases. This is due to the piggybacking of information in messages: each message conveys not only information related to the read and write operations (e.g., *tag*, *value*, *cmap*, *confirmed*) but also information related to the reconfiguration process (e.g., *ballot*, *pxs*, *voted-ballot*).

Moreover, all messages contain fields common to operations and reconfiguration: the set of processes ids *world* the sender process knows of, and the current configuration map *cmap*. When process i receives a message, provided i is not failed or idle, it sets its status to active—completing the join protocol, if it has not already done so. It also updates its information with the message content: i starts participating in a new reconfiguration if the ballot received is larger than its ballot, i updates some of its *pxs* subfield (lines 123–128) if i discovers that a pending consensus focuses on a larger indexed configuration than the one it is aware of (line 121). That is, during a stale reconfiguration i might catch up with the actual reconfiguration while aborting the stale one. The receiver also progresses in the reconfiguration (adding the sender id to its *pxs.acc* subfield, lines 132, 135, 138) if the sender uses the same ballot (line 134), and responds to the right message of i (line 131). Observe that if i discovers another consensus instance aiming at

Specification 30 RDS_i – Transitions 1

1: **Input read**$_i$	41: **Precondition:**
2: **Effect:**	42: $\neg failed \wedge status =$ active
3: **if** $\neg failed \wedge status =$ active **then**	43: $op.type \in \{$read, write$\}$
4: $pnum1 \leftarrow pnum1 + 1$	44: $op.phase =$ prop
5: $op.pnum \leftarrow pnum1$	45: $\forall k \in \mathbb{N}, c \in C : op.cmap(k) = c \implies$
6: $op.type \leftarrow$ read	46: $(\exists W \in write\text{-}quorums(c) : W \subseteq op.acc$
7: $op.phase \leftarrow$ query	47: **Effect:**
8: $op.cmap \leftarrow cmap$	48: $op.phase \leftarrow$ done
9: $op.acc \leftarrow \emptyset$	49: $confirmed \leftarrow confirmed \cup op.tag$
	// optimization
10: **Input write**$(v)_i$	
11: **Effect:**	50: **Output read-ack**$_i$
12: **if** $\neg failed \wedge status =$ active **then**	51: **Precondition:**
13: $pnum1 \leftarrow pnum1 + 1$	52: $\neg failed \wedge status =$ active
14: $op.pnum \leftarrow pnum1$	53: $op.type =$ read
15: $op.type \leftarrow$ write	54: $op.phase =$ done $\vee$ *// two–phase read*
16: $op.phase \leftarrow$ query	55: $(op.phase =$ prop $\wedge op.tag \in confirmed)$
17: $op.cmap \leftarrow cmap$	*// 1 phase*
18: $op.acc \leftarrow \emptyset$	56: $v = op.value$
19: $op.value \leftarrow v$	57: **Effect:**
	58: $op.phase \leftarrow$ idle
20: **Internal query-fix**$_i$	
21: **Precondition:**	59: **Output write-ack**$_i$
22: $\neg failed \wedge status =$ active	60: **Precondition:**
23: $op.type \in \{$read, write$\}$	61: $\neg failed \wedge status =$ active
24: $op.phase =$ query	62: $op.type \leftarrow$ write
25: $\forall k \in \mathbb{N}, c \in C : op.cmap(k) = c \implies$	63: $op.phase =$ done
26: $(\exists R \in read\text{-}quorums(c) : R \subseteq op.acc$	64: **Effect:**
27: **Effect:**	65: $op.phase \leftarrow$ idle
28: **if** $op.type =$ read **then**	
29: $op.value \leftarrow value$	66: **Input join**$(W)_i$
30: $op.tag \leftarrow tag$	67: **Effect:**
31: **else**	68: $status \leftarrow$ joining
32: $value \leftarrow op.value$	69: $world \leftarrow world \cup W$
33: $tag \leftarrow \langle tag.counter + 1, i \rangle$	
34: $op.tag \leftarrow tag$	70: **Output join-ack**$_i$
35: $pnum1 \leftarrow pnum1 + 1$	71: **Precondition:**
36: $op.pnum \leftarrow pnum1$	72: $status =$ active
37: $op.phase \leftarrow$ prop	73: $joined =$ false
38: $op.cmap \leftarrow cmap$	74: **Effect:**
39: $op.acc \leftarrow \emptyset$	75: $joined \leftarrow$ true
40: **Internal prop-fix**$_i$	

installing a configuration at a larger index, or if i discovers a larger ballot than its, then i sets its *pxs.phase* to idle. Thus, i stops participating in the reconfiguration.

In the meantime, i updates fields related to the read/write operations and either continues the phase of the current operation or restarts it depending on the current phase and the incoming phase number (lines 110–116). Node i compares the incoming tag t to its own *tag*. If t is strictly greater, it represents a more recent version of the object; in this case, i sets its *tag* to t and its value to the incoming value v. Node i updates its configuration map *cmap* with the incoming *cm*, using the update operator defined in Chapter 7.1. Furthermore, process i updates its *pnum2(j)* component for the sender j to reflect new information about the phase number of the sender,

Specification 31 RDS_i – Transitions 2

76: **Input** leader$(b)_i$	107: $cmap \leftarrow$ update$(cmap, cm)$
77: **Effect:**	108: $pnum2(j) \leftarrow$ max$(pnum2(j), pns)$
78: $isLeader \leftarrow b$	109: **if** $op.phase \in \{$query, prop$\} \wedge$
	110: $pnr \geq op.num$ **then**
79: **Input** fail$(W)_i$	111: $op.cmap \leftarrow$ extend$(op.cmap, cm)$
80: **Effect:**	112: **if** $op.cmap \in Truncated$ **then**
81: $failed \leftarrow$ true	113: $op.acc \leftarrow op.acc \cup \{j\}$
	114: **else**
82: **Output** send$(W, v, t, cnf, cm, pns, pnr, b, p, vb)_{i,j}$	115: $op.acc \leftarrow \emptyset$
83: **Precondition:**	116: $op.cmap \leftarrow cmap$
84: $\neg failed \wedge status \neq$ idle	117: **if** $b.id > ballot.id$ **then**
85: $j \in world$	118: $ballot \leftarrow b$
86: $W = world$	119: $pxs.phase \leftarrow$ idle
87: $v = value$	120: $pxs.acc \leftarrow \emptyset$
88: $t = tag$	121: **if** $p.conf\text{-}index > pxs.conf\text{-}index$ **then**
89: $cnf = confirmed$ // optimization	122: **if** $recon\text{-}in\text{-}progress =$ false **then**
90: $cm = cmap$	123: $pxs.conf\text{-}index \leftarrow p.conf\text{-}index$
91: $pns = pnum1$	124: $pxs.conf \leftarrow p.conf\text{-}index$
92: $pnr = pnum2$	125: $pxs.conf \leftarrow p.conf$
93: $b = ballot$ // Paxos ballot number	126: $pxs.old\text{-}conf \leftarrow p.old\text{-}conf$
94: $p = pxs$ // Paxos instance information	127: $pxs.phase \leftarrow$ idle
95: $vb = voted\text{-}ballots$	128: $pxs.acc \leftarrow \emptyset$
96: $joined =$ false	129: $voted\text{-}ballots \leftarrow voted\text{-}ballots \cup vb$
97: **Effect:**	130: **if** $pxs.phase =$ prepare **then**
98: None	131: **if** $pnr \geq pxs.pnum$ **then**
99: **Input** recv$(W, v, t, cnf, cm, pns, pnr, b, p, vb)_{j,i}$	132: $pxs.acc \leftarrow pxs.acc \cup \{j\}$
100: **Effect:**	133: **else if** $pxs.phase =$ propose **then**
101: **if** $\neg failed \wedge status \neq$ idle **then**	134: **if** $ballot \in vb \wedge ballot = b$ **then**
102: $status \leftarrow$ active	135: $pxs.acc \leftarrow pxs.acc \cup \{j\}$
103: $world \leftarrow world \cup W$	136: **else if** $pxs.phase =$ propagate **then**
104: $confirmed \leftarrow confirmed \cup cnf$	137: **if** $cm(ballot.conf\text{-}index) = ballot.conf$ **then**
105: **if** $t > tag$ **then**	138: $pxs.acc \leftarrow pxs.acc \cup \{j\}$
106: $\langle value, tag \rangle \leftarrow \langle v, t \rangle$	

which appears in the *pns* component of the message. If process i is currently conducting a phase of a read or write operation, it verifies that the incoming message is "recent," in the sense that the sender j sent it after j received a message from i that was sent after i began the current phase. Node i uses the phase number to perform this check: if the incoming phase number *pnr* is at least as large as the current operation phase number (*op.pnum*), then process i knows that the message is recent.

If i is currently in a query or propagate phase and the message effectively corresponds to a fresh response from the sender (line 110) then i extends its *op.cmap* record used for its current read and write operations with the *cmap* received from the sender. Next, if there is no gap in the sequence of configurations of the extended *op.cmap*, meaning that *op.cmap* $\in$ *Truncated*, then process i takes notice of the response of j (lines 112 and 113). In contrast, if there is a gap in the sequence of configuration of the extended *op.cmap*, then i infers that it was running a phase using an out-of-date configuration and restarts the current phase by emptying its field *op.acc* and updating its *op.cmap* field (lines 114–116).

Specification 32 RDS_i – Transitions 3

139: **Input recon**$(c, c')_i$
140:   **Effect:**
141:     **if** $\neg failed \wedge status \neq$ idle **then**
142:       let $k = \max(\ell : cmap(\ell) \in C)$
143:       $pxs.conf\text{-}index \leftarrow k + 1$
144:       $pxs.old\text{-}conf \leftarrow c$
145:       $pxs.conf \leftarrow c'$
146:       $pxs.phase \leftarrow$ idle
147:       $pxs.acc \leftarrow \emptyset$
148:       $recon\text{-}in\text{-}progress \leftarrow$ true

149: **Internal init**$_i$
150:   **Precondition:**
151:     $\neg failed \wedge status =$ active
152:     $c = pxs.conf \neq \perp$
153:     $k = pxs.conf\text{-}index \neq \perp$
154:     $cmap(k) = \perp$
155:     $cmap(k\text{-}1) = pxs.old\text{-}conf \neq \perp$
156:     **if** $k > 1$ **then**
157:       $cmap(k - 2) = \pm$
158:     $isLeader \leftarrow$ true
159:   **Effect:**
160:     $pxs.phase \leftarrow$ idle
161:     $pxs.acc \leftarrow \emptyset$
162:     $ballot.conf \leftarrow c$
163:     $ballot.conf\text{-}index \leftarrow k$

164: **Internal prepare**$(b)_i$
165:   **Precondition:**
166:     $\neg failed \wedge status =$ active
167:     $isLeader =$ true
168:     $b = ballot$
169:     $pxs.phase =$ idle
170:   **Effect:**
171:     $pnum1 \leftarrow pnum1 + 1$
172:     $pxs.pnum \leftarrow pnum1$
173:     $pxs.acc \leftarrow \emptyset$
174:     $ballot.i \leftarrow \langle ballot.id.counter + 1, i \rangle$
175:     $pxs.phase \leftarrow$ prepare

176: **Output recon-ack**$(r)_i$
177:   **Precondition:**
178:     $\neg failed \wedge status =$ active
179:     $recon\text{-}in\text{-}progress =$ true
180:     let $k = pxs.conf\text{-}index$
181:     $cmap(k) \in C \vee$
182:       $cmap(k - 2) \neq \pm \vee$
183:       $cmap(k - 1) \neq pxs.old\text{-}conf$
184:     **if** $cmap(k) = pxs.conf$ **then**
185:       $r \leftarrow$ ok
186:     **else** $r \leftarrow$ failed
187:   **Effect:**
188:     $pxs.conf \leftarrow \perp$
189:     $pxs.conf\text{-}index \leftarrow \perp$
190:     $recon\text{-}in\text{-}progress \leftarrow$ false

191: **Internal prepare-done**$(b)_i$
192:   **Precondition:**
193:     $\neg failed \wedge status =$ active
194:     $isLeader \leftarrow$ true
195:     $b = ballot$
196:     $pxs.phase =$ prepare
197:     let $k = ballot.conf\text{-}index$
198:     let $c = cmap(k - 1)$
199:     $c \in C$
200:     $\exists R \in read\text{-}quorum(c) : R \subseteq pxs.acc$
201:   **Effect:**
202:     $pxs.prepared\text{-}id \leftarrow ballot.id$
203:     $pxs.acc \leftarrow \emptyset$
204:     $pxs.phase \leftarrow$ idle

8.3.4   RECONFIGURATION

The pseudocode for reconfiguration appears in Specifications 32 and 33. When a client wants to change the set of replicas, it initiates a reconfiguration, specifying a new configuration. The processes then initiate a consensus protocol, ensuring that everyone agrees on the active configuration, and that there is a total ordering on configurations. The resulting protocol is more complicated than typical consensus, since at the same time, the reconfiguration operation propagates information from the old configuration to the new configuration.

The reconfiguration protocol uses an optimized variant of Paxos. The reconfiguration initialization is presented in Specification 32. The reconfiguration is requested at some process through the recon action. If the requested process is not the leader the request is forwarded to

Specification 33 RDS_i – Transitions 4

205: **Internal init-propose**$(k)_i$
206:    **Precondition:**
207:      $\neg failed \wedge status =$ active
208:      $isLeader \leftarrow$ true
209:      $ballot.conf\text{-}index = k \neq \bot$
210:      $ballot.id = pxs.prepared\text{-}id$
211:      $pxs.conf\text{-}index = ballot.conf\text{-}index$
212:      $pxs.conf = ballot.conf$
213:    **Effect:**
214:      $pxs.phase \leftarrow$ idle
215:      let $S = \{b \in voted\text{-}ballots : b.conf\text{-}index = k\}$
216:      if $S \neq \emptyset$ then
217:        let $b' = b'' : b''.id = \text{argmax}_{b \in S}(b.id)$
218:        $ballot.conf \leftarrow b'.conf$
219:      $voted\text{-}ballots \leftarrow voted\text{-}ballots \cup \{ballot\}$

220: **Internal propose**$(k)_i$
221:    **Precondition:**
222:      $\neg failed \wedge status =$ active
223:      $ballot.conf\text{-}index = k \neq \bot$
224:      $ballot = voted\text{-}ballots$
225:    **Effect:**
226:      $pxs.phase \leftarrow$ propose
227:      $pnum1 \leftarrow pnum1 + 1$
228:      $pxs.pnum \leftarrow pnum1$
229:      $pxs.acc \leftarrow \emptyset$

230: **Internal propagate**$(k)_i$
231:    **Precondition:**
232:      $\neg failed \wedge status =$ active
233:      $k = ballot.conf\text{-}index$
234:      $cmap(k) \in C$
235:    **Effect:**
236:      $pxs.phase \leftarrow$ propagate
237:      $pnum1 \leftarrow pnum1 + 1$
238:      $pxs.pnum \leftarrow pnum1$
239:      $pxs.acc \leftarrow \emptyset$

240: **Internal propose-done**$(k)_i$
241:    **Precondition:**
242:      $\neg failed \wedge status =$ active
243:      $pxs.phase =$ propose
244:      let $k = ballot.conf\text{-}index$
245:      let $c = cmap(k-1)$
246:      $c \in C$
247:      $\exists R_1 \in read\text{-}quorums(c):$
248:        $R_1 \subseteq pxs.acc$
249:        $\exists W_1 \in write\text{-}quorums(c):$
250:        $W_1 \in pxs.acc$
251:    **Effect:**
252:      $pxs.phase \leftarrow$ idle
253:      $cmap(k) \leftarrow ballot.conf$
254:      $pxs.pnum \leftarrow pnum1$
255:      $pxs.acc \leftarrow \emptyset$

256: **Internal propagate-done**$(k)_i$
257:    **Precondition:**
258:      $\neg failed \wedge status =$ active
259:      $pxs.phase =$ propagate
260:      $k = ballot.conf\text{-}index$
261:      let $c = cmap(k-1)$
262:      let $c' = cmap(k)$
263:      $c \in C$
264:      $c' \in C$
265:      $\exists W_2 \in write\text{-}quorums(c):$
266:        $W_2 \subseteq pxs.acc$
267:        $\exists R_2 \in read\text{-}quorums(c):$
268:        $R_2 \in pxs.acc$
269:    **Effect:**
270:      $cmap(k-1) \in \pm$
271:      $pxs.phase \leftarrow$ idle
272:      $pxs.acc \leftarrow \emptyset$

the leader via the generic information exchange. Then, the leader starts the reconfiguration by executing an init event, and the reconfiguration completes by a recon-ack event. More precisely, the recon(c, c') event is executed at some process i starting the reconfiguration aiming to replace configuration c by c'. This event records the reconfiguration information in the *pxs* field, that is, process i records the c and c' in *pxs.old-conf* and *pxs.conf*, respectively. Node i selects the index of its *cmap* that immediately succeeds the index of the latest installed configuration and records it in *pxs.conf-index* as a possible index for c' (Specification 32, line 142). Finally, i starts participating in the reconfiguration by reinitializing its *pxs.acc* field. The leader ℓ sets its reconfiguration information either during a recon event or when it receives this information from another process, as described in Section 8.3.3. The leader executes an init event and starts a new consensus instance to decide upon the kth configuration, only if the *pxs* field is correctly set (e.g., *pxs.old-conf* must be equal to *cmap*($k - 1$)). If so, the *pxs.acc* is emptied, the configuration of this consensus instance is recorded as the ballot configuration with k, its index.

The leader coordinates the reconfiguration, which consists of three phases: a *prepare* phase in which a ballot is made ready (Specification 32), a *propose* phase, in which the new configuration is proposed, and a *propagate* phase, in which the results are distributed.

1. The prepare phase, specified in Specification 32, sets a new ballot identifier larger than any previously seen ballot identifier, accesses a read quorum of the old configuration (Specification 32, line 200), thus learning about any earlier ballots, and associates the largest encountered ballot to this consensus instance. But, if a larger ballot is encountered indicating that the tentatively prepared ballot was actually not the largest, then *pxs.phase* becomes idle (Specification 32, line 119). When the leader concludes the prepare phase, it chooses a configuration to propose through an init-propose event: if no configurations have been proposed to replace the current old configuration, the leader can propose its own preferred configuration; otherwise, the leader must choose the previously proposed configuration with the largest ballot (Specification 33, line 217).

2. The propose phase, specified in Specification 33, then begins by a propose event, accessing both a read and a write quorum of the old configuration (Specification 33, lines 247–250). This serves two purposes:

   - it requires that the processes in the old configuration vote on the new configuration, and

   - it collects information on the tag and value from the old configuration.

3. Finally, the propagate phase, specified in Specification 33, begins by a propagate event and accesses a read and a write quorum from the old configuration (Specification 33, lines 265–268); this ensures that enough processes are aware of the new configuration to ensure that any concurrent reconfiguration requests obtain the desired result.

Optimizations.   There are two optimizations included in the protocol. First, if a process has already prepared a ballot as part of a prior reconfiguration, it can continue to use the same ballot for the new reconfiguration, without redoing the prepare phase. This means that if the same process initiates multiple reconfigurations, only the first reconfiguration has to perform the prepare phase. Second, the propose phase can terminate when *any* process, even if it is not the leader, discovers that an appropriate set of quorums has voted for the new configuration. If all the processes in a quorum send their responses to the propose phase to all the processes in the old configuration, then all the replicas can terminate the propose phase at the same time, immediately sending out propagate messages. Again, when any process receives a propagate response from enough processes, it can terminate the propagate phase. This saves the reconfiguration one message delay. Together, these optimizations mean that when the same process is performing repeated reconfigurations, it only requires three message delays:

1. the leader sending the propose message to the old configuration,

2. the processes in the old configuration sending the responses to the processes in the old configuration, and

3. the processes in the old configuration sending a propagate message to the initiator, which can then terminate the reconfiguration.

8.4   CONSENSUS OF RDS

In this section, we focus on the proof of agreement of RDS. We do not present the proof of atomicity of reads and writes that follows from the same argument as the correctness proof of RAMBO presented in Chapter 7. One distinction though is that RDS features optimal reads while RAMBO does not. The reader can look at Chapter 5 for details on how the confirmed tag optimization of RDS can be exploited in the static model. The proof of validity is straightforward, while termination of consensus requires the assumption that the system stabilizes for long enough for messages to be delivered (without losses).

We show that nodes agree on the active configuration(s). Observe that there is a single default configuration c_0 in the *cmap* field of every node of the system when the algorithm starts, as indicated at line 10 of Specification 29. For index ℓ, we say that the configuration of index ℓ is well-defined if there exists a configuration, *config*, such that for all nodes i, at all points in α, $cmap(\ell)_i$ is either undefined ($\bot$), removed ($\pm$), or equal to *config*. In particular, no other configuration is ever installed in slot ℓ of the *cmap*. We first show, inductively, that configuration ℓ is well-defined for all ℓ.

Theorem 8.1   *For any execution α, for all ℓ, for any $i, j \in I$, if $cmap(\ell)_i$, $cmap(\ell)_j \in C$ then $cmap(\ell)_i = cmap(\ell)_j$ at any point in α.*

Proof sketch.   First, initially $cmap(0)_i = cmap(0)_j = c_0$ for any $i, j \in I$, by definition. We proceed by induction: assume that for all $\ell' \leq \ell$, $cmap(\ell')_i = cmap(\ell')_j$ (so that we can omit the index i and j and denote this by $cmap(\ell')$). We show that $cmap(\ell)_i = cmap(\ell)_j$. Assume, by contradiction, that there exist two propose-done(ℓ) events, ρ_1 and ρ_2 at nodes i and j, respectively, that install two different configurations in slot ℓ of i and j's *cmap* in Specification 30, line 253. Let $b = ballot_i$ immediately after ρ_1 occurs and $b' = ballot_j$ immediately after ρ_2 occurs. The ballot when the two operations complete must refer to different configurations: $b.conf \neq b'.conf$. Without loss of generality, assume that $b.id < b'.id$. (Ballot identifiers are uniquely associated with configurations, so the two ballots cannot have the same identifier.) At some point, a *prepare(b')* action must have occurred at some node—we say in this case that ballot b' has been prepared.

1. Consider the case where b' was prepared as part of a recon operation installing configuration ℓ. Let R be a read-quorum of configuration $cmap(\ell - 1)$ accessed by the prepare-done

of ballot b', and let W_1 be a write-quorum of $cmap(\ell - 1)$ accessed by the propose-done associated with b. Since $cmap(\ell - 1)_i = cmap(\ell - 1)_j$ for any $i, j \in I$ by the inductive hypothesis, there is some node $i' \in R \cap W_1$. There are two sub-cases to consider: i' processed either the prepare first or the propose first.

- If i' processed the prepare first, then the propose would have been aware of ballot b', and hence the ballot identifier at the end of the proposal could have been no smaller than $b'.id$, contradicting the assumption that $b.id < b'.id$.

- Otherwise, if i' processed the propose first, then ballot b ends up in $voted\text{-}ballots'_i$, and eventually in $voted\text{-}ballots_j$. This ensures that j proposes the same configuration as i, again contradicting our assumption that ρ_1 and ρ_2 result in differing configurations for ℓ.

2. Consider the case, then, where b' was prepared as part of a recon operation installing a configuration $\ell' \leq \ell$. In this case, we can show that $b.id \geq b'.id$, contradicting our assumption. In particular, some recon for ℓ' must terminate prior to the ρ_1 and ρ_2 beginning reconfiguration for ℓ. By examining the quorum intersections, we know that the identifier associated with ballot b' must have been passed to the propose for this recon for ℓ', and from there to the propose of a recon for $\ell' + 1$, and so on, until it reaches the propose for ρ_1, leading to the contradiction.

We can therefore conclude that if two reconfigurations complete for configuration ℓ, then they must both install the same configuration, and hence $cmap(\ell - 1)_i = cmap(\ell - 1)_j$ for any $i, j \in I$. □

8.5 CONDITIONAL PERFORMANCE ANALYSIS

In this section, we analyze the performance of the reconfiguration of RDS. To ensure progress of the algorithm we make a series of assumptions about the network delays, the connectivity, and the failure patterns.

In a nutshell, assuming that eventually the network stabilizes at time τ and delivers messages with a delay of d, we show that the algorithm stabilizes within $e + 2d$ after τ, where e is the time required for new nodes to fully join the system and notify old nodes about their existence. We also show that after the algorithm stabilizes, reconfiguration completes in $5d$ time; if a single node performs repeated reconfigurations, then after the first, each subsequent reconfiguration completes in $3d$ time, reads and writes complete in $8d$ time, reads complete in $4d$ time if there is no interference from ongoing writes, and in $2d$ if no reconfiguration is pending.

Assumptions. We assume that at time τ the following hold: (i) all local clocks progress at the same rate; (ii) messages are not lost and are received in at most d time, where d is a constant unknown to the algorithm; (iii) nodes respond to protocol messages as soon as they receive them and they broadcast messages every d time to all service participants; and (iv) all enabled actions are processed with zero time passing on the local clock.

For a reconfiguration to complete, we assume that at least one quorum does not fail prior to a reconfiguration replacing it. We thus assume *configuration-viability*: at least one read quorum and one write quorum from each installed configuration do not fail for $4d$ time after (i) the network stabilizes, which occurs at time τ, and (ii) a following successful reconfiguration operation completes.

We also place some restrictions on reconfiguration. We assume *recon-readiness*: each node in a new configuration has completed the joining protocol at least time e prior to the configuration being proposed, for a fixed constant e. We also assume *recon-spacing*: that for any k, the propose-done(k) events and the propose-done($k + 1$) are at least $5d$ time apart.

Finally, after stabilization, we assume that nodes, once they have joined, learn about each other quickly, within time e. We refer to this as *join-connectivity*. A leader election service informs a node that it is currently the leader through a leader action. We assume that, at time $\tau + e$, this leader election service chooses a single leader ℓ and that ℓ remains active (i) until the next leader is chosen and (ii) for a sufficiently long time for a reconfiguration to complete.

Bounding reconfiguration and read and write operations latency.   First, we show that reconfiguration attempts complete, after the system stabilizes, within three message delays in some executions but always within at most five message delays. In particular, now that the reconfiguration is intergrated, the reconfiguration completion guarantees both the installation of a new configuration and the garbage collection of old configurations.

Theorem 8.2   *Assume that ℓ starts the reconfiguration process, initiated by recon(c, c'), at time $t \geq \tau + e + 2d$. Then the corresponding reconfiguration completes no later than $t + 5d$.*

In addition, if ℓ successfully conducted the last reconfiguration to c', then the next reconfiguration from c' to c'', initiated by ℓ at time $t' > t + 5d$, completes at the latest at time $t' + 3d$.

Proof.   First, if the init(c)$_\ell$ occurs at time t then the prepare phase ends by $t + 2d$. By *join-connectivity* and *recon-readiness*, ℓ sends to the members of the current configuration and receive responses no later than time $t + 2d$. Second, the propose phase ends before time $t + 4d$ because it starts with no time passing and the members of the configuration sends a message no later than $t + 3d$ that is received by $t + 4d$. Third, the propose phase ends no later than time $t + 5d$ because propagate(k) occurs at all these nodes at time $t + 4d$ and their messages are exchanged no later than time $t + 5d$.

Finally, if ℓ successfully conducted the last reconfiguration and initiates a new reconfiguration at time $t' > t + 5d$, then the prepare phase of the reconfiguration can be skipped. Since the propose phase takes $2d$ and the propagation phase takes d time, the reconfiguration completes by time $t' + 3d$.   □

Second, we show the bounds on the duration of read and write operations. In particular, we show that after the system stabilizes, read operations complete within two message delays in some executions and that all operations complete within eight message delays.

Theorem 8.3   *Consider a read operation that starts at node i at time t and denote t' by $max(t, \tau + e + 2d)$.*

1. *If no write propagation is pending at any node and no reconfiguration is ongoing, then it completes at the latest at time $t' + 2d$.*

2. *If no write propagation is pending, then it completes no later than time $t' + 8d$.*

Consider a write operation that starts at node i at time t. Then it completes at the latest at time $t' + 8d$.

Proof. When a read$_i$ or write$_i$ event occurs at time t', the phase is set to query. Let c be the last configuration at time $t' - d$. Because of *configuration-viability*, the members of c are active during the reconfiguration. Moreover, because of *join-connectivity* and since join-ack$_j$ occurs prior to time $t' - e - d$, we know that j is connected to members of c at time t' and j knows about this configuration. The phase takes at least two message delays but if a reconfiguration is concurrent, then j might learn about a new configuration and the phase might be delayed an additional $2d$ time since j has now to contact a quorum of the new configuration and the phase completes at the latest at time $t' + 2d$ without concurrent configuration and at the latest at time $t' + 4d$.

The current *phase$_i$* becomes prop no later than time $t' + 4d$. If the operation is a write, then a new *tag$_i$* is set that does not belong to the exchanged *confirmed* tags set yet. If the operation is a read, the *tag$_i$* is the highest received one. This tag was maintained by a member of the read quorum queried, and it was confirmed only if the phase that propagated it to this member has completed.

From this point on, if the tag appears not to be confirmed to i, then in any operation the propagation phase fix-point has to be reached. The propagation phase fix-point is reached in at most $4d$ time and any operation terminates at the latest at time $t' + 8d$.

But, if the tag is already confirmed and i learns it (either by receiving a confirmed set containing it or by having propagated it itself) then the read operation can terminate directly by executing a read-ack$_i$ event without any time passing, after a single phase, which occurs prior to time $t' + 4d$ and at time $t' + 2d$ if no reconfiguration is concurrent. □

8.6   BIBLIOGRAPHIC NOTES

Consensus is a fundamental problem of distributed computing [100], known to be unsolvable in an asynchronous system in the presence of failures [38]. Lamport's Paxos algorithm first appeared in a technical report [72], and published several years later [73]. Chandra and Toueg presented the weakest failure detector to solve consensus with crash failures [23]. Paxos was later deconstructed into a round-based register, a round-based consensus and a weak leader election [16], and using read-modify-write objects [25]. Several Paxos optimizations similar to the one RDS exploits were mentioned in the literature [17, 74, 79]. The viewstamped replication method was concomitantly proposed to solve the same problem [97]. Paxos differs from the viewstamped replication in that its leader is simply used to coordinate distributed processes that all decide as if they were actively replicating, whereas in viewstamped replication its leader (or primary) decides and other processes replicate passively the decision.

The first full-fledged integration of Paxos in RAMBO is RAMBO III [50]. RDS, presented in this chapter, optimizes RAMBO III in multiple ways. First, it integrates existing Paxos optimizations presented in Cheap Paxos [78] and Fast Paxos [75, 76] to reach consensus in three messages delays, which is optimal [24].

Second, it reuses the confirmation optimization of GeoQuorums [30] to allow for optimal atomic read operations [34] that terminate after two message delays instead of the original read operations that terminate after four message delays.

The resulting RDS protocol was shown theoretically efficient to reconfigure a distributed storage in only three message delays [24]. RDS inspired other algorithms such as DSR that maintains the virtual synchrony property [14] and found applications in dynamic read/write storage [15], collaborative telemedicine [32], and software upgrade [53].

In recent years, Paxos experienced an important research interest among the distributed system community: LinkedIn and IBM exploited Paxos to implement a distributed key-value store [101], Google used it to implement a distributed locking service and databases [8, 26]. There are so many variants of Paxos that we could not cite all of them without possible omissions, but most use a traditional majority quorum system.

An interesting area of research is reconfigurable State Machine Replication (SMR) [77]. An SMR protocol that exploits a consensus protocol similar to Paxos is the viewstamped replication [97]. In contrast with SMR, RDS does not totally order all commands with respect to each other but rather distinguishes read/write operation requests from reconfiguration requests, hence totally ordering only reconfigurations with each other. This optimization allows RDS to ensure the independence of read/write operations from reconfigurations so that the termination of a read or a write operation does not depend on the termination of any reconfiguration.

Yahoo! developed Zookeeper [62, 66], an SMR protocol for managing a cluster of distributed machines based on primary-backup [67] similar to the viewstamped replication algorithm. It was later extended with a reconfiguration service also relying on the primary to decide on a new configuration [105]. A recent simplifying alternative to Paxos, called Raft, attracted lots of attention at it was implemented in various languages [98]. Raft shares the viewstamped replication model of Zookeeper and proposes a reconfiguration for cluster membership changes. During reconfiguration, Raft may use a "joint consensus" configuration that results from the union of the two configurations that are both active, similarly to the way RDS may transiently use two configurations in the course of a reconfiguration. A significant difference is that Raft requires a stronger leader than Paxos, whose reconfiguration may transiently disrupt the service [53], however, Raft is generally simpler to understand and implement [98].

CHAPTER 9

DynaStore: Incremental Reconfigurations

In this chapter we present a different approach to implementing reconfiguration, where changes to a configuration are done incrementally, adding and removing individual nodes, instead of replacing the entire configuration as presented in the previous two chapters. The algorithm, called DynaStore, implements a dynamic atomic memory service for multi-writer/multi-reader objects with such an incremental changes to the configuration. DynaStore, as earlier implementations, builds on the ABD algorithm approach in its read and write operations, and its incremental reconfiguration is accomplished without the use of consensus.

Here the participants start with a default local configuration, that is, some common set of replica hosts. The algorithm supports three kinds of operations: *read*, *write*, and *reconfig*. The read and write operations involve two phases, and in the absence of reconfigurations, the protocol is similar to ABD: it uses majorities of replicas, where each replica maintains the value of the object and the associated tag.

If a participant wishes to introduce a configuration change, it uses the *reconfig* operation and supplies with it a set of incremental changes with elements of the form $\langle +, i \rangle$, indicating the addition of replica host i, and $\langle -, j \rangle$, indicating the removal of host j. The implementation of *reconfig* consists of two phases (described in more detail later) and uses a distributed *weak snapshot* service to announce the locally-originating changes by means of the *update* primitive, and obtain the changes submitted by other members of the configuration by means of the *scan* primitive. The snapshot itself is not atomic as it does not globally order updates, and because *scan* is not guaranteed to reflect all previously completed updates. Yet, the snapshot service is sufficient for establishing a certain directed acyclic graph (DAG) that is stored locally as part of the state of each participant. Vertices of the graph correspond to configurations that can be produced by means of *changes* that in turn correspond to the edges.

The implementation of *reconfig* involves traversals of such DAG's, representing possible sequences of changed configurations. In each traversal the DAG may be revised to reflect multiple changes, submitted at different hosts, to the same configuration. The assumption that a majority of the involved hosts are not removed and do not crash ensures that there is a path through the DAG that is guaranteed to be common among all hosts. Interestingly, the hosts themselves do not learn of this common path, however, traversing all paths ensures that the common path is also traversed. The traversal terminates when a sink node is reached. An additional assumption

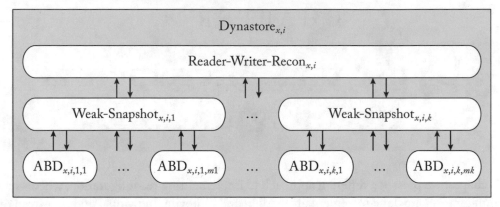

Figure 9.1: The architecture of DynaStore for object x at process i comprising the *Reader-Writer-Recon* automaton, the *WeakSnapshot* automata, and the ABD register automata; communication *Ch* automata between the DynaStores of two processes have been omitted for simplicity with k configurations and m_i members in configuration i.

that there is a finite number of configuration changes ensures termination of read and write operations.

The architecture of DynaStore at a process i and for a given object x is depicted in Figure 9.1. In a nutshell, DynaStore comprises of an integrated *Reader-Writer-Recon* automaton that interacts with as many *WeakSnapshot* automata as the number of configurations (i.e., vertices) on the DAG. We fix the number of configurations in the DAG to k for simplicity in the presentation. Each of these k *WeakSnapshot* automata interacts with $|\mathcal{I}|$ SWMR atomic registers, one per process. The implementation of such a register in a distributed system is denoted $ABD_{x,i,k,n}$ and it is given in Specification 2. Next, we proceed with the *WeakSnapshot* and the *Reader-Writer-Recon* algorithms.

9.1   PRELIMINARIES

One main distinction from previous algorithms is that DynaStore does not involve the use of consensus in order for a set of concurrent *reconfig* operations to agree on the next configuration in the system. Instead, *reconfig* operations may concurrently propose *incremental* changes on the membership of replica hosts (either by adding or removing hosts), and each process maintains a local *estimate* (possibly different from other processes) of the current configuration in the system. Those local estimates eventually converge to a single configuration when no new configurations are proposed for a sufficiently long time. Therefore, this new approach allows, on one hand, a *reconfig* operation to terminate without any synchrony assumptions on the underlying communication medium (as opposed to consensus need for partial synchrony); on the other hand, a reconfig can terminate only when it is concurrent with a finite number of other reconfigurations and thus eventually reach a merged configuration.

9.1.1 INCREMENTAL RECONFIGURATION

DynaStore allows its participants to add members to and remove from an existing configuration. We assume a non-empty initial configuration that is known to every process $i \in \mathcal{I}$. We first define of *configuration changes*, or simply changes.

Definition 9.1 Change. A *configuration change* (or simply *change*) *chg* is a tuple from the set $chg \in \{+, -\} \times \mathcal{I}$.

Here a change $\langle +, i \rangle$ denotes the addition of process i, and a change $\langle -, j \rangle$ denotes the removal of process j. Using changes we can define configurations (or *views* as used by DynaStore).

Definition 9.2 Views. A *view* (or *configuration*) c is a set of changes, such that $c \subseteq \{+, -\} \times \mathcal{I}$.

We assume that all the processes start with an initial configuration c_0. An *incremental reconfiguration* operation takes as a parameter a set of changes. Changes are used during reconfigurations, to add/remove processes to/from the service. We say that a change *chg* is *proposed* in an execution if a reconfig(c) action occurs at some process i, such that $chg \in c$.

9.1.2 ACTIVITY OF PROCESSES

We assume that any value written on the atomic object of DynaStore is unique (this is solely for simplicity). For an execution ξ of DynaStore, we introduce the notion of active processes that is a refinement of the notion of correct processes used previously.

Definition 9.3 Active Process. A process i is *active* in an execution ξ if the following properties hold:

- process i is correct in ξ (does not fail), i.e., ξ does not contain a fail step for i,

- ξ contains a reconfig(c) action such that $\langle +, i \rangle \in c$ or $\langle +, i \rangle \in c_0$, and

- ξ does not contain any reconfig(c') action such that $\langle -, i \rangle \in c'$.

In other words, a process i is active in an execution, if i is correct, it is added by a reconfiguration operation, and is not removed by any reconfiguration. Any active process is assumed to take infinitely many steps.

For a set of changes c we define the *removal-set* of c as the set $c.remove = \{i \,|\, \langle -, i \rangle \in c\}$. Similarly the *join-set* of c is the set $c.join = \{i \,|\, \langle +, i \rangle \in c\}$. Using those two sets we can determine the *members* of c, such that $c.members = c.join \setminus c.remove$. Note that node removals are permanent, and hence a process i that is removed can never be a member again. In practical terms, this requirement can be relaxed by letting processes re-enter the service with a new identifier.

9.1.3   MAJORITY ASSUMPTION

At a high level, to guarantee the termination of any *read/write/reconfig* operation, and thus liveness of the service, DynaStore assumes that a majority of processes in any future pending configuration remains correct and are not proposed for removal.

Let us consider an execution ξ of DynaStore. For a given state σ in ξ, we refer to ξ_σ as the execution fragment that starts with the first state of ξ, say σ_0, and ends with σ. We now define the following notation: (i) $V(\sigma)$ denotes the union of all configurations c such that the response step of reconfig(c) appears in ξ_σ; (ii) $P(\sigma)$ denotes the union of all configurations c' such that reconfig(c') is invoked in ξ_σ but has not yet completed; and (iii) $F(\sigma)$ denotes the set of all processes that fail in ξ_σ. Liveness of the service can be defined as follows.

Definition 9.4   Service Liveness (termination). If at each state σ of an execution ξ of *DynaStore*, we have $|F(\sigma) \cup P(\sigma).remove| < |V(\sigma).members|/2$, then every *read/write/reconfig* operation invoked in ξ eventually completes.

In DynaStore, processes can concurrently propose changes to an existing configuration without requiring agreement, these multiple incremental changes are executed concurrently without being totally ordered. These changes can be represented as a DAG (directed acyclic graph), where vertices represent configurations and edges represent a partial order defined by the changes. An example is depicted in Figure 9.2. The advantage of the total order is to easily identify the current configuration of the system as the latest one. With the partial order, one can reconstruct the current configuration of the system, but vertices of the DAG need to be traversed first. To this end, DynaStore executes a breadth-first search traversal that is detailed in Section 9.3.1.

9.2   THE WEAK SNAPSHOT AUTOMATON

Given a current configuration c, DynaStore does not require that participants agree on a single configuration to replace c as in earlier approaches. Instead, DynaStore guarantees that among all candidate configurations to replace c, there exist at least one configuration in common among all these participants. To this end, DynaStore maps each configuration c to a weak snapshot object that maintains the information about the set of possible configurations to replace c. In short, the

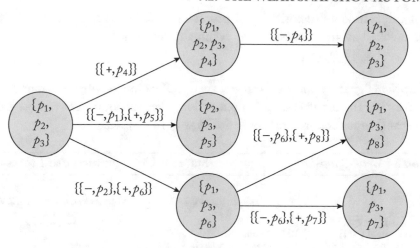

Figure 9.2: An example of partially ordered configurations, represented as a directed acyclic graph (DAG) whose vertices are configurations and edges are incremental changes, where the initial configuration is the set of processes $\{p_1, p_2, p_3\}$ and whose current global configuration $\{p_3, p_5, p_7, p_8\}$ can be deduced by traversing all incremental changes.

weak snapshot object exports operations update(chg), to propose a change chg to configuration c, and scan() to retrieve a set of changes applied to configuration c.

A weak snapshot object maintains the current state of a configuration by allowing processes to update a configuration change in a single-writer/multiple-reader (SWMR) register and to scan all SWMR registers to obtain the current set of configuration changes.

Definition 9.5   Weak Snapshot Object.   The weak snapshot object guarantees the five following properties.

1. Integrity: Let π be a scan action that returns $chgs$. For each $change \in chgs$, an update($change$)$_j$ is invoked by some process $j \in \mathcal{I}$ prior to the completion of π.

2. Validity: Let π be a scan operation that is invoked after the completion of an update($change$)$_j$ action where $change \neq \bot$. The set of changes $chgs$ returned by scan is non-empty.

3. Monotonicity of scan: Let π, π' be two scan operations that return $chgs$ and $chgs'$, respectively, such that π' is invoked after π completes. The set of changes returned by π is included in the set of changes returned by π', i.e., $chgs \subseteq chgs'$.

4. Non-empty intersection: There exists some $change$ such that for every scan operation that returns $chgs \neq \bot$, $change \in chgs$.

5. Termination: If some majority M of processes in $\mathcal{I}$ does not crash then every *scan* and *update* invoked by any process $i \in M$ eventually completes.

The *WeakSnapshot* signature and states are give in Specification 34 while its transitions are given in Specification 35. The update(*change*) input action takes the argument *change* $\in \{+, -\} \times \mathcal{I}$, whereas the scan() input action returns a set of *chgs* $\subseteq \{+, -\} \times \mathcal{I}$.

Specification 34 *Weak-Snapshot$_{i,c}$* – Signature/State for Configuration c at Process i

---

1: **Signature:**	8: write-ack()$_{i,c}$, $i \in I$	14: read$_{i,c,j}$, $i,j \in I, c \in C$
2: **Input:**	9: fail$_i$, $i \in I$	15: write(v)$_{i,c,j}$, $i,j \in I, c \in C$,
3: scan$_{i,c}$, $i \in I, c \in C$		16: $v \in \{+, -\} \times I$
4: update(*change*)$_{i,c}$, $i \in I$,	10: **Output:**	
5: $c \in C$, *change* $\in \{+, -\} \times I$	11: scan-ack(*changes*)$_{i,c}$, , $i \in I$,	17: **Internal:**
6: read-ack(val)$_{i,c}$, $i \in I$,	12: $c \in C$, *change* $\in \{+, -\} \times I$	18: collect-fix$_{i,c}$, $i \in I, c \in C$
7: $c \in C, v \in \{+, -\} \times I$	13: update-ack$_{i,c}$, $i \in I, c \in C$	19: recollect-fix$_{i,c}$, $i \in I, c \in C$

20: **State:**	25: *rcvd* $\subseteq$ *c.members*, received ids, initially $\emptyset$	
21: *chgs* $\subseteq \{+, -\} \times I$, set of collected changes,		
22: initially $\emptyset$	26: *phase* $\in \{$scan-collect, recollect, scan-fix,	
23: *upd-chg* $\subseteq \{+, -\} \times I$, the update change,	27: upd-collect, upd-write, upd-ack, idle$\}$, initially idle	
24: initially $\emptyset$	28: *op-type* $\in \{$read, write$\}$, initially read, initially read	

Auxiliary service: interface. Finally, we define a third kind of automata, called *Interface$_i$*, for each process i, that is omitted here for the sake of simplicity of the presentation. It has: (a) read()$_{i,c,j}$ and write(*message*)$_{i,c,j}$ input actions, and read-ack(*message*)$_{i,c,j}$ and write-ack()$_{i,c,j}$ output actions that interact with the *WeakSnapshot* automaton; (b) send(*message*)$_{i,j}$ output action and recv(*message*)$_{i,j}$ input action that interact with the underlying communication channel automata; and (c) read()$_i$ and write(*message*)$_i$ output actions, and read-ack(*message*)$_i$ and write-ack()$_i$ input actions that interact with the ABD$_{i,c,j}$ automaton (see Figure 9.1 and Section 4.1).

Once an input action read()$_{i,c,j}$ is received from the *WeakSnapshot$_i$*, *Interface$_i$* sends a message to process j's *Interface$_j$* automaton through the channel $Ch_{i,j}$ with output action send(*message*)$_{i,j}$. The corresponding recv(*message*)$_{j,i}$ input action enables the precondition for *Interface$_j$* to read()$_j$ from ABD$_{j,i,c}$. The read-ack(*message*)$_j$ input action at *Interface$_j$* resulting from the output of ABD$_{j,i,c}$ disables the same precondition and enables the sending of the response of the read/write operation through the $Ch_{i,j}$ automaton to *Interface$_i$*. The reception of the response by *Interface$_i$* enables its read-ack(*message*)$_i$ output action that triggers the corresponding input action of the *WeakSnapshot$_i$* automaton. The write(*message*)$_{i,j,c}$ action of *WeakSnapshot$_i$* proceeds similarly across *WeakSnapshot$_j$*, $Ch_{i,j}$, and ABD$_{j,i,c}$ to result into the write-ack()$_i$ at *WeakSnapshot$_i$*.

Specification 35 *Weak-Snapshot$_{i,c}$* – Transitions for Configuration c at Process i

29: **Transitions:**
30:   **Input scan()$_{i,c}$**
31:     **Effect:**
32:       **if** $\neg$*failed* $\wedge$ *status* = active **then**
33:         *chgs* $\leftarrow \emptyset$
34:         *phase* $\leftarrow$ scan-collect
                            // read others' register

35:   **Internal collect-fix()$_{i,c}$**
36:     **Precondition:**
37:       $\neg$*failed* $\wedge$ *status* = active
38:       *phase* $\in$ {scan-collect, upd-collect}
39:       *c.members* $\subseteq$ *rcvd*
                            // collecting from all
40:     **Effect:**
41:       *op-type* $\leftarrow$ read
42:       *rcvd* $\leftarrow \emptyset$
43:       **if** *chgs* $\neq \emptyset$ **then**
                            // some changes were collected
44:         **if** *phase* = upd-collect **then**
45:           *phase* $\leftarrow$ upd-ack
46:         **if** *phase* = scan-collect **then**
47:           *phase* $\leftarrow$ recollect
48:       **else**
49:         **if** *phase* = upd-collect **then**
50:           *phase* $\leftarrow$ upd-write
51:           *op-type* $\leftarrow$ write
52:         **if** *phase* = scan-collect **then**
53:           *phase* = scan-fix

54:   **Internal recollect-fix()$_{i,c}$**
55:     **Precondition:**
56:       $\neg$*failed* $\wedge$ *status* = active
57:       *phase* = recollect
58:       *c.members* $\subseteq$ *rcvd*
59:     **Effect:**
60:       *phase* = scan-fix
61:       *rcvd* $\leftarrow \emptyset$

62:   **Output scan-ack(*changes*)$_{i,c}$**
63:     **Precondition:**
64:       $\neg$*failed* $\wedge$ *status* = active
65:       *phase* = scan-fix
66:       *changes* = *chgs*
67:     **Effect:**

68:       *phase* = idle
69:   **Input update(*change*)$_{i,c}$**
70:     **Effect:**
71:       **if** $\neg$*failed* $\wedge$ *status* = active **then**
72:         *op-type* $\leftarrow$ read
73:         *upd-chg* $\leftarrow$ *change*
74:         *rcvd* $\leftarrow \emptyset$
75:         *phase* $\leftarrow$ upd-collect

76:   **Output read()$_{i,c,j}$**
77:     **Precondition:**
78:       $\neg$*failed* $\wedge$ *status* = active
79:       *phase* $\in$ {scan-collect, recollect, upd-collect}
80:       *op-type* = read
81:       $j \in$ *c.members*
                            // read the register of all j of c
82:     **Effect:** none

83:   **Input read-ack(*v*)$_{i,c,j}$**
84:     **Effect:**
85:       **if** $\neg$*failed* $\wedge$ *status* = active **then**
86:         *rcvd* $\leftarrow$ *rcvd* $\cup \{j\}$
87:         *chgs* $\leftarrow$ *chgs* $\cup \{v\}$

88:   **Output write(*v*)$_{i,j,c}$**
89:     **Precondition:**
90:       $\neg$*failed* $\wedge$ *status* = active
91:       *phase* = upd-write
92:       *op-type* = write
93:       v = *upd-chg*
94:       $j = i$ *// write to the local register*
95:     **Effect:** none

96:   **Input write-ack()$_{i,c}$**
97:     **Effect:**
98:       **if** $\neg$*failed* $\wedge$ *status* = active **then**
99:         *phase* $\leftarrow$ upd-ack

100:   **Output update-ack()$_{i,c}$**
101:     **Precondition:**
102:       $\neg$*failed* $\wedge$ *status* = active
103:       *phase* = upd-ack
104:     **Effect:**
105:       *phase* $\leftarrow$ idle
106:       *upd-chg* $\leftarrow \bot$

Correctness of Weak Snapshot   Lemma 9.6   *The Weak-Snapshot automaton implements a weak snapshot object.*

Proof sketch. The integrity property follows from the initial emptiness of the registers (as we saw at line 15 of Specification 2 in Chapter 4) and that a *change* can only be recorded during an update action because this is the only action to enable a write to a register (line 50 of Specification 35). The validity follows from that any register to which an update records its *change* is necessarily read by a subsequent scan (cf. line 58 of Specification 35). The monotonicity of scan follows from that an update writes to a register only if no change was previously recorded on the same register (line 43 of Specification 35) and that any register from which a scan reads some *change* is necessarily read by a subsequent scan (cf. line 58 of Specification 35). The non-empty intersection property follows from the two collect phases of a scan returning some changes. As each collect reads all ABD registers (of the corresponding view) by consulting and propagating to a majority of processes (cf. Section 5.1 for further details), even among two concurrent scans (of the same view) one propagates its change to a majority of processes in its first collect before the other one consults from another majority (and observe necessarily the same change) during its second consultation. Termination follows from the fact that ABD's read and write actions return if a majority of processes are correct.   □

Specification 36 Dynastore *Reader-Writer-Recon$_i$*: Signature and State

---

1: **Signature:**
2:    **Input:**
3:      read$_i$, $i \in I$
4:      write$(v)_i$, $i \in I$, $v \in V$
5:      reconfig$(c)_i$, $i \in I$, $c \subset$
6:        $\{+,-\} \times I$
7:      recv$(m)_{j,i}$, $m \in Msgs$, $j,i \in I$
8:      scan-ack$(changes)_i$, $i \in I$,
9:        $changes \subset \{+,-\} \times I$
10:     update-w-ack$()_i$, $i \in I$
11:     fail$_i$, $i \in I$

12:   **Output:**
13:     read-ack$(v)_i$, $v \in V$, $i \in I$
14:     write-ack$_i$, $i \in I$
15:     recon-ack$_i$, $i \in I$
16:     send$(m)_{i,j}$, $m \in Msgs$, $i,j \in I$
17:     scan$()_{i,w}$, $i \in I$, $w \in C$
18:     update$(d)_{i,w}$, $d \subseteq$
19:       $\{+,-\} \times I$, $i \in I$, $w \in C$

20:   **Internal:**

21:     init$_i$
22:     traverse$_i$
23:     breadth-first-search$_i$
24:     set-desired-view$_i$
25:     propagate$_i$
26:     traverse-fix$_i$
27:     write-in-view$_i$
28:     contactq$_i$
29:     contactq-fix$_i$
30:     notifyq-fix$_i$

31: **State:**
32:    $value \in V \cup \{\bot\}$, initially $\bot$
33:    $tag \in T$, a tag containing
34:      $timestamp \in \mathbb{N}$, initially 0
35:      $id \in I$, initially i
36:    $maxV \in V \cup \{\bot\}$, initially $\bot$
37:    $maxTag \in T$, initially $(0, i)$
38:    $curview \subseteq \{+,-\} \times I$, initially $InitView$
39:    $desiredview \subseteq \{+,-\} \times I$, initially $InitView$
40:    $replySet \subseteq I \times \mathbb{N}$, initially $\emptyset$
41:    $acc \subset I \times M$, initially $\emptyset$
42:    $changesets \subseteq \{+,-\} \times I$, initially $\emptyset$

43:    $newconfig \subseteq \{+,-\} \times I$, initially $\emptyset$

44:    $pnum \in \mathbb{N}$, initially 0
45:    $op\text{-}type \in \{\text{read, write, reconfig}\}$, initially $\bot$
46:    $status \in \{\text{idle, active}\}$, initially idle
47:    $stage \in \{\text{idle, traverse, traverse-rec1, traverse-rec2,}$
48:      $\text{traverse-fix, pick-new-ts, update,}$
49:      $\text{update-done, scan, scan-done,}$
50:      $\text{contactq-start, contactq, notifyq, notifyq-done}\}$
51:      initially idle
52:    $phase \in \{\text{query, propagate}\}$, initially query
53:    $failed \in \{\text{true, false}\}$, initially false

9.3   THE READER-WRITER-RECON AUTOMATON

The *Reader-Writer-Recon* automaton specifies the client level actions of DynaStore. The signature of the *Reader-Writer-Recon* automaton is given in Specification 36 and its transitions are given in Specifications 37, 38, and 39. In particular, the signature of automaton *Reader-Writer-Recon* incorporates the external signature of DynaStore, namely the read, write and reconfig actions. DynaStore exports a multi-writer/multi-reader service through actions read

Specification 37 Dynastore *Reader-Writer-Recon$_i$*: Transitions 1

```
 1:   Internal init_i
 2:     Precondition:
 3:        ¬failed ∧ status = active
 4:        i ∈ InitView.members
 5:     Effect:
 6:        status ← active

 7:   Input fail_i
 8:     Effect:
 9:        failed ← true

10:   Input read_i
11:     Effect:
12:        if ¬failed ∧ status = active then
13:           op-type ← read
14:           newconfig ← ∅
15:           stage ← traverse

16:   Output read-ack(v)_i
17:     Precondition:
18:        ¬failed ∧ status = active
19:        op-type = read
20:        stage = notifyq-done
21:        v = maxV
22:     Effect:
23:        stage ← idle

24:   Input write(v)_i
25:     Effect:
26:        if ¬failed ∧ status = active then
27:           value ← v
28:           op-type ← write
29:           newconfig ← ∅
30:           stage ← traverse

31:   Output write-ack_i
32:     Precondition:
33:        ¬failed ∧ status = active
34:        op-type = write
35:        stage = notifyq-done
36:     Effect:
37:        stage ← idle

38:   Input reconfig(c)_i
39:     Effect:
40:        if ¬failed ∧ status = active then
41:           op-type ← recon
42:           newconfig ← c
43:           stage ← traverse

44:   Output recon-ack()_i
45:     Precondition:
46:        ¬failed ∧ status = active
47:        op-type = reconfig
48:        stage = notifyq-done
49:     Effect:
```

```
50:        stage ← idle

51:   Output send(⟨mtype, ph, view, pn, v, t⟩)_{i,j}
52:     Precondition:
53:        ¬failed ∧ status = active
54:        [stage = contactq ∧ j ∈ w.members ∧
55:         ⟨mtype, ph, view, pn, v, t⟩ =
56:         ⟨ REQUEST, phase, ⊥, pnum, maxV, maxTag⟩]
57:                      // send read/write request
58:        [⟨j, num⟩ ∈ replySet ∧
59:         ⟨mtype, ph, view, pn, v, t⟩ =
60:         ⟨ REPLY, ⊥, ⊥, num, value, tag⟩]
61:                      // reply to read/write request
62:        [notify-v ∈ notifySet ∧ j ∈ notify-v.members ∧
63:         ⟨mtype, ph, view, pn, v, t⟩ =
64:         ⟨ NOTIFY, ⊥, notify-v, ⊥, ⊥, ⊥⟩]
65:                      // send notify for a view
66:     Effect:
67:        None

68:   Input recv(⟨mtype, ph, view, pn, v, t⟩)_{j,i}
69:     Effect:
70:        if ¬failed ∧ status = active then
71:           if mtype = REPLY then
72:              acc ← acc ∪ {j, ⟨mtype, ph, pn, v, t⟩}
73:           if mtype = REQUEST then
74:              if ph = propagate ∧ t > tag then
75:                 (value, tag) ← (v, t)
76:              replySet ← replySet ∪ {⟨j, pn⟩}
77:           if mtype = NOTIFY then
78:              if stage = notifyq then
79:                      // collect the replies
80:                 rcvd-notify ← rcvd-notify ∪ {⟨j, view⟩}
81:              else
82:                      // received notify while stage ≠ notifyq
82:                 if view ∉ notifySet then
83:
84:                      // add the view the first time we receive it
84:                    notifySet ← notifySet ∪ {view}
85:                    if curView ⊂ view then
86:                       curView ← view
87:                       if i ∈ view.join then
88:                          status ← active
89:                          stage ← traverse
90:                                        // restart traverse

91:   Internal notifyq-fix_i
92:     Precondition:
93:        ¬failed ∧ status = active
94:        stage = notifyq
95:        rcvdP = {j : ⟨j, curview⟩ ∈ rcvd-notify, j ∈ I}
96:        majority(curview.members) ⊆ rcvdP
97:     Effect:
98:        stage ← notifyq-done
```

and write and corresponding acknowledgments. Initially, each object has a special value $v_0 \in V$. After a read() action is invoked, the service responds with read-ack(v) action returning a value v. After a write(v) action with value $v \in V$ is invoked, the service responds with write-ack() action. Finally, after a reconfig() operation the service responds with a recon-ack() action.

We now describe the operations at high level, starting with the two-phase structure of *reconfig*. The goal of the first phase is similar to the query phase of ABD: discover the latest value-tag pair for the object. The goal of the second phase is similar to the propagate phase of ABD: convey the latest value-tag pair to a suitable majority of replica hosts. The main difference is that these two phases are performed in the context of applying the incremental changes to the configuration, while at the same time discovering the changes submitted by other participants. This essentially "bootstraps" possible new configurations. Given that all of this is done by traversing all possible paths—and thus configurations—in the DAG ensures that the common path is also traversed.

Finally, we provide additional details for the read and write operations. The *read* follows the implementation of *reconfig*, with the differences being: (a) the set of configuration changes is empty; and (b) the discovered value is returned to the client. The *write* also follows the implementation of *reconfig*, with the differences being: (a) the set of changes is empty; (b) a new, higher tag is produced upon the completion of the first phase; and (c) the new value-tag pair is propagated in the second phase. Note that while the set of configuration changes is empty for *read* and *write*, both operations may discover changes submitted elsewhere, and help with the bootstrapping of revised configurations. As with *reconfig*, stable majorities ensure that nothing blocks the protocols from progressing, and the finite number of reconfigurations guarantees termination.

9.3.1 PARTIALLY ORDERED CONFIGURATIONS

In the following, we use interchangeably the terms *configuration* and *view*. Each *read* and *write* operation executes in a series of two stages: *read-in-view* and *write-in-view* that comprise, respectively, the *query* and *prop* phases similar to other MRMW memory algorithms we presented earlier. In each phase, a majority quorum is contacted through the use of a contactq action (lines 166–172). The *read* and *write* operations proceed by catching up with the most recent view. As this view is defined by the initial configuration and potentially concurrent configuration changes, it is represented as a directed acyclic graph (DAG) whose nodes are views and whose edges are the changes applied to the source view to obtain the target view.

Each read(), write(v) or reconfig(c) action determines the current configuration by traversing the DAG using a breadth-first search strategy (lines 11–50). The traversal executes recursively through actions traverse, breadth-first-search and set-desired-view, propagate, traverse-fix as seen in lines 100–148. The idea behind the traversal of the DAG configurations is to record all membership changes of the system into a *desiredview* variable which represents the new configuration that must be added to a corresponding weak snapshot, so that all further operations will eventually catch up with this configuration. The traversal starts at the root of the DAG called the *front* configuration. A *desiredview* is different from the *curview* only if the traversal is part of a reconfiguration, in which case it is set to the union of the *curview* and *newconfig*, which corresponds to the set of changes c parameter given to the reconfig action. The traversal can only be executed by a member of the current configuration, otherwise the traversal stops. This check occurs at lines 113 and 114. The traversal starts by picking the closest configuration (indicated by the minimal set of changes recorded in the current view *curview* at line 111). This corresponds to following the corresponding outgoing link of the current view in the DAG.

9.3.2 ADDING NEW CONFIGURATIONS

It might be the case that the current view does not include all membership changes, typically if $w \neq desiredview$ (line 116), in which case these changes are installed as a new view of the DAG linked from the current view through the update action (lines 199–204). The same process cannot install another outgoing edge from the current view. Only concurrently traversing processes might, hence the DAG structure.

If a process cannot install another outgoing edge from the current view (because all membership changes are included), a *read-in-view* stage starts to query a majority quorum of the weak snapshot to determine the set of outgoing links the traversal must follow. This process is repeated at all new encountered views, until no new edges leading to other views are found. At that point, the *write-in-view* stage starts propagating the latest known value to this *desiredview*: typically this transfers the state found during the traversal to the latest known view. The *query* phase performs a scan action to the current state of the view, to return potential changes recorded in the weak snapshot of this view (lines 150–164) before contacting a majority quorum through a contactq action (lines 166–188).

The *propagate* phase proceeds differently as it first picks a new timestamp (action pick-new-ts) before executing a contactq and then a scan actions. This is done to ensure that any written value is propagated to the latest view. To illustrate the problem, consider an execution fragment ξ that contains: (i) a reconfiguration request reconfig(c), from c_1 to c_2 (where $c_2 = c_1 \cup c$) from process i_1; (ii) a write(v) action that is invoked concurrently with the reconfig(c) from i_2; and (iii) a read() action that succeeds both the reconfig(c) and write(v) actions from i_1. According to atomicity the read action in ξ has to return v, the value written by the latest preceding *write* action. Furthermore, since the *read* succeeds the *reconfig* action, the query phase of the read operation will operate in c_2—the latest view known to i_1. Thus, the *read* may return v, only if v is written in c_2. Now consider that the *reconfig* operation was invoked after the read phase of the *write* operation. Also consider that the *write* operation executes the scan action before the contactq in *propagate* phase. Then the following execution fragment is possible:

- i_2 executes scan on c_1 (lines 150–164);

- i_1 invokes reconfig(c) (lines 39–45);

- i_1 executes all the actions up to update(c_1, c) (lines 199–209);

- i_1 executes scan on c_1 (lines 150–164);

- i_1 executes contactq on c_1 (query phase) (lines 166–188); and

- i_2 executes contactq on c_1 (propagation of v) (lines 166–188).

In the above scenario, on the one hand, the *write* operation scans for changes on the view before the *reconfig* action propagates any changes (using the update action) so it is not aware of the existance of c_2. On the other hand, the reconfig action queries c_1 but does not observe the value v as it is written in c_1 after the *reconfig* contacts a quorum in c_1. Since the *write* is not aware of the configuration c_2, and since the *reconfig* is not aware of v, then none of the operations is going to transfer (write) the new value v in c_2. Thus, the succeeding *read* operation will not observe v and is going to return an older value, violating atomicity. Instead, if the *write* operation contacts a quorum in c_1 before scanning then the above scenario becomes:

- i_2 executes contactq on c_1 (propagation of v) (lines 166–188);

- i_1 invokes reconfig(c) (lines 39–45);

- i_1 executes all the actions up to update(c_1, c) (lines 199–209);

- i_1 executes scan on c_1 (lines 150–164);

- i_1 executes contactq on c_1 (query phase) (lines 166–188); and

- i_2 executes scan on c_1 (lines 150–164).

So in this case both the *write* and the *reconfig* actions are aware of the update and the new value v. Also notice that no matter how we interleave the actions of i_1 and i_2 (always preserving the order of actions locally in each process), either the *write* is going to be aware of c_2 or the *reconfig* is going to observe v. So, in either case, v is going to be written in c_2 and the succeeding read operation will observe it.

9.3.3   CONTACTING QUORUMS

The contactq action, resets the accumulator field *acc*, sets the *stage* to contactq and increments the phase number *pnum* to indicate that the operation has moved to a new phase. The messages received through the recv action (lines 69–90) for the corresponding phase *ph* and phase number *pn* are collected in the accumulator *acc* (line 72). Once a message is received from all members of a majority quorum, the contactq-fix (lines 174–188) action is enabled to update the appropriate local tag *t* and value *v* to the highest tag and the associated value, received from the majority quorum. Finally, if we are in the query phase then we proceed to the propagation phase, otherwise we scan the weak snapshot for possible configuration changes. If changes are discovered then the operation restarts.

Specification 38 Dynastore *Reader-Writer-Recon$_i$*: Transitions 2

99: **Internal traverse()$_i$**
100:   **Precondition:**
101:    ¬*failed* ∧ *status* = active
102:    *stage* = traverse
103:   **Effect:**
104:    *front* ← *curview*
105:    *desiredview* ← *curview* ∪ *newconfig*
106:    *stage* ← traverse-rec1

107: **Internal breadth-first-search()$_i$**
108:   **Precondition:**
109:    ¬*failed* ∧ *status* = active
110:    *stage* = traverse-rec1
111:    $w = \ell$ s.t. $|\ell| = \min_{\ell' \in front}\{|\ell'|\}$
112:   **Effect:**
113:    **if** $i \notin w.members$ **then**
114:     *status* ← idle
                      // halt if not a member of the view
115:    **else**
116:     **if** $w \neq desiredview$ **then**
117:      *to-be-updated* ← $(w, desiredview \setminus w)$
118:      *stage* ← update
119:     **else**
120:      *phase* ← query
121:      *stage* ← scan

122: **Internal set-desired-view()$_i$**
123:   **Precondition:**
124:    ¬*failed* ∧ *status* = active
125:    *stage* = traverse-rec2
126:    *changesets* ≠ ∅
127:   **Effect:**
128:    *front* ← *front* \ {w}
129:    **for** all $c \in changesets$ **do**
130:     *desiredview* ← *desiredview* ∪ *c*
131:     *front* ← *front* ∪ {$w \cup c$}

132:    *stage* ← traverse-rec1
133: **Internal propagate()$_i$**
134:   **Precondition:**
135:    ¬*failed* ∧ *status* = active
136:    *stage* = traverse-rec2
137:    *changesets* = ∅
138:   **Effect:**
139:    *phase* ← propagate
140:    **if** (*op-type* = write) **then** *stage* ← pick-new-ts
141:    **else** *stage* ← contactq-start   *// same ts for reads*

142: **Internal traverse-fix()$_i$**
143:   **Precondition:**
144:    ¬*failed* ∧ *status* = active
145:    *stage* = traverse-fix
146:   **Effect:**
147:    *curview* ← *desiredview*
148:    *stage* ← notifyq

149: **Output scan()$_{i,w}$**
150:   **Precondition:**
151:    ¬*failed* ∧ *status* = active
152:    *stage* = scan
153:   **Effect:** None

154: **Input scan-ack(*changes*)$_{i,w}$**
155:   **Effect:**
156:    **if** ¬*failed* ∧ *status* = active **then**
157:     *changesets* ← *changes*
158:     **if** *phase* = query **then**
159:      *stage* ← contactq-start
160:     **else**   *// phase* = propagate
161:      **if** *changesets* ≠ ∅ **then**
162:       *stage* ← traverse-rec1
163:      **else**
164:       *stage* ← traverse-fix

To give a graphical representation of how the states of the automaton evolve, we represented the state of *stage* field as vertices and the actions that modify its states as edges in Figure 9.3. Initially, the *Reader-Writer-Recon* automaton starts with *stage* set to idle, then actions read(), write(v) and reconfig(c) sets it to traverse. The rectangles indicate the *WeakSnapshot* automata with which *Reader-Writer-Recon* interacts before modifying the state of *stage*.

9.4 CORRECTNESS

We need to show that the automaton presented implements correctly an atomic read/write memory object. We first discuss why DynaStore satisfies liveness property by showing that any correct process eventually terminates, and then we present a proof sketch that shows that the algorithm satisfies the safety property by satisfying all the conditions of atomicity.

Specification 39 Dynastore *Reader-Writer-Recon$_i$*: Transitions 3

165: **Internal** contactq$_i$
166:   **Precondition:**
167:     $\neg failed \wedge status =$ active
168:     $stage =$ contactq-start
169:   **Effect:**
170:     $acc \leftarrow \emptyset$
171:     $pnum \leftarrow pnum + 1$
172:     $stage \leftarrow$ contactq

173: **Internal** contactq-fix$_i$
174:   **Precondition:**
175:     $\neg failed \wedge status =$ active
176:     $stage =$ contactq
177:     $repliedP = \{j : \langle j, m \rangle \in acc \wedge m.pn = pnum\}$
178:     $majority(w.members) \subseteq repliedP$
179:   **Effect:**
180:     **if** $op\text{-}type =$ read **then**
181:       $t \leftarrow \max_{\langle j,m \rangle \in acc}\{m.tag\}$
182:       $v \leftarrow v' : \langle t, v' \rangle \in acc$
183:       **if** $t > maxtag$ **then**
184:         $(maxV, maxtag) \leftarrow (t, v)$
185:     **if** $phase =$ query **then**
186:       $stage \leftarrow$ traverse-rec2
187:     **else**   // $phase =$ propagate

188:       $stage \leftarrow$ scan
189: **Internal** pick-new-ts()$_i$
190:   **Precondition:**
191:     $\neg failed \wedge status =$ active
192:     $stage =$ pick-new-ts
193:     $changesets = \emptyset$
194:   **Effect:**
195:     $maxtag \leftarrow \langle maxtag.timestamp + 1, i \rangle$
196:     $maxv \leftarrow value$
197:     $stage \leftarrow$ contactq-start

198: **Output** update(d)$_{i,w}$
199:   **Precondition:**
200:     $\neg failed \wedge status =$ active
201:     $\langle w, d \rangle =$ to-be-updated
202:     $stage =$ update
203:   **Effect:**
204:     $to\text{-}be\text{-}updated \leftarrow \perp$

205: **Input** update-ack()$_{i,w}$
206:   **Effect:**
207:     **if** $\neg failed \wedge status =$ active **then**
208:       $phase \leftarrow$ query
209:       $stage \leftarrow$ scan

Termination (liveness property). Termination requires that an operation terminates in an execution of the algorithm if it is invoked by a correct process. Operations (*read*, *write*, and *reconfig*) in DynaStore restart when a new view is detected. A *read* or *write* operation may detect a new view in the system only when it is concurrent with a reconfiguration operation. Thus, in DynaStore we assume that only a *finite* number of reconfigurations are invoked concurrently with any other operation.

Liveness, on the other hand, guarantees progress of the service regardless of any process failures or departures. Action notify (lines 92–98) sends messages to the members of a view and serves three purposes: (a) it notifies added processes that are part of the system to enable their actions and start participating; (b) it notifies current members of the view about the latest known view; and (c) it notifies removed processes that are not part of the system so they can terminate any pending operations (and lead them to termination). Notice that DynaStore assumes that the majority of processes are alive in the latest view. Thus, a process that is a member of the latest view may stall trying to complete an operation in an older view where more than a majority of processes were removed. Thus, (b) ensures that once such processes are notified, they are able to restart their operation in the new view to achieve both the liveness of the service and the termination of the operation.

Atomicity (safety property). To prove atomicity we need to show that DynaStore satisfies property **A1**, **A2**, and **A3** of Definition 2.16. According to the algorithm each read or write

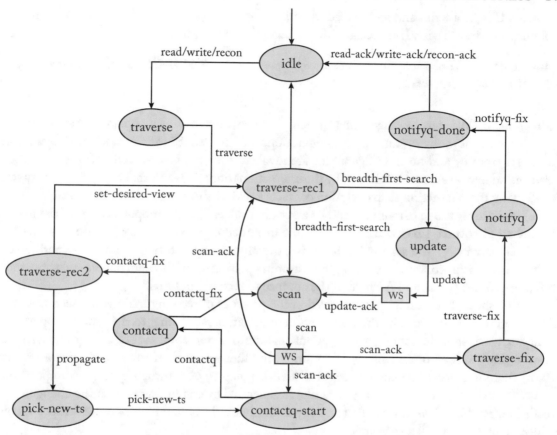

Figure 9.3: The state of the *stage* field of the *Reader-Writer-Recon* automaton and the actions that modify it.

operation consists of two phases: (i) a query phase in which the operation discovers the latest tag written on the atomic object; and (ii) a propagation phase in which an operation propagates a tag and the associated value to the majority of the replicas. During the propagation phase a read propagates the maximum tag discovered during the query phase and its associated value, whereas a write increments the maximum tag discovered in the query phase and propagates the new tag along with the value to be written. When reconfigurations are invoked concurrently with read and write operations these phases are repeated until no new configuration (view) is discovered.

Similar to the approach presented for other algorithms, we define the partial ordering $\prec$ on read and write operations in terms of tags. Let tag_π be the tag of each operation at the traverse-fix event. For two operations π_1 and π_2 we say that $\pi_1 \prec \pi_2$ if $tag_{\pi_1} < tag_{\pi_2}$ and π_2 is a write. If π_1 is a write and π_2 is a read, then $\pi_1 \prec \pi_2$ if $tag_{\pi_1} \leq tag_{\pi_2}$. The rest of the order is obtained by transitivity. Here reads with the same tags are not ordered.

Theorem 9.7 *The DynaStore automaton implements an atomic MWMR read/write shared memory in a dynamic environment.*

Proof sketch. We start by considering the simple case where read/write operations are executed on the same view, say c_1, and no reconfigurations are invoked. Since any read/write operation π starts from c_1 and no reconfigurations are invoked, then the traverse action (lines 100–106) returns no new *view* and is followed by the scan action (lines 150–153 that returns an empty set. Following the scan action each operation contacts a majority in c_1 via contactq action (lines 166–172) to discover the maximum tag and its associated value. Next, π propagates either the maximum tag discovered (in case π is a read) or the incremented maximum tag (in case π is a write) to a majority in c_1. The scan action following the propagation returns an empty set and hence π terminates immediately. Following the reasoning presented in Theorem 5.1 we can show that all properties **A1, A2**, and **A3** hold in the absence of reconfigurations.

To show that atomicity is preserved in the presence of reconfigurations we need to recall the properties guaranteed by the *WeakSnapsot* automaton. According to the fourth property of the weak snapshot the set of scan operations that return a non empty set of changes on a single view c_i have at least one change e_c in common. In other words from any view c_i (vertex on the DAG) there is at least one change (edge) e_c that is going to be returned by any scan operation on c_i. The view (or vertex) $c_n = c_i \cup e_c$ that is generated by combining c_i with the change e_c is called an *established view*. Note that any operation that visits c_i and obtains a non-empty set by the scan operation will also visit c_n.

According to action set-desired-view (lines 123–132), which is reached at the end of the query phase (lines 185–186), a process p examines all the changes (outgoing edges) returned by the scan operation of the query phase in the set *ChangeSets*, and generates a new view (*desiredView*) which is the union of all the changes $e \in ChangeSets$ and the view c_i (line 130). More formally:

$$desiredView = (\bigcup_{e \in ChangeSets} e) \cup c_i. \tag{9.1}$$

Moreover, the set with the views to be queried (*front*) is augmented with all the sets generated from the union of c_i with any returned change set (line 131). Formally:

$$\forall e \in ChangeSets, e \cup c_i \in front. \tag{9.2}$$

Notice that by Equations (9.1) and (9.2) any view $c_f \in front$ is a subset of the *desiredView*, i.e., $c_f \subseteq desiredView$. Also notice that since at least a single change $e_c \in ChangeSets$ is common and the view $c_i \cup e_c$ is an established view by definition, then the set *front* always includes at least one established view. At the end of the action set-desired-view (lines 123–132), the *stage* changes to traverse-rec1 where the smallest view in the set *front* is next selected, say c_n. Note that since c_n is the smallest set in the set *front* and $c_n \subseteq desiredView$, then $c_n = desiredView$ iff c_n is the only member in the set *front*. Since, however, the set *front* always contains an established view then the *desiredView* is also an established view.

In the case where $c_n \neq desiredView$, a process p performs an update action (line 117) writing the change $desiredView \setminus c_n$ to the weak snapshot object of c_n. By the update action in the *WeakSnapshot* automaton (line 199) if another change is discovered on c_n then this change is returned and the update is omitted. In other words, the update behaves like a scan action in such a case. Following the update each process performs a query phase which includes a scan and a contactq actions. During those actions the process p observes any changes on the view c_n and collects the value of the register from the majority of the members of the view, c_n.*members*.

A process repeats the traversal until it reaches a view (*desiredView*) such that the action scan does not return any change on that view (line 161). So, if a process p starts at a view *curView*, it encounters *all* the established views, between *curView* and the *desiredView* returned in action traverse-fix (line 147).

Although the query phase of each read or write operation π is performed on every established view the propagation phase of π is performed at least on the *desiredView* returned in action traverse-fix. Thus, the propagation phase is performed on an established view. Now we reason that properties **A1, A2**, and **A3** hold.

A1: If for operations π_1 and π_2 in Π, $\pi_1 \rightarrow \pi_2$, then it cannot be the case that $\pi_2 \prec \pi_1$.

Let operation π_1 complete and propagate its value (new or maximum discovered) on an established view c_{π_1}. Let π_2 be a read or write operation that succeeds π_1. There are two cases to consider regarding the starting view $curView$ of π_1: (i) either $curView$ is a descendant of c_{π_1} in the DAG, or (ii) c_{π_1} is a descendant of or equal to $curView$. Notice that in any case the view c_{π_1} is a subset of the *desiredView* reached by π_2 due to the incremental nature of the views.

In Case (i), since π_2 examines all the established views from $curView$ to its own *desiredView*, then it will also examine c_{π_1}, which is an established view in that segment. When π_2 performs contactq on c_{π_1} there will be at least a single member of c_{π_1} that will send the value propagated by π_1 to π. Thus, as shown in the case without reconfigurations $tag_{\pi_2} \geq tag_{\pi_1}$.

If Case (ii) holds it means that the process invoking π_2, say p, received a notify message about a view c_n that is also established and newer or equal to c_{π_1}. As view changes are incremental, $c_{\pi_1} \subseteq c_n$. Also since a notify message is sent only if an operation reached c_n as its *desiredView* it means that there exists a process that started from a descendant of c_{π_1} and reached c_n. So we need to show that the value propagated by π_1 in c_{π_1} will be transferred to c_n. This is ensured by the order in which the scan and contactq actions are performed in query and propagation phases.

Let π' be the first operation that sent the notify message about view c_n. Any operation π' that is concurrent with π_1 will execute actions update, scan and then contactq. The operation π_1 executes contactq before scan (during its write phase), writing the value before checking for any view change. Thus, if the process executing π_1 does not observe any change then the action scan during π_1 is executed before the update action during π'. Thus, the contactq (query phase) of π' will be executed after the contactq of π_1 and thus π' will observe the value propagated. If π' does not observe the value written it means that its contactq action was executed before the contactq (and thus scan) action of π_1 and hence π_1 will observe any change made by π' and will restart the traversal. In any case, the value written will be transferred to the next established view and hence eventually will be transferred to c_n. Thus, operation π_2 will observe the value written on c_n and will return a tag $tag_{\pi_2} \geq tag_{\pi_1}$. Notice that if π_2 is a write operation then π_2 will increment the maximum tag discovered before propagating. As the maximum tag will be greater or equal to tag_{π_1}, then $tag_{\pi_2} > tag_{\pi_1}$.

A2: If ω is a write operation and π is any operation, then either $\omega \prec \pi$ or $\pi \prec \omega$.

If $tag_\omega > tag_\pi$ (or $tag_\omega < tag_\pi$) then $\pi \prec \omega$ (resp. $\omega \prec \pi$) follows directly. If $tag_\omega = tag_\pi$ then it must be that π is a read and cannot be the case that π is a write operation. Each writer increments the maximum discovered tag before propagating its value. If the max tag discovered by ω is not equal to the max tag discovered by π then either $tag_\omega > tag_\pi$ or $tag_\omega < tag_\pi$ as both tags are generated from the increment of their respective max tags. If the max tags discovered are equal, then assuming that the writer identifiers are comparable and unique, the tags generated can be ordered lexicographically and either $tag_\omega > tag_\pi$ and $\pi \prec \omega$, or $tag_\omega < tag_\pi$ and $\omega \prec \pi$.

A3: The value returned by a read operation is the value written by the last preceding write operation according to $\prec$ (or the initial value if there is no such write).

A read operation ρ returns a value associated with the max tag discovered during its phase 1. Let ω be the last preceding write of ρ. If $tag_\rho = tag_\omega$ then ρ did not discover a tag larger than tag_ω during its phase 1. Also, it cannot be the case that there exists operation ω' such that $tag_{\omega'} > tag_\omega$, which appears in a view not examined by ρ as ρ terminates only when no more changes are discovered and the view reached contains any previous view. If, on the other hand, $tag_\rho > tag_\omega$ then ω is not the latest preceding write, since ρ returns values written by some writer, leading to contradiction.

This completes the proof sketch.   □

9.5 IMPLEMENTATION AND PERFORMANCE CONSIDERATIONS

In this chapter we presented a different approach to reconfiguration that introduces incremental configuration changes instead of replacing the entire configuration. Such incremental changes consist of additions and removals of individual nodes, and the target configuration is build incrementally from the current configuration by incorporating the changes proposed concurrently by different participants. This is in contrast with the approaches in RDS and RAMBO, where only one of the proposed new configurations is agreed upon by the participants. The incremental reconfiguration in DynaStore obviates the need for consensus, while guaranteeing operation liveness as long as each operation is concurrent with a finite number of reconfigurations and the relevant majorities of processes do not fail. One would expect that elimination of consensus would boost operation performance. However, practical studies like [64, 104] show that this strategy may actually have a negative impact on the latency of operations in certain realistic scenarios as compared to implementations that use consensus.

The DynaStore algorithm was used as the basis for developing an evaluation implementation, called DynaDisc [104]. The implementation was tested in a local area network and it adopts the data-centric approach, where the replica hosts are passive network storage devices. The implementation was designed to reconfigure the service either asynchronously without the use of consensus, or partially-synchronously with the help of consensus. The evaluation showed that in the absence of reconfigurations the two versions of the algorithm have similar read and write operation latencies. When multiple reconfigurations occur concurrently, it was observed that the asynchronous, consensus-free approach has a significant negative effect on the latency of read and write operations that are concurrent with reconfigurations. The explanation here is that the consensus-free algorithm must examine multiple possible evolutions of configurations, whereas an algorithm that incorporates reconfiguration with consensus normally deals with a single configuration on which all clients agree. Reconfiguration latency on the other hand is somewhat better in the consensus-free version of DynaDisk when many reconfigurations occur simultaneously. In such situations, the consensus-based DynaDisk may take longer to reach a decision.

Another study evaluated several algorithms for reconfigurable atomic storage, both with and without consensus. The study encompassed several algorithm implementations, including DynaStore, RAMBO, an optimized version of RAMBO, and two other specialized implementations [64]. Set in the context of a data-centric model under different environment assumptions, the results do not reveal dramatic differences in performance between implementations using consensus in reconfiguration and those not using consensus. One interesting finding is the observation that implementations that separate memory access operations and reconfigurations can have advantage. The DynaStore algorithm use read and write operations to "help" [21] with the concurrent reconfigurations. In the experiments it was observed that helping with reconfiguration generally increases the overhead on read and write operations. Conversely, in implementations where read and write operations do not help with concurrent reconfigurations, the overhead can be significantly reduced. Not surprisingly, the study also suggests that the difference in performance of various algorithms substantially depends on network settings where the systems are deployed. For example, in the WAN setting the incremental nature of reconfiguration in DynaStore does not prevent it from completing reconfigurations substantially faster than RAMBO, yet the memory access operations in RAMBO generally have lower latency in the same setting. In experiments where reconfigurations are "batched" together, DynaStore had overall slightly higher latencies for both reconfigurations and memory access.

Remark 9.8   On algorithms and real system performance: Implementors of distributed systems know well the adage that "one can always achieve worse performance when deploying algorithms in real systems." The point here is that in building distributed systems one cannot optimize algorithms in the abstract without considering the parameters of the target networked platforms, and expect the optimizations to be reflected in the performance of real systems. This is in stark contrast with the sequential (von Neumann) paradigm of computation where the algorithms can be analyzed abstractly, and where the scalability and performance properties of algorithms are generally preserved in real implementations (as observed by Valiant [110]). **End remark**

9.6   BIBLIOGRAPHIC NOTES

The evaluation [104] by Shraer et al. of the performance of reconfigurable storage with and without consensus showed that one may be better suited than the other depending on environment and system settings. The observations were briefly discussed in the previous section, where we also discussed some findings from the performance study of Jehl and Meling [64] of several reconfigurable memory implementations. It is worth noting that consensus-based reconfigurations also proved practical in the Byzantine fault-tolerant setting, for example, to change the membership of Byzantine consensus protocols [12, 102] and to update deterministically the set of participants of a Byzantine fault-tolerant blockchain [112].

As already observed [2], the consensus-free solution remains interesting from a theoretical point of view because consensus protocols are not guaranteed to complete in an asynchronous failure-prone environment. Moreover, some improvements over DynaStore, like SmartMerge [65], were proposed to handle the installation of conflicting incremental configurations, hence preventing the system from reaching an empty configuration.

Vukolić [113] presents a survey of quorum systems, including probabilistic quorum systems [86] and Byzantine quorum systems [85] and explained how some could be used for storage, including with RAMBO. Dynamic (or adaptive) quorum systems [96], whose members are determined one after another while being contacted, are not discussed here but have been used in SQUARE [52] for implementing a dynamic storage on a large number of replicas where reconfigurations involving a constant number of nodes are frequent. Since then, some results implemented quorum systems in a continuously dynamic model where the *churn* is modeled as the number of nodes leaving and entering the system during a unit of time [55]. Reconfiguration in this churn model is an active topic of research [6]. Reconfiguration has more recently found applications to change the processes with the permissions to run the consensus of a blockchain service while assuming synchrony [1, 99] or partial synchrony [11, 112].

CHAPTER 10

Concluding Remarks and Looking Ahead

We presented a representative collection of algorithms that emulate read/write memory objects with atomic guarantees on a set of asynchronous message-passing computing devices. The first five chapters deal with algorithms for *static environments* where the collection of participating nodes is fixed and known *a priori* to every service participant, and where a certain number of crashes may occur at arbitrary times. Whereas such algorithms may not be practical in more dynamic settings, studying algorithms for static environments allows to introduce fundamental algorithmic techniques and reason about performance lower bounds. Algorithms built for the static environment can be used as building blocks for solutions in more dynamic or adversarial environments.

The next four chapters dealt with algorithms for *dynamic environments*. In such systems the collections of participating nodes may evolve over time due to failures, voluntary or planned departures of nodes, and new nodes may join the computation. Due to the changes in the system such algorithms are more complex while having the promise of being more practical in real implementations. The participating nodes are not aware a priori of the dynamic changes in the membership of the service, and thus sophisticated techniques are used to transfer the system state from one set of members to the next. Given the highly dynamic nature of the environments, it is not surprising that the performance here is degraded relative to the performance of consistent memory implementations for static systems.

With the advent of cloud services, distributed storage services are attracting more attention. The technical challenges and performance overheads may be the reasons why the existing distributed storage solutions shy away from atomic consistency guarantees. Commercial solutions, such as Google's File System (GFS) [44], Amazon's Dynamo [29], and Facebook's Cassandra [70] provide less intuitive guarantees. The concepts discussed in this book are echoed in the design decisions of production systems. For instance, consensus is used in GFS [44] to ensure agreement on system configurations as it is done in RAMBO; global time is used in Spanner [26] as it is done in GeoQuorums [31], a variation of RAMBO in ad-hoc mobile networks; replica access protocols in Dynamo [29] use quorums as the majority of approaches presented in this book. These examples provide motivation for pursuing rigorous algorithmic approaches in the study of consistent data services for both static and dynamic networked systems.

Consistent storage systems continue to be an area of active research and advanced development, and there are good reasons to believe that as high-performance dynamic memory systems with superior fault-tolerance become available, they will play a significant role in the construction of sophisticated distributed applications. The demand for implementations providing atomic read/write memory will ultimately be driven by the needs of distributed applications that require provable consistency and performance guarantees. Through the algorithms we presented here one may identify the key aspects that distributed shared memory algorithms would have to address in order to improve over the previous approaches.

Redundancy.   *Can we achieve fault-tolerance with reduced storage demands?* Replication of information is used in the algorithms presented in this book to allow data survivability in the case of failures. As the strongest redundancy scheme, replication maintains an exact copy of the data (data mirror) at the replica hosts and ensures that the data maybe recovered even if a single copy may be accessed. Although replication is sufficient for basic objects, like registers, it becomes very costly when dealing with large data objects: each object requires storage equal to the object size times the number of replicas. *Erasure codes*, as introduced in information theory, provide a natural way of redundancy while at the same time reduce the storage cost. Briefly, an erasure coded algorithm takes as an input a string of B bits, splits those bits into k fragments of size $\frac{B}{k}$ bits. Then it generates m additional fragments of the same size, for a total of $n = k + m$ fragments, for $k < m$. An erasure coded algorithm decodes the value of the object if any k of those fragments are collected. Replication is a special case of an erasure coded algorithm where $k = 1$ and $m = n - 1$.

Recent studies focused in the exploitation of erasure codes for implementing fault-tolerant atomic shared memory emulations [20, 33, 69]. However, as shown in [107], asynchronous fault-prone systems introduce inherent limitations on the space requirements of a shared storage algorithm, independent from the erasure coding algorithm they use. It is interesting to understand those limitations and design algorithms that will provide a tight trade-off between storage usage and fault-tolerance.

Redundancy is also widely used in commercial systems to guarantee fault tolerance. Systems like Hadoop Distributed File System (HDFS) [106], Facebook's Cassandra [70] and GFS [44] are some examples. However, storage efficiency and speed of retrieval, pushes many of the leading tech companies to revise their redundancy strategies. For example, Facebook introduced f4 [91], to improve over their previous storage system Haystack [10]. f4 introduces the idea of "hot" and "warm" data, i.e., data that are accessed very often and those that are not requested frequently, respectively.

Communication and latency.   *What are the communication requirements in providing a consistent shared storage?* In a message-passing environment information is transferred through asynchronous communication channels, and there are two associated costs: the total number of messages, and the number of communication rounds. Algorithms presented here focus as the first priority on reducing latency by minimizing the number of communication rounds an operation needs to perform before terminating. In some cases doing so comes with a significant cost, e.g., to reduce the communication latency of memory access operations to a single round requires placing stiff upper bounds on the number of participants using the service [34], and involves substantial local processing [4]. In other cases, reducing latency comes at a cost of an increase in the total number of messages [59]. While the communication costs of atomic memory have already been substantially studied in static environments, much work remains in investigating the communication costs in dynamic environments.

New challenges also arise in dealing with large objects or large sets of objects. In a resent study for Facebook [10, 91] the authors posit that the major bottleneck in retrieving a single file in their storage system is the number of metadata operations (input/output) performed per object. That includes the time to look up a particular object on a replica host. And so moving around large objects may reduce the relative cost of metadata, but will increase the communication cost, while fragmenting large objects will benefit communication but increase local computation demands. This leads to tradeoffs between the number and size of fragments per shared object.

Reconfiguration.   *When and how to reconfigure an atomic memory service?* To achieve scalability and longevity of the service it is important to allow new participants to join the service and the existing participants to depart or fail. Newly joined participants are unaware of the state of the object and they need to be carefully integrated. Sufficiently many failures and departures may prevent joining processes from retrieving the value of the object. Hence, the service must evolve, and migrate the state of the object to the new participants, preferably fast (as done in RDS). The main challenges that need to be addressed are: (a) decide when to reconfigure, (b) establish the next configuration of the system, and (c) allow the service progress (i.e., allow operations to be invoked and terminate) during the reconfiguration.

Regardless of how the reconfiguration of the set of replica hosts is done, any practical implementation must address the challenge of deciding *when* to reconfigure. Here one may delegate the decision to individual hosts (as done in DynaStore). In particular, a node joining the service causes reconfiguration, also a node implicitly causes reconfiguration when its failure is detected. Although such approaches may be simple and effective when perturbations are infrequent and the set of replicas is small, they may cause undue overheads when nodes continue joining and leaving the service even though some core set of hosts is stable and sufficient for providing good service. Another approach is to leave the decision for when to reconfigure to another distributed service that monitors the performance of the memory system and decides when to reconfigure based on these observations and on speculative forecasts (this approach aligns with RAMBO where reconfiguration requests issued by its environment). Implementing such external service is has the potential of providing superior quality of service. Additional consideration is selecting a suitable set of hosts. Just because a node is interested in serving as a replica host does not mean that its wish must be granted. Here the external service that decides when to reconfigure can also decide on the target set of nodes. Note that no agreement on the target set is required—all memory services we presented here are able to deal with the situations when several target sets or changes are proposed.

When an external service is used to determine the next configuration, in addition to fault-tolerance considerations it can also include performance issues. For example, the behavior of the participants in RAMBO can be observed, gossiped, and used as predictors for future behaviors, with the goal of finding quorum configurations that minimize read and write operation delays without affecting correctness and fault-tolerance properties of the system [89]. The resultant performance improvements allow more reasonably sized systems to be reconfigured online in a way that optimizes hosting of quorums with respect to relevant performance criteria [90].

A direct approach to guaranteeing consistency is to ensured that all operations access the current at the time configuration. Thus, strong primitives, like consensus, are used with approaches such as RDS to allow participants to agree explicitly on the next established configuration. On the other hand, DynaStore offer a more fluid solution without the use of consensus where the notion of a configuration being current is implicit, but that guarantees that operations access the right collection hosts in read and write operations.

Finally, reconfiguration needs to be transparent to the clients of the service, thus enabling them to perform read and write operations as if reconfigurations did not exist. In particular, the service must provide the same safety (atomicity) and liveness (termination) guarantees to the operations, even while operations are invoked concurrently with a reconfiguration. As the participation changes, it is critical that the object state is transferred from one configuration to the next. It is also important that participants learn about the new configuration as older configurations may be obsolete and prevent an operation from terminating. A conservative approach that suspends (or even aborts) operations during a reconfiguration to transfer the state of the object to the next configuration, and then resume the operations appears to be inadequate. Although this could be acceptable when reconfigurations are infrequent and are relatively fast. A more general approach should allow the operations to continue during reconfiguration, but ensure that a sufficient collection of object replicas is accessed, from multiple relevant configurations, when a reconfiguration is concurrent with the operations. This is the approach adopted by all dynamic algorithms presented here.

Bibliography

[1] Ittai Abraham, Dahlia Malkhi, Kartik Nayak, Ling Ren, and Alexander Spiegelman. Solida: A blockchain protocol based on reconfigurable Byzantine consensus. In *Proc. of the 21st International Conference on Principles of Distributed Systems, OPODIS*, page 25:1–25:19, 2017. 154

[2] Marcos K. Aguilera, Idit Keidar, Dahlia Malkhi, Jean-Philippe Martin, and Alexander Shraer. Reconfiguring replicated atomic storage: A tutorial. *Bulletin of the EATCS*, 102:84–108, 2010. 79, 154

[3] Jeannie R. Albrecht and Yasushi Saito. RAMBO for dummies. *HP Labs Tec. Report HPL-2005-39*, 2005. 111, 113

[4] Antonio Fernández Anta, Theophanis Hadjistasi, Nicolas Nicolaou, Alexandru Popa, and Alexander A. Schwarzmann. Tractable low-delay atomic memory. *Distributed Computing*, 34(1):33–58, 2021. DOI: 10.1007/s00446-020-00379-y 46, 157

[5] Hagit Attiya, Amotz Bar-Noy, and Danny Dolev. Sharing memory robustly in message-passing systems. *Journal of the ACM*, 42(1):124–142, 1995. DOI: 10.1145/200836.200869 45, 81, 83

[6] Hagit Attiya, HyunChul Chung, Faith Ellen, Saptaparni Kumar, and Jennifer L. Welch. Simulating a shared register in an asynchronous system that never stops changing. In Yoram Moses, Ed., *Distributed Computing*, vol. 9363 of *Lecture Notes in Computer Science*, pages 75–91, Springer Berlin Heidelberg, 2015. DOI: 10.1007/978-3-662-48653-5_6 154

[7] Hagit Attiya and Jennifer L. Welch. Sequential consistency versus linearizability. *ACM Transactions on Computer Systems*, 12(2):91–122, 1994. DOI: 10.1145/176575.176576 2

[8] Jason Baker, Chris Bond, James C. Corbett, J. J. Furman, Andrey Khorlin, James Larson, Jean-Michel Leon, Yawei Li, Alexander Lloyd, and Vadim Yushprakh. Megastore: Providing scalable, highly available storage for interactive services. In *Proc. of the Conference on Innovative Data system Research, CIDR*, pages 223–234, 2011. 132

[9] Jacob Beal and Seth Gilbert. Rambonodes for the metropolitan ad hoc network. In *Proc. of DIWANS Workshop, International Conference on Dependable Systems and Networks*, Florence, Italy (see also MIT Tech. Report AIM-2003-027), 2004. 110

[10] Doug Beaver, Sanjeev Kumar, Harry C. Li, Jason Sobel, and Peter Vajgel. Finding a needle in haystack: Facebook's photo storage. In *Proc. of the 9th USENIX Conference on Operating Systems Design and Implementation, OSDI*, pages 1–8, USENIX Association, Berkeley, CA, 2010. 156, 157

[11] Alysson Bessani, Eduardo Alchieri, João Sousa, André Oliveira, and Fernando Pedone. From Byzantine replication to blockchain: Consensus is only the beginning. In *50th Annual IEEE/IFIP International Conference on Dependable Systems and Networks, DSN*, pages 424–436, June 2020. DOI: 10.1109/dsn48063.2020.00057 154

[12] Alysson Bessani, João Sousa, and Eduardo E. P. Alchieri. State machine replication for the masses with BFT-smart. In *Proc. of the 44th Annual IEEE/IFIP International Conference on Dependable Systems and Networks, DSN*, pages 355–362, 2014. DOI: 10.1109/dsn.2014.43 154

[13] Ken Birman. A history of the virtual synchrony replication model. In *Replication: Theory and Practice*, pages 91–120, 2010. DOI: 10.1007/978-3-642-11294-2_6 81

[14] Ken Birman. *Guide to Reliable Distributed Systems: Building High-Assurance Applications and Cloud-Hosted Services*. Springer, 2012. DOI: 10.1007/978-1-4471-2416-0 132

[15] Ken Birman, Dahlia Malkhi, and Robbert Van Renesse. Virtually synchronous methodology for dynamic service replication. *Technical Report MSR-TR-2010-151*, Microsoft Research, 2010. 81, 132

[16] Romain Boichat, Partha Dutta, Svend Frølund, and Rachid Guerraoui. Deconstructing paxos. *SIGACT News*, 34(1):47–67, March 2003. DOI: 10.1145/637437.637447 132

[17] Romain Boichat, Partha Dutta, Svend Frolund, and Rachid Guerraoui. Reconstructing paxos. *SIGACT News*, 34(2):42–57, 2003. DOI: 10.1145/637437.637447 132

[18] Eric A. Brewer.   Towards robust distributed systems, July 2000. DOI: 10.1145/343477.343502 2

[19] Eric A. Brewer. Pushing the CAP: Strategies for consistency and availability. *IEEE Computer*, 45(2):23–29, 2012. 3

[20] Viveck R. Cadambe, Nancy Lynch, Muriel Médard, and Peter Musial. A coded shared atomic memory algorithm for message passing architectures. In *Proc. of the 13th IEEE International Symposium on Network Computing and Applications, NCA*, pages 253–260, August 2014. DOI: 10.1109/MC.2012.37 156

[21] Keren Censor-Hillel, Erez Petrank, and Shahar Timnat. Help! In *Proc. of the ACM Symposium on Principles of Distributed Computing, Donostia-San Sebastián, Spain, PODC*, pages 241–250, July 2015. DOI: 10.1145/2767386.2767415 153

[22] Tushar Deepak Chandra, Vassos Hadzilacos, and Sam Toueg. The weakest failure detector for solving consensus. *Journal of the ACM*, 43(4):685–722, July 1996. DOI: 10.1145/234533.234549 80

[23] Tushar Deepak Chandra and Sam Toueg. Unreliable failure detectors for asynchronous systems (preliminary version). In *Proc. of the 10th Annual ACM Symposium on Principles of Distributed Computing, PODC*, pages 325–340, 1991. DOI: 10.1145/112600.112627 132

[24] Gregory Chockler, Seth Gilbert, Vincent Gramoli, Peter M. Musial, and Alexander A. Shvartsman. Reconfigurable distributed storage for dynamic networks. *Journal of Parallel and Distributed Computing*, 69(1):100–116, January 2009. DOI: 10.1016/j.jpdc.2008.07.007 77, 111, 132

[25] Gregory Chockler and Dahlia Makhi. Active disk paxos with infinitely many processes. *Distributed Computing*, 18(1):73–84, 2005. DOI: 10.1007/s00446-005-0123-x 132

[26] James C. Corbett, Jeffrey Dean, Michael Epstein, Andrew Fikes, Christopher Frost, J. J. Furman, Sanjay Ghemawat, Andrey Gubarev, Christopher Heiser, Peter Hochschild, Wilson Hsieh, Sebastian Kanthak, Eugene Kogan, Hongyi Li, Alexander Lloyd, Sergey Melnik, David Mwaura, David Nagle, Sean Quinlan, Rajesh Rao, Lindsay Rolig, Yasushi Saito, Michal Szymaniak, Christopher Taylor, Ruth Wang, and Dale Woodford. Spanner: Google's globally-distributed database. In *Proc. of the 10th USENIX Conference on Operating Systems Design and Implementation, OSDI'12*, pages 251–264, USENIX Association, Berkeley, CA, 2012. 132, 155

[27] Roberto De Prisco, Alan D. Fekete, Nancy A. Lynch, and Alexander A. Shvartsman. A dynamic primary configuration group communication service. In *Proc. of the 13th International Symposium on Distributed Computing, DISC*, pages 64–78, 1999. DOI: 10.1007/3-540-48169-9_5 81

[28] Roberto De Prisco, Nancy Lynch, Alexander Shvartsman, Nicole Immorlica, and Toh Ne Win. A formal treatment of Lamport's paxos algorithm, 2002. Manuscript https://groups.csail.mit.edu/tds/papers/DePrisco/Paxos2002-manuscript.pdf 101, 105, 106, 113

[29] Giuseppe DeCandia, Deniz Hastorun, Madan Jampani, Gunavardhan Kakulapati, Avinash Lakshman, Alex Pilchin, Swaminathan Sivasubramanian, Peter Vosshall, and Werner Vogels. Dynamo: Amazon's highly available key-value store. In *Proc. of 21st ACM SIGOPS Symposium on Operating Systems Principles, SOSP*, pages 205–220, New York, 2007. DOI: 10.1145/1323293.1294281 155

[30] Shlomi Dolev, Seth Gilbert, Nancy A. Lynch, Alexander A. Shvartsman, and Jennifer L. Welch. GeoQuorums: Implementing atomic memory in mobile ad hoc networks. In *Proc. of the 17th International Conference on Distributed Computing, DISC*, pages 306–320, Springer, 2003. DOI: 10.1007/978-3-540-39989-6_22 77, 132

[31] Shlomi Dolev, Seth Gilbert, Nancy A. Lynch, Alexander A. Shvartsman, and Jennifer L. Welch. GeoQuorums: Implementing atomic memory in mobile ad hoc networks. *Distributed Computing*, 18(2):125–155, 2005. DOI: 10.1007/s00446-005-0140-9 111, 114, 155

[32] Lionel Droz-Bartholet, Jean-Christophe Lapayre, Fabrice Bouquet, Eric Garcia, and Alexander Heinisch. Ramos: Concurrent writing and reconfiguration for collaborative systems. *Journal of Parallel and Distributed Computing*, 72(5):637–649, May 2012. DOI: 10.1016/j.jpdc.2012.02.012 132

[33] Partha Dutta, Rachid Guerraoui, and Ron R. Levy. Optimistic erasure-coded distributed storage. In *Proc. of the 22nd International Symposium in Distributed Computing, DISC*, pages 182–196, Springer Berlin Heidelberg, Arcachon, France, September 2008. DOI: 10.1007/978-3-540-87779-0_13 156

[34] Partha Dutta, Rachid Guerraoui, Ron R. Levy, and Arindam Chakraborty. How fast can a distributed atomic read be? In *Proc. of the 23rd Annual ACM Symposium on Principles of Distributed Computing, PODC*, pages 236–245, ACM Press, New York, 2004. DOI: 10.1145/1011767.1011802 45, 46, 60, 77, 132, 157

[35] Partha Dutta, Rachid Guerraoui, Ron R Levy, and Marko Vukolic. Fast access to distributed atomic memory. *SIAM Journal on Computing*, 39(8):12, December 2010. 2010. DOI: 10.1137/090757010 45

[36] Burkhard Englert, Chryssis Georgiou, Peter M. Musial, Nicolas Nicolaou, and Alexander A. Shvartsman. On the efficiency of atomic multi-reader, multi-writer distributed memory. In *Proc. of the 13th International Conference on Principle of Distributed Systems, OPODIS*, pages 240–254, 2009. DOI: 10.1007/978-3-642-10877-8_20 17, 77

[37] Alan D. Fekete, Nancy A. Lynch, and Alexander A. Shvartsman. Specifying and using a partitionable group communication service. *ACM Transactions on Computer Systems*, 19(2):171–216, 2001. DOI: 10.1145/377769.377776 81

[38] Michael J. Fischer, Nancy A. Lynch, and Michael S. Paterson. Impossibility of distributed consensus with one faulty process. *Journal of ACM*, 32(2):374–382, 1985. DOI: 10.1145/3149.214121 80, 131

[39] Chryssis Georgiou, Theophanis Hadjistasi, Nicolas C. Nicolaou, and Alexander A. Schwarzmann. Unleashing and speeding up readers in atomic object implementations. In *Proc. of the 6th International Conference on Networked Systems, Revised Selected Papers, NETYS*, pages 175–190, Essaouira, Morocco, May 9–11, 2018. DOI: 10.1007/978-3-030-05529-5_12 77

[40] Chryssis Georgiou, Peter M. Musial, and Alexander A. Shvartsman. Developing a consistent domain-oriented distributed object service. In *Proc. of the 4th IEEE International Symposium on Network Computing and Applications, NCA*, pages 149–158, 2005. DOI: 10.1109/nca.2005.16 110, 113

[41] Chryssis Georgiou, Peter M. Musial, and Alexander A. Shvartsman. Long-lived RAMBO: Trading knowledge for communication. *Theoretical Computer Science*, 383(1):59–85, 2007. DOI: 10.1016/j.tcs.2007.03.052 96, 109, 113

[42] Chryssis Georgiou, Nicolas C. Nicolaou, Alexander Russell, and Alexander A. Shvartsman. Towards feasible implementations of low-latency multi-writer atomic registers. In *Proc. of The 10th IEEE International Symposium on Networking Computing and Applications, NCA*, pages 75–82, IEEE Computer Society, 2011. DOI: 10.1109/nca.2011.18 77

[43] Chryssis Georgiou, Nicolas C. Nicolaou, and Alexander A. Shvartsman. Fault-tolerant semifast implementations of atomic read/write registers. *Journal of Parallel and Distributed Computing*, 69(1):62–79, 2009. DOI: 10.1016/j.jpdc.2008.05.004 46, 77

[44] Sanjay Ghemawat, Howard Gobioff, and Shun-Tak Leung. The Google file system. *SIGOPS Operating Systems Review*, 37(5):29–43, October 2003. DOI: 10.1145/1165389.945450 155, 156

[45] David K. Gifford. Weighted voting for replicated data. In *Proc. of the 7th ACM Symposium on Operating Systems Principles, SOSP*, pages 150–162, ACM Press, 1979. DOI: 10.1145/800215.806583 17

[46] Seth Gilbert. RAMBO II: Rapidly reconfigurable atomic memory for dynamic networks. Master's thesis, MIT, 2003. DOI: 10.1109/dsn.2003.1209936 101, 107

[47] Seth Gilbert and Nancy Lynch. Brewer's conjecture and the feasibility of consistent, available, partition-tolerant web services. *SIGACT News*, 33:51–59, June 2002. DOI: 10.1145/564585.564601 2

[48] Seth Gilbert, Nancy A. Lynch, and Alexander A. Shvartsman. RAMBO II: Rapidly reconfigurable atomic memory for dynamic networks. In *Proc. of the IEEE/IFIP International Conference on Dependable Systems and Networks, DSN*, pages 259–268, 2003. DOI: 10.1109/dsn.2003.1209936 109, 113

[49] Seth Gilbert, Nancy A. Lynch, and Alexander A. Shvartsman. RAMBO: A robust, reconfigurable atomic memory service for dynamic networks. *Distributed Computing*, 23(4):225–272, 2010. DOI: 10.1007/s00446-010-0117-1 101, 109, 113

[50] Vincent Gramoli. RAMBO III: Speeding up the reconfiguration of an atomic memory service in dynamic distributed system. Master's thesis, University Paris-Sud 11, 2004. 111, 113, 132

[51] Vincent Gramoli. Distributed shared memory for large-scale dynamic systems. Ph.D. thesis, University of Rennes, 2007. 17

[52] Vincent Gramoli, Emmanuelle Anceaume, and Antonino Virgillito. SQUARE: Scalable quorum-based atomic memory with local reconfiguration. In *Proc. of the ACM Symposium on Applied Computing, SAC*, pages 574–579, 2007. DOI: 10.1145/1244002.1244133 154

[53] Vincent Gramoli, Len Bass, Alan Fekete, and Daniel Sun. Rollup: Non-disruptive rolling upgrade with fast consensus-based dynamic reconfigurations. *IEEE Transactions on Parallel and Distributed Systems*, 27(9):2711–2724, 2016. DOI: 10.1109/tpds.2015.2499772 132, 133

[54] Vincent Gramoli, Peter M., and Alexander A. Shvartsman. Operation liveness and gossip management in a dynamic distributed atomic data service. In *Proc. of the ISCA 18th International Conference on Parallel and Distributed Computing Systems, PDCS*, pages 206–211, 2005. 96, 109, 113

[55] Vincent Gramoli and Michel Raynal. Timed quorum systems for large-scale and dynamic environments. In *Proc. of the 11th International Conference on Principles of Distributed Systems, PODC*, pages 429–442, 2007. DOI: 10.1007/978-3-540-77096-1_31 154

[56] Rachid Guerraoui, Ron R. Levy, and Marko Vukolic. Lucky read/write access to robust atomic storage. In *Proc. of the IEEE/IFIP International Conference on Dependable Systems and Networks, DSN*, pages 125–136, IEEE Computer Society, Washington, DC, 2006. DOI: 10.1109/dsn.2006.50 46

[57] Rachid Guerraoui and Luís Rodrigues. *Introduction to Reliable Distributed Programming*. Springer-Verlag New York, Inc., Secaucus, NJ, 2006. DOI: 10.1007/3-540-28846-5 4

[58] Rachid Guerraoui and Marko Vukolic. Refined quorum systems. *Distributed Computing*, 23:1–42, 2010. DOI: 10.1007/s00446-010-0103-7 17, 46

[59] Theophanis Hadjistasi, Nicolas C. Nicolaou, and Alexander A. Schwarzmann. Oh-RAM! one and a half round atomic memory. In *Proc. of the 5th International Conference on Networked Systems, Proceedings, NETYS*, pages 117–132, Marrakech, Morocco, May 17–19, 2017. DOI: 10.1007/978-3-319-59647-1_10 46, 157

[60] Maurice Herlihy. A quorum-consensus replication method for abstract data types. *ACM Transactions on Computer Systems*, 4(1):32–53, February 1986. DOI: 10.1145/6306.6308 113

[61] Maurice Herlihy and Jeannette M. Wing. Linearizability: A correctness condition for concurrent objects. *ACM Transactions on Programming Languages and Systems*, 12(3):463–492, 1990. DOI: 10.1145/78969.78972 2, 5, 17

[62] Patrick Hunt, Mahadev Konar, Flavio P. Junqueira, and Benjamin Reed. Zookeeper: Wait-free coordination for internet-scale systems. In *USENIX Annual Technical Conference, ATC*, page 11, 2010. 132

[63] Tomasz Imieliński and Julio C. Navas. GPS-based geographic addressing, routing, and resource discovery. *Communications of the ACM*, 42(4):86–92, April 1999. DOI: 10.1145/299157.299176 112

[64] Leander Jehl and Hein Meling. The case for reconfiguration without consensus: Comparing algorithms for atomic storage. In *Proc. of the 20th International Conference on Principles of Distributed Systems*, vol. 70 of *OPODIS*, page 31:1–31:17, Schloss Dagstuhl-Leibniz-Zentrum für Informatik, Madrid, Spain, December 13–16, 2016. DOI: 10.4230/LIPIcs.OPODIS.2016.31 108, 153, 154

[65] Leander Jehl, Roman Vitenberg, and Hein Meling. Smartmerge: A new approach to reconfiguration for atomic storage. In *Proc. of the 29th International Symposium on Distributed Computing, DISC*, pages 154–169, 2015. DOI: 10.1007/978-3-662-48653-5_11 154

[66] Flavio Junqueira and Benjamin Reed. *ZooKeeper: Distributed Process Coordination*. O'Reilly Media, November 2013. 132

[67] Flavio Paiva Junqueira, Benjamin C. Reed, and Marco Serafini. Zab: High-performance broadcast for primary-backup systems. In *Proc. of the IEEE/IFIP International Conference on Dependable Systems and Networks, DSN*, pages 245–256, 2011. DOI: 10.1109/dsn.2011.5958223 132

[68] Kishori M. Konwar, Peter M. Musial, Nicolas C. Nicolaou, and Alexander A. Shvartsman. Implementing atomic data through indirect learning in dynamic networks. In *6th IEEE International Symposium on Network Computing and Applications, NCA*, pages 223–230, IEEE Computer Society, Cambridge, MA, July 2007. DOI: 10.1109/nca.2007.30 110

[69] Kishori M. Konwar, N. Prakash, Erez Kantor, Nancy A. Lynch, Muriel Médard, and Alexander A. Schwarzmann. Storage-optimized data-atomic algorithms for handling erasures and errors in distributed storage systems. In *IEEE International Parallel and Distributed Processing Symposium, IPDPS*, pages 720–729, IEEE Computer Society, Chicago, IL, May 2016. DOI: 10.1109/ipdps.2016.55 156

[70] Avinash Lakshman and Prashant Malik. Cassandra: A decentralized structured storage system. *SIGOPS Operating Systems Review*, 44(2):35–40, April 2010. DOI: 10.1145/1773912.1773922 17, 155, 156

[71] Leslie Lamport. On interprocess communication, part I: Basic formalism. *Distributed Computing*, 1(2):77–85, 1986. DOI: 10.1007/bf01786227 2, 5, 17

[72] Leslie Lamport. The part-time parliament. *Technical Report 49*, DEC Systems Research Center, 1989. 17, 101, 115, 131

[73] Leslie Lamport. The part-time parliament. *ACM Transactions on Computer Systems*, 16(2):133–169, May 1998. DOI: 10.1145/279227.279229 17, 80, 81, 84, 111, 113, 131

[74] Leslie Lamport. Paxos made simple. *ACM SIGACT News (Distributed Computing Column)*, 32(4):18–25, December 2001. 132

[75] Leslie Lamport. Fast paxos. *Distributed Computing*, 19(2):79–103, 2006. DOI: 10.1007/s00446-006-0005-x 132

[76] Leslie Lamport. Lower bounds for asynchronous consensus. *Distributed Computing*, 19(2), October 2006. DOI: 10.1007/s00446-006-0155-x 132

[77] Leslie Lamport, Dahlia Malkhi, and Lidong Zhou. Reconfiguring a state machine. *SIGACT News*, 41(1):63–73, March 2010. DOI: 10.1145/1753171.1753191 132

[78] Leslie Lamport and Mike Massa. Cheap paxos. In *Proc. of the International Conference on Dependable Systems and Networks, DSN*, page 307, IEEE Computer Society, 2004. DOI: 10.1109/dsn.2004.1311900 132

[79] Butler W. Lampson. How to build a highly available system using consensus. In *Proc. of the 10th International Workshop on Distributed Algorithms, WDAG*, pages 1–17, Springer-Verlag, London, UK, 1996. DOI: 10.1007/3-540-61769-8_1 132

[80] Nancy Lynch. *Distributed Algorithms*. Morgan Kaufmann Publishers, 1996. 18, 80, 105

[81] Nancy Lynch and Alex Shvartsman. RAMBO: A reconfigurable atomic memory service for dynamic networks, 2002. *Technical Report MIT-LCS-TR-856*, MIT Laboratory for Computer Science, Cambridge, MA. 101, 107

[82] Nancy Lynch and Alexander A. Shvartsman. RAMBO: A reconfigurable atomic memory service for dynamic networks. In *Proc. of the 16th International Symposium on Distributed Computing, DISC*, pages 173–190, 2002. DOI: 10.1007/3-540-36108-1_12 113

[83] Nancy A. Lynch and Alexander A. Shvartsman. Robust emulation of shared memory using dynamic quorum-acknowledged broadcasts. In *Proc. of Symposium on Fault-Tolerant Computing*, pages 272–281, 1997. DOI: 10.1109/ftcs.1997.614100 77

[84] Nancy A. Lynch and Mark R. Tuttle. An introduction to input/output automata. *CWI Quarterly*, 2:219–246, 1989. 17

[85] Dahlia Malkhi and Michael Reiter. Byzantine quorum systems. In *Proc. of the 29th Annual ACM Symposium on Theory of Computing, STOC*, pages 569–578, 1997. DOI: 10.1145/258533.258650 154

[86] Dahlia Malkhi, Michael Reiter, and Rebecca Wright. Probabilistic quorum systems. In *Proc. of the 16th Annual ACM Symposium on Principles of Distributed Computing, PODC,* pages 267–273, 1997. DOI: 10.1145/259380.259458 154

[87] Jean-Philippe Martin and Lorenzo Alvisi. A framework for dynamic Byzantine storage. In *Proc. of the 34th Annual IEEE/IFIP International Conference on Dependable Systems and Networks, DSN,* 2004. DOI: 10.1109/dsn.2004.1311902 4

[88] Hosame H. Abu-Amara and Michael C. Loui. Memory requirements for agreement among unreliable asynchronous processes. *Advances in Computing Research*, 4:163–183, 1987. 80

[89] Laurent Michel, Martijn Moraal, Alexander A. Shvartsman, Elaine L. Sonderegger, and Pascal Van Hentenryck. Online selection of quorum systems for RAMBO reconfiguration. In Ian P. Gent, Ed., *Principles and Practice of Constraint Programming—CP, 15th International Conference, Proceedings,* vol. 5732 of *Lecture Notes in Computer Science,* pages 88–103, Springer, Lisbon, Portugal, September 20–24, 2009. DOI: 10.1007/978-3-642-04244-7_10 158

[90] Laurent Michel, Alexander A. Shvartsman, Elaine L. Sonderegger, and Pascal Van Hentenryck. Load balancing and almost symmetries for RAMBO quorum hosting. In *Proc. of the 16th International Conference of Principles and Practice of Constraint Programming, CP,* pages 598–612, Springer, St. Andrews, Scotland, UK, September 6–10, 2010. DOI: 10.1007/978-3-642-15396-9_47 158

[91] Subramanian Muralidhar, Wyatt Lloyd, Sabyasachi Roy, Cory Hill, Ernest Lin, Weiwen Liu, Satadru Pan, Shiva Shankar, Viswanath Sivakumar, Linpeng Tang, and Sanjeev Kumar. f4: Facebook's warm blob storage system. In *11th USENIX Symposium on Operating Systems Design and Implementation, OSDI,* pages 383–398, USENIX Association, Broomfield, CO, October 2014. 156, 157

[92] Peter Musial. From high level specification to executable code: Specification, refinement, and implementation of a survivable and consistent data service for dynamic networks, 2007. Ph.D. Thesis, University of Connecticut. 109, 110, 114

[93] Peter M. Musial, Nicolas C. Nicolaou, and Alexander A. Shvartsman. Implementing distributed shared memory for dynamic networks. *Communications of the ACM*, 57(6):88–98, 2014. DOI: 10.1145/2500874 79

[94] Peter M. Musial and Alexander A. Shvartsman. Implementing a reconfigurable atomic memory service for dynamic networks. In *18th International Parallel and Distributed Processing Symposium, IPDPS,* page 208b, IEEE Computer Society, Santa Fe, New Mexico, April 2004. DOI: 10.1109/IPDPS.2004.1303237 109, 110

[95] A. Muthitacharoen, S. Gilbert, and R. Morris. Etna: A fault-tolerant algorithm for atomic mutable DHT data, 2005. *MIT-LCS Technical Report MIT-LCS-TR-993.* 110

[96] Moni Naor and Udi Wieder. Scalable and dynamic quorum systems. *Distributed Computing*, 17(4):311–322, 2005. DOI: 10.1007/s00446-004-0114-3 154

[97] Brian M. Oki and Barbara Liskov. Viewstamped replication: A general primary copy. In *Proc. of the 7th ACM Symposium on Principles of Distributed Computing, PODC*, pages 8–17, Toronto, August 1988. DOI: 10.1145/62546.62549 132

[98] Diego Ongaro and John Ousterhout. In search of an understandable consensus algorithm. In *USENIX Annual Technical Conference, ATC*, pages 305–319, USENIX Association, Philadelphia, PA, 2014. 132, 133

[99] Rafael Pass and Elaine Shi. Hybrid consensus: Efficient consensus in the permissionless model. In *Proc. of the 31st International Symposium on Distributed Computing, DISC*, page 39:1–39:16, 2017. 154

[100] Marshall Pease, Robert Shostak, and Leslie Lamport. Reaching agreement in the presence of faults. *Journal of the ACM*, 27(2):228–234, April 1980. DOI: 10.1145/322186.322188 131

[101] Jun Rao, Eugene J. Shekita, and Sandeep Tata. Using paxos to build a scalable, consistent, and highly available datastore. *Proc. of VLDB Endowment*, 4(4):243–254, January 2011. DOI: 10.14778/1938545.1938549 132

[102] Rodrigo Rodrigues, Barbara Liskov, Kathryn Chen, Moses Liskov, and David Schultz. Automatic reconfiguration for large-scale reliable storage systems. *IEEE Transactions on Dependable and Secure Computing*, 9(2):145–158, 2012. DOI: 10.1109/tdsc.2010.52 4, 154

[103] Yasushi Saito, Svend Frølund, Alistair Veitch, Arif Merchant, and Susan Spence. FAB: Building distributed enterprise disk arrays from commodity components. *SIGARCH Computer Architecture News*, 32(5):48–58, October 2004. DOI: 10.1145/1037947.1024400 111

[104] Alexander Shraer, Jean-Philippe Martin, Dahlia Malkhi, and Idit Keidar. Data-centric reconfiguration with network-attached disks. In *Proc. of the 4th International Workshop on Large Scale Distributed Systems and Middleware, LADIS*, pages 22–26, 2010. DOI: 10.1145/1859184.1859191 153, 154

[105] Alexander Shraer, Benjamin Reed, Dahlia Malkhi, and Flavio Junqueira. Dynamic reconfiguration of primary/backup clusters. In *Proc. of the USENIX Conference on Annual Technical Conference, ATC*, pages 39–39, USENIX Association, Berkeley, CA, 2012. 132

[106] Konstantin Shvachko, Hairong Kuang, Sanjay Radia, and Robert Chansler. The hadoop distributed file system. In *Proc. of the 26th IEEE Symposium on Mass Storage Systems and Technologies, MSST*, pages 1–10, IEEE Computer Society, Washington, DC, 2010. DOI: 10.1109/msst.2010.5496972 156

[107] Alexander Spiegelman, Yuval Cassuto, Gregory Chockler, and Idit Keidar. Space bounds for reliable storage: Fundamental limits of coding. *Technical Report, ArXiv:1507.05169v1*, 2015. DOI: 10.1145/2933057.2933104 156

[108] Robert Thomas. A majority consensus approach to concurrency control for multiple copy databases. *ACM Transactions on Database Systems*, 4(2):180–209, 1979. DOI: 10.1145/320071.320076 17

[109] Eli Upfal and Avi Wigderson. How to share memory in a distributed system. *Journal of the ACM*, 34(1):116–127, 1987. DOI: 10.1145/7531.7926 45

[110] Leslie G. Valiant. A bridging model for parallel computation. *Communications of the ACM*, 33(8):103–111, 1990. DOI: 10.1145/79173.79181 154

[111] Paolo Viotti and Marko Vukolić. Consistency in non-transactional distributed storage systems. *ACM Computer Survey*, 49(1), June 2016. DOI: 10.1145/2926965 2

[112] Guillaume Vizier and Vincent Gramoli. ComChain: A blockchain with Byzantine fault tolerant reconfiguration. *Concurrency and Computation, Practice and Experience*, 32(12), May 2020. DOI: 10.1002/cpe.5494 154

[113] Marko Vukolić. *Quorum Systems: With Applications to Storage and Consensus*. Synthesis Lectures on Distributed Computing Theory. Morgan & Claypool Publishers, 2012. DOI: 10.2200/s00402ed1v01y201202dct009 17, 154

Authors' Biographies

VINCENT GRAMOLI

Vincent Gramoli is a Future Fellow of the Australian Research Council at the University of Sydney, Australia and a Visiting Professor at EPFL, Switzerland. Vincent started his research on the topic of reconfigurable atomic memory while visiting the University of Connecticut and MIT (USA). He then worked in the area of large-scale distributed systems at INRIA (France) and on the slicing problem at Cornell University (USA). He moved to the University of Neuchâtel and EPFL (Switzerland), where he contributed to the development of the Transactional Memory stack. He obtained his Ph.D. from Université de Rennes and his Habilitation from Sorbonne University. His interest lies in the security and fault tolerance of distributed computing.

NICOLAS NICOLAOU

Nicolas Nicolaou is a co-founder and a senior scientist and algorithms engineer at Algolysis Ltd. He held various academic positions as a visiting faculty until 2014, as an IEF Marie Curie Fellow at IMDEA Networks Institute (2014-2016), a short-term scholar at MIT (2017), and a PostDoc Researcher at the KIOS Research Center of Excellence (2017-2019) before departing for an industrial position in 2019. He holds a Ph.D. (2011) and a M.Sc. (2006) from the University of Connecticut and a B.Sc. (2003) from the University of Cyprus. His main research interests lie in the areas of distributed systems, design and analysis of fault-tolerant distributed algorithms, distributed ledgers (blockchains), security for embedded devices and critical infrastructures, and sensor networks.

ALEXANDER A. SCHWARZMANN

Alexander A. Schwarzmann is the Dean of the School of Computer and Cyber Sciences at Augusta University in Georgia, USA. He holds a Ph.D. from Brown University (1992), M.S. from Cornell University (1981), and a B.S. from Stevens Institute of Technology (1979), all in Computer Science, and he did his post-doctoral work at MIT (USA). Previously, he worked at Bell Labs, Digital Equipment Corp., and the University of Connecticut, where he was the Head of Computer Science & Engineering, and the Founding Director of the Center for Voting Technology Research. His professional interests are in Distributed Computing, Fault-tolerance, and Security and Integrity of Electronic Voting Systems. He authored over 150 technical articles, 3 books, and 1 patent. He is also a Vigneron d'Honneur of Jurade de Saint-Emilion.

Index

n-wise quorum system, 11, 60
    k-wise quorum system, 12
    2-wise quorum system, 12

actions, 7, 8
    input, 8
    internal, 8
    output, 8
active process, 137
ad hoc mobile networks, 111
adversary, 9
algorithm
    ABD, 23, 27, 30, 43, 47, 79, 83, 135
    CwFr, 51
        iterative technique, 52, 54
    Fast, 30, 37, 38, 40
    Rambo, 83, 86, 116, 153
        garbage collection, 83, 84, 92, 99, 109
        reconnaissance, 83, 88
    SfW, 66
        server side ordering, 67
    Sliq, 38, 40
    mwABD, 48, 51
    DynaStore, 135
        change, 137
        view, 137, 144
    RDS, 153
asynchronous channels, 11
asynchrony, 3, 7, 19, 52, 153
atomic memory, 12, 23, 47
atomic object, 34, 49, 51, 61

atomicity, 2, 4, 13, 15, 25, 32, 35, 44, 47, 49, 74, 88, 148
    serialization point, 4, 15
Attiya, Bar-Noy, and Dolev, 23
automaton, 8

biquorum, 11, 13, 84
    read quorums, 84, 98, 99
    write quorums, 84, 98, 99

CAP conjecture, 2
channel, 30, 40, 52, 102
    reliable, 19
channel automaton, 11
churn, 4
communication complexity, 47
communication round, 20, 21, 23, 29, 32, 39, 41, 53, 100
composition, 8, 14, 16
computation time, 20
concurrent, 14, 25, 47, 51, 66
configuration, 82, 83, 85, 118
configuration changes, 135, 137
configuration consistency, 90
configuration map, 83, 85, 120
    truncate, 85, 96, 98
    usable, 85
configuration uniqueness, 87, 90
configuration validity, 87, 90
confirmed tag, 70, 112, 122
consensus, 80, 82, 118, 125

    agreement, 80

    termination, 80

    validity, 80

consensus service, 100

consistency, 2, 12, 13

contact, 20

coordination, 11

correct, 12

correctness, 27

coteries, 11

crash, 3, 7, 10, 13, 19, 23, 30, 37, 83, 86

dag traversal, 135

    breadth first search, 144

data, 2

    availability, 2

    longevity, 2

    replication, 2

    sustainability, 2

directed acyclic graph, 135, 138

distributed networked system, 4

    dynamic, 4

    static, 4

domains, 110

dynamic environment, 7, 79

dynamic memory, 4

DynaStore

    desiredview, 144

    join set, 138

    member set, 138

    removal set, 138

elasticity, 82

Etna, 110

execution, 9, 14, 25, 32, 34, 44

    admissible timed, 105

    configuration viable, 106, 130

    good, 9, 115

execution fragment, 9

failure detector, 80

failure model, 10, 29, 30, 37

fast implementation, 21, 30, 37

fast operation, 21, 23, 30, 41, 51, 66

Fast Paxos, 117

fault-tolerance, 23, 82

federated array of bricks, 111

FIFO, 11

GeoQuorums, 111

    focal points, 112

    get quorums, 112

    put quorums, 112

global ordering, 68

Global Positioning System, 112

global time, 15

gossip, 109

gossip communication, 99

group communication service, 81, 82

incomplete write, 40

incremental reconfiguration, 135, 153

indirect learning, 110

initial configuration, 84, 137

initial value, 40

inprogress set, 70

Input/Output Automata, 7

integrated reconfiguration, 115

intersection degree, 12, 60, 63

invocation, 13

IOA, 11

join-connectivity, 130

latency, 20, 29, 105, 153

leader election, 119, 130

lexicographical order, 48, 51, 68

linearizability, 2, 5, 15

liveness, 15, 27, 34, 44, 49, 57, 74, 138, 148

local broadcast service, 112

local clock, 105, 129

local ordering, 68
long-lived, 109
lower bound, 37, 60

majority, 11, 24, 27, 29, 48, 135, 138
message, 10
    in transit, 11
message delay, 29, 105, 127, 129
multiple-writers multiple-readers, 7
MWMR, 7, 47, 51, 142

network partition, 2
number of messages, 29

Part-Time Parliament, 116
partial order, 15, 35, 48, 84
partial synchrony, 153
Paxos, 84, 101, 115, 116, 125
    acceptors, 116
    ballot, 116
    learners, 116
    proposers, 116
point-to-point, 7, 19, 20, 95, 122
precedes, 14
predicate, 20, 32, 33, 72
prepare phase, 127
previous value, 30, 34
process, 7
propagate phase, 127
propagation, 24, 43, 48, 96, 98, 121, 144
propose phase, 127
protocol, 4

query, 24, 48, 67, 96, 98, 121, 144
quorum, 12, 29, 40, 51, 144
quorum intersection, 51
quorum switching, 60, 64
quorum system, 11, 29, 40, 44, 52, 62, 82, 84
quorum system failure , 12
quorum views, 39, 40, 51, 54

read operation, 14, 24, 25, 32, 39, 51, 92
read-modify-write, 3
recon-readiness, 130
recon-spacing, 130
reconfigurable atomic memory, 83, 86, 88
reconfiguration, 82, 83, 107, 125
reconfiguration service, 90, 100
register, 4
    atomic, 5
    regular, 5
    safe, 5
reliable channels, 11
replica, 25, 43
replica host, 4
replication, 7, 19
response, 13

safety, 15, 27, 34, 44, 57, 74, 86
seen set, 34
sensor network, 110
sequence of configurations, 89
server, 4
set system, 12
shared memory, 1, 4, 13, 14, 23
    read operation, 1
    write operation, 1
shared object, 7, 19, 23
shared storage service, 1
signature, 8
single round, 30, 34
single-writer multiple-readers, 7
slow operation, 21, 23, 41
software update, 82
split-vote, 118
state, 8
state machine, 7
static environment, 7, 19
static memory, 4
step, 8, 9
succeeds, 14

SWMR, 7, 23, 30
synchronization, 11

tag, 25, 30, 48, 51, 119
tag distribution, 39, 41
termination, 16, 27, 34, 49, 138, 148
total order, 23, 51, 61, 89, 112, 125
transitions, 8

variables, 8
virtual synchrony, 81

voted-ballot set, 121

weak snapshot, 135, 138
    integrity, 139
    monotonicity of scan, 139
    non-empty intersection, 139
    termination, 140
    validity, 139
well formedness, 52, 60, 87, 89, 115
world set, 120
write operation, 14, 24, 25, 30, 39, 48, 92